D1451949

ART AND DEATH AT THE SPANISH HABSBURG COURT

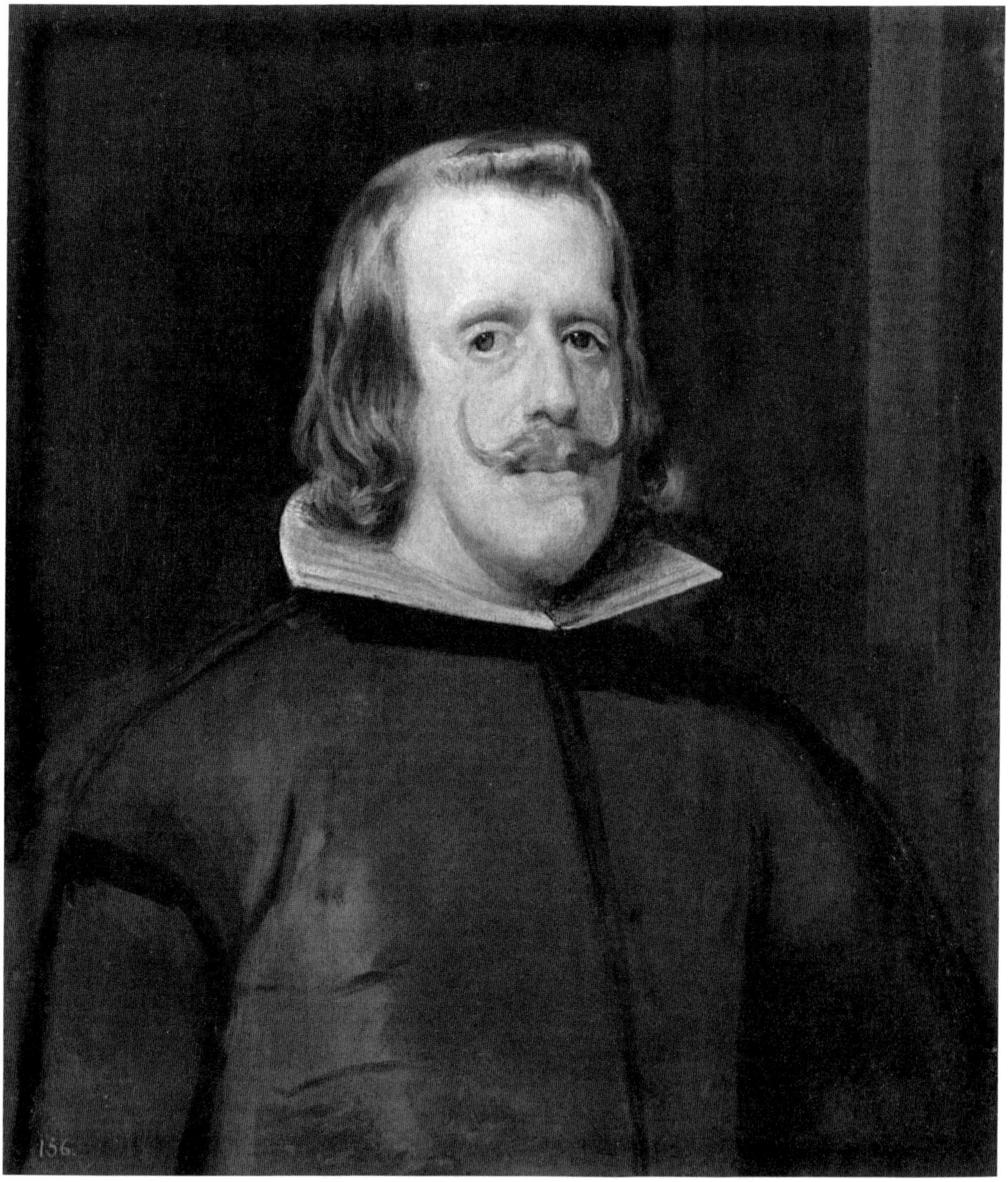
156.

Art and Death at the Spanish Habsburg Court

The Royal Exequies for Philip IV

Steven N. Orso

University of Missouri Press
Columbia

DP
185
.O77
1989

Copyright © 1989 by
The Curators of the University of Missouri
University of Missouri Press, Columbia, Missouri 65211
Printed and bound in the United States of America
All rights reserved

Library of Congress Cataloging-in-Publication Data
Orso, Steven N., 1950–
    Art and death at the Spanish Habsburg court : the royal exequies for Philip IV / Steven N. Orso
        p.   cm.
    Bibliography: p.
    Includes index.
    ISBN 0-8262-0710-3 (alk. paper)
    1. Philip IV, King of Spain, 1605–1665—Death and burial. 2. Art and state. 3. Habsburg, House
of—Art patronage. 4. Spain—Kings and rulers—
Death and burial. I. Title DP185.077   1989
946'.052—dc19   89-4745
                                                                                CIP

♾ This paper meets the minimum requirements of the American National Standard for Permanence
of Paper for Printed Library Materials, Z39.48, 1984.

This book was brought to publication with the generous assistance of the Program for Cultural
Cooperation Between Spain's Ministry of Culture and United States' Universities.
All photographs reproduced in this volume have been provided by the owners of the works, except as
noted.
Frontispiece illustration of *Philip IV of Spain* by Diego de Velázquez (Madrid, Museo del Prado, all
rights reserved).

3 3001 00750 1934

IN MEMORY OF MY GRANDMOTHER
ELIN NORGAARD OLIVER

Contents

Preface

Like so many affairs of the Spanish Habsburg court, my work on this book has proceeded at an erratic pace in which periods of intense effort have alternated with lengthy spells of inactivity. Over the years I have benefitted from the advice and encouragement of several friends and institutions, whose contributions I gladly acknowledge here.

I am especially grateful to five friends who read different versions of this book as it evolved and who offered invaluable suggestions for its improvement: A. Stephen Arbury, who generously shared the fruits of his unpublished research on the evolution of Spanish catafalques; Carol Bolton Betts, whose editorial criticisms of my text have spared my readers numerous infelicities; Jonathan Brown, whose pioneering studies of Habsburg patronage have decisively shaped my own approach to the subject; Narciso G. Menocal, who provided sensitive advice on problems of Spanish translation; and James J. O'Donnell, who contributed the Latin translations found throughout this book and who put his considerable knowledge of Church history at my disposal.

I am indebted as well to Rocío Arnáez, J. H. Elliott, John B. Friedman, Gail L. Geiger, William B. Jordan, Richard L. Kagan, P. David Lagomarsino, Vicente Lleó Cañal, John Rupert Martin, James L. Miller, Stephen Polcari, Sarah Schroth, Ignacio Vicens y Hualde, and Howard D. Weinbrot for aiding my work in a variety of ways. Of the staffs of the many archives and libraries that accommodated my research, I would be remiss if I failed to mention in particular those of the Archivo del Palacio Real, Madrid and the Archivo General de Simancas.

Several institutions have facilitated my research and writing with generous financial assistance. I first began gathering material on Spanish royal exequies as a graduate student in 1975–1976, when I spent nine months in Spain on a grant funded by the Samuel H. Kress Foundation and awarded by the Department of Art and Archaeology, Princeton University. In the summer of 1982, a grant from the Research Board of the University of Illinois at Urbana–Champaign enabled me to return to Spain to carry out archival and library research that proved critical to my work. Upon my return to the United States, I enjoyed a rewarding year as a postdoctoral fellow at the Institute for Research in the Humanities at the University of Wisconsin at Madison, where I devoted much of my appointment to writing the first draft of this book. My financial support from the Institute was supplemented by an overlapping fellowship awarded by the American Council of Learned Societies, which enabled me to return to Spain in the summer of 1983 for additional research.

During the academic year 1986–1987 a sabbatical leave granted by the University of Illinois at Urbana–Champaign enabled me to return to the Institute as an honorary fellow and to revise my manuscript extensively. Finally, thanks are due to the Program for Cultural Cooperation Between Spain's Ministry of Culture and United States' Universities for providing a generous subvention for the publication of this study.

ABBREVIATIONS

AGS	Archivo General de Simancas
AGS, CM3	———, Contaduría Mayor, 3ª época
AGS, CM3, leg. 756	———, legajo 756, Pagador Francisco de Villanueva, 1645–1648
AGS, CM3, leg. 1,362	———, legajo 1,362, Pagador Francisco de Arce, 1665–1675
AGS, CM3, leg. 1,461	———, legajo 1,461, Pagador Francisco de Villanueva, 1640–1644
AGS, CM3, leg. 1,810(2)	———, legajo 1,810(2), Pagador Francisco de Arce, 1661–1665
AHN	Archivo Histórico Nacional, Madrid
APM	Archivo del Palacio Real, Madrid
APM, SH	———, Sección Histórica
APM, SH, Hf	———, Honras fúnebres
APM, SH, Libro de pagos	Archivo del Palacio Real, Sección Histórica, Reinados, Felipe IV, I^{bis}, legajo 2,916
BLL	British Library, London
BNM	Biblioteca Nacional, Madrid
BPM	Biblioteca del Palacio Real, Madrid
leg.	legajo
RAH	Real Academia de la Historia, Madrid

Books of the Bible are named and numbered following the Vulgate.

ART AND DEATH AT THE SPANISH HABSBURG COURT

INTRODUCTION

When death claimed Philip IV of Spain (frontispiece), he was released from a life of public cares and private griefs. As the sovereign of a mighty empire, he had proved a manifest failure at the arts of statecraft, for under his forty-four-year rule Spain had suffered a devastating string of political, military, and economic setbacks. As an individual, his life was punctuated by the deaths of those he loved. By the time Philip himself prepared to die, he had survived the deaths of his parents, three brothers, two of three sisters (a fourth had died before he was born), the first of two wives, and nine of his twelve legitimate children (see Table 1). Less is known of his bastards, whose number is commonly put at from five to eight (although some contemporary rumors put the number at twenty-three or thirty-two), but at least two preceded him to the grave.[1] As the years passed, his public failures and private losses inexorably broke his spirit.

Philip lay in his deathbed for less than a week, but he had suffered poor health for years.[2] In 1658, while he had been

hunting at Aranjuez, exposure to the cold and wet had broken his health and had palsied his right arm and leg, which he could move thereafter only with forceful effort. He bore that affliction for seven years. Then, in 1665, he endured a six-month period in which he suffered uncontrollable, sometimes bloody, and sometimes painful evacuations of his bowels and bladder. On the evening of September 11, another pronounced, but bloodless, evacuation of the bowels signaled the onset of his final illness. Philip took to his bed in the summer apartments of the Alcázar of Madrid, but he spent the night with little sleep. On September 12

---

1. R. A. Stradling, *Philip IV and the Government of Spain 1621–1665*, 330; and José Deleito y Piñuela, *El Rey se divierte (recuerdos de hace tres siglos)*, 85–87. We are not fully informed about royal miscarriages, but they, too, added to Philip's woes; for example, see *Cartas de algunos PP. de la Compañía de Jesus sobre los sucesos de la monarquía entre los años de 1634 y 1648*, 5:452.

2. For the following account of events from Philip IV's decline through his entombment, the most important sources are José María Caparrós, "Enfermedad, muerte y entierro del Rey D. Felipe IV de España"; Gregorio Díaz de Ylarraza, *Relacion diaria de la enfermedad, y mverte del gran Rey Don Felipe IIII. Nuestro Señor...*; and Pedro

Rodríguez de Monforte, *Descripcion de las honras qve se hicieron a la Catholica Mag^d de D. Phelippe quarto Rey de las Españas...*, fols. 6–50.

See also Jerónimo de Barrionuevo, *Avisos*, ed. A. Paz y Mélia, 4:57, 68, and 108–9; "Breue Relacion De la muerte del Rey Catholico Phelipe Quarto...," fols. 4–5^v; María del C. Cayetano Martín, Pilar Flores Cuerrero, and Cristina Gállego Rubio, "El Concejo de Madrid y las honras fúnebres en memoria del rey Don Felipe IV, Año 1665," 727; Deleito y Piñuela, *El Rey se divierte*, 308–16; "Dia en q^e murio nŕo Rey q^e Dios tiene el Gran Don filipo quarto"; "Enfermedad, Muerte y Entierro, del Catolico Rey Don Phelipe quarto. Año de 1665"; Anne, Lady Fanshawe, *Memoirs... To Which are Added Extracts from the Correspondence of Sir Richard Fanshawe*, 258–65 and 352–54; Gabriel, Duque de Maura y Gamazo, *Vida y reinado de Carlos II*, 1:51–52; *Négociations relatives à la succession d'Espagne sous Louis XIV...*, ed. François A. A. Mignet, 372–90; *Relacion de la enfermedad, mverte, y entierro del Rey Don Felipe Quarto nuestro Señor...*; "Tratado de las ceremonias, o, culto, qve se dà a Dios en la Real Capilla de los Reyes Catholicos Nuestros Señores (Dios los guarde) Dividido en Dos partes," 1: fols. 113–13^v; and an untitled *gaceta* of 1665 in "Sucesos del año 1665," BNM, Ms. 2,392, fols. 237–38^v.

Table 1
The Family of Philip IV

	Birth	Death
Parents		
Philip III	April 14, 1578	March 31, 1621
Margarita of Austria	December 25, 1584	October 3, 1611
Siblings		
Ana	September 22, 1601	January 21, 1666
María	February 1, 1603	March 1, 1603
PHILIP IV	April 8, 1605	September 17, 1665
María	August 18, 1606	May 13, 1646
Carlos	September 15, 1607	July 30, 1632
Fernando	May 16, 1609	November 9, 1641
Margarita Francisca	May 24, 1610	March 11, 1617
Alfonso	September 22, 1611	September 16, 1612
Wives		
Isabella of Bourbon	November 22, 1602	October 6, 1644
Mariana of Austria	December 22, 1634	May 16, 1696
Legitimate Children		
María Margarita	August 14, 1621	August 16, 1621
Margarita María Catalina	November 25, 1623	December 22, 1623
María Eugenia	November 21, 1625	July 21, 1627
Isabel María Teresa de los Santos	October 31, 1627	November 1, 1627
Baltasar Carlos	October 17, 1629	October 9, 1646
María Antonia	January 16, 1635	December 5, 1636
María Teresa	September 20, 1638	July 30, 1683
Margarita María	July 12, 1651	March 12, 1673
María Ambrosia	December 7, 1655	December 20, 1655
Felipe Próspero	November 28, 1657	November 1, 1661
Fernando Tomás	December 21, 1658	October 23, 1659
Charles II	November 6, 1661	November 1, 1700
Natural Child		
Juan José (acknowledged in 1642)	April 7, 1629	September 17, 1679

his evacuations turned bloody and persisted uncontrollably. A fever that would worsen over the course of his remaining days set in, and he passed the night as painfully as he had the day. The symptoms continued on September 13, and his weakness prevented his doctors from applying "violent remedies" (bleeding him?) to relieve his fever. By nightfall they concluded that the disease was mortal, but they judged it was not yet necessary to send for the Viaticum or to tell the king their prognosis. Nonetheless, Philip recognized that he was in danger and summoned Blasco de Loyola, the senior secretary of the Council of State and a secretary of the Universal Dispatch (the king's private office), to receive instructions concerning additions that he wished to make to his will. That night the king's condition continued to deteriorate.

September 14 saw no mitigation of the king's attacks, and his doctors concluded early that morning that the Viaticum should be sent for. Preparations for conveying the Sacrament to him were undertaken in the Royal Chapel, and Fray Juan Martínez, the king's Dominican confessor, informed him of his doctors' conclusion, which news he received calmly. Philip then confessed and heard Mass, which Martínez celebrated at an altar that had been set up in the king's bedroom. Shortly after 9:00 A.M. the king gave the order for the Viaticum, and when asked whether he wished it brought to him in secret or in public procession, he chose the latter. An hour later a solemn procession of clerics, nobility, and royal servants set out from the Royal Chapel. Alonso Pérez de Guzmán, Patriarch of the Indies, carried the monstrance containing the Blessed Sacrament and walked the route to the king's bedroom beneath a canopy supported by six of the king's chaplains. The procession grieved the courtiers who saw it, for it confirmed rumors that the king was dying. After placing the monstrance on the altar in the king's bedroom, the patriarch aspersed, performed the customary absolution, and posed the questions of the Protestation of the Faith, to which Philip responded by confessing his faith in the mysteries and sacraments of the Church. Because he was physically unable to pay reverence to the Host, he asked that the monstrance be placed upon his bed, whereupon he demonstrated his devotion to it with words and tears. When he received the ritual lavation, the monstrance was returned to the altar. The patriarch next asked the king whether he wished to receive Extreme Unction, to which he replied that he would request it when the need was at hand and receive it then with pleasure. The sacramental procession then returned the Host to the Royal Chapel by the same public route by which it had come.

Later that day Philip authorized the codicil to his will he had instructed Loyola to prepare the night before, but he was so debilitated that the Count of Castrillo, one of the witnesses to the codicil, had to sign it on his behalf. Meanwhile, the king's illness had become public knowledge, and prayers and supplicatory demonstrations for his rescue were undertaken throughout the capital. In the Royal Chapel the Blessed Sacrament was exposed to view, and for two hours the choir sang the Psalms of David in the presence of the queen, Mariana of Austria, and her two children, Charles and Margarita María. Devotional appeals were made to miraculous images of the Virgin, and at 6:00 P.M. the town of Madrid staged a procession in which the cathedral chapter carried the body of Saint Isidro from its chapel in the church of San Andrés to the parish church of Santa María. Three times that afternoon and evening the king asked for Extreme Unction, but each time his doctors concluded that he would live another day and that he could defer it to the following morning if there were no further complications.

On September 15, having spent another fatiguing night, Philip heard Mass at 9:00

A.M. His subjects' appeals for divine intercession continued, and at 10:00 A.M. the body of Saint James of Alcalá, which had been brought from its resting place in Alcalá by order of the Father General of the Franciscans, was carried into the king's bedroom and placed on the temporary altar. Also that morning the miraculous image of the Virgin of Atocha was carried past the Alcázar in a procession from its chapel at the Dominican monastery of Nuestra Señora de Atocha to the convent of the Descalzas Reales. These actions were to no avail, and Philip's condition continued to deteriorate. He ate badly, and he continued to lose blood. Owing to his weakness, it was decided that he should receive Extreme Unction, which the Patriarch of the Indies administered at 4:00 P.M.

The queen had sent for permission to visit her husband with their children, and at 4:30 Philip received Charles, Margarita María, and Mariana in succession for the last time. Having given them his blessing, he desired to devote whatever life remained to him to spiritual matters. To that end, Fray Antonio del Castillo, a Franciscan who was the Commissary General of Jerusalem, had the grandees, the Council of State, and other senior ministers who were waiting in the king's apartments summoned to the royal bedroom. There Castillo showed them the crucifix that Charles I, Philip II, and Philip III had adored at their deaths, which had already been brought to the dying king. Addressing them in Philip's name, Castillo exhorted them to peace and to serve the future Charles II and the queen, his mother. On behalf of the king, Castillo asked for the pardon of any whom he had treated unjustly, and he declared the king's pardon of those who had done him offense. These words reduced the assembled noblemen to tears, and kneeling before the king, they took their leave of him.[3] Asked whether he wished to have the body of Saint Isidro brought to his room, Philip declined, saying that the place where the saint's body lay (Santa María) had greater propriety, and that for what he would ask of the saint, the distance between them would prove no impediment. For the same reason, no other relics or miraculous images were brought to his bedside.

The morning of September 16 found his condition unchanged, and he asked to receive Communion once more. Philip was extremely weak, and in order to receive the Sacrament with propriety, he had the Count of Tajara prop him up with a pillow. Besides adoring the crucifix that his predecessors had held at their deaths, Philip took comfort in his final hours from images of Christ on the Cross and the Virgin Mary that he had ordered to be hung on the canopy of his bed. At 4:00 P.M. he summoned the papal nuncio to ask for absolution and for any Graces or Indulgences that the nuncio and the pope might grant him. At 6:30 he suffered a paroxysm that prompted the Patriarch of the Indies, the royal chaplains, and other religious to return for the Recommendation of the Soul. The rite was to be performed several more times before the king died. Over the course of the night, five or six more paroxysms interrupted his devotions until the end came shortly after 4:15 A.M. on Thursday, Sep-

3. Caparrós, "Enfermedad," 176, gives the more detailed account of Castillo's address but dates it to September 14. I am inclined to follow Rodríguez de Monforte, *Descripcion*, fols. 14–14ᵛ, who dates it to September 15, because his is the official chronicle of the king's death.

tember 17, 1665. Philip IV had lived sixty years, five months, and nine days, and he had ruled the Spanish Monarchy for forty-four years, five months, and seventeen days. When his doctors embalmed his body so that it could lie in state, they discovered the cause of his death to have been a stone in his right kidney.

After the doctors had finished with the corpse, it was dressed for a lying-in-state in a suit of pearl-colored camlet with silver embroidery, a white beaver hat, a cape, a sword, and a collar of the Order of the Golden Fleece. The court initially planned a lying-in-state for a single day, September 18, in the Great Hall of the Alcázar, but public grief was too great. The crowds of mourners who forced their way past the royal guards into the hall made it necessary to extend the observance through September 19 so that delegations from all the monastic communities in Madrid could celebrate Masses there for the repose of his soul, as was customary. That night a royal funeral procession set out for El Escorial under the joint direction of the Patriarch of the Indies and the king's majordomo of the week, Luis Francisco Núñez de Guzmán, Marquis of Monte-Alegre. The cortege reached the royal monastery of San Lorenzo at 7:30 the following morning, and the Hieronymite community there received the body for interment with all the solemnities appropriate to a king of Spain.

Philip's subjects joined the royal family in mourning his demise. In part, this reflected the popularity of the Habsburg dynasty within Spain, for even when the public held the government in contempt, its loyalty to the royal family was generally strong. Furthermore, the people recognized that a death in the royal family

threatened the security of their own lives because the Habsburg dynasty was the keystone of political order within the *monarquía*, or Monarchy, as the Spanish empire was commonly called. God was held to have granted the king his place on the throne for the good of Spain and the Catholic faith, and the power and authority to govern were vested in his person. As a result, the well-being of the king and his family was essential to political stability within the Monarchy, and anything that disrupted that well-being threatened the entire social fabric. Death was inevitable, even for kings, but knowing that did not lessen public dismay when a Spanish Habsburg died.

A king's death plunged the Monarchy into crisis. The accession of his heir usually proceeded without incident, but that did not preclude a period of political uncertainty. Because princes stood in the shadows of their fathers, their talents and intentions were not well known when they ascended the throne. More often than not, their fathers had permitted them some participation in the affairs of state, but their skills had not been tested seriously. Furthermore, new kings tended to promulgate new policies and to replace their fathers' counselors with men of their own choosing. While the government underwent such upheavals, the king's subjects anxiously awaited the first signs of what the future was to bring. Such a situation had prevailed when Philip IV ascended the throne in 1621.[4] In 1665 the situation was even more unsettled: Philip's heir, Charles II, was still a minor, which meant that a temporary regency

4. On the circumstances attending the accession of Philip IV, see J. H. Elliott, *The Count-Duke of Olivares: The Statesman in an Age of Decline,* 3–127 passim.

would have to govern in his name. Not only would rumor and speculation about the new king's capabilities flourish, but so, too, would the regent come under apprehensive scrutiny.

The potential for political instability in the aftermath of a royal demise was not confined to the deaths of kings. In some circumstances, the death of a queen could also inspire public anxiety. If she were to die without having provided her husband with an heir, the continuity of the royal line would stand in jeopardy. The kingship of Spain was hereditary, and the existence of an acknowledged heir apparent within the immediate royal family ensured an orderly transition of power. In the absence of such an heir, the Spanish crown might pass to another royal house, and a dynastic change could bring far greater upheavals in the government than did ordinary royal accessions. Such crises were averted when at least one son survived the queen. Under the fundamental law of Spain a daughter could inherit in the absence of a son, but the accession of a daughter would pose other difficulties. If she failed to marry and have children, the royal line might die out. If she did marry, however, whom would she take as a husband? Unless her groom was another Habsburg (that is, a prince from the German branch of the family), the dreaded prospect of a dynastic change on the throne would loom large. To avoid such outcomes, the customary practice when a queen died without leaving a son was for the king to remarry. Arranging a suitable match could entail years of negotiation with foreign courts, and in the meantime the continuity of the royal line would remain under a cloud.

In like fashion, the death of an heir apparent could arouse public despair.

If a brother survived the deceased, then the line of succession would remain clear and unthreatened, but royal brothers were seldom abundant in Habsburg Spain. In the absence of a male sibling, a sister could inherit, but as already noted, that possibility was fraught with risk. More likely the king and queen would try to have another son (assuming, of course, that the queen had not predeceased the late heir).

Thus, the death of a Spanish Habsburg presented his or her survivors with a formidable array of public and private tasks that did not end when the royal corpse was delivered to El Escorial. The passing of Philip IV was no exception. Familial duty required his survivors to render appropriate honors to his memory and to have Masses celebrated for the Christian salvation of his soul. Public responsibility required them to console the people's grief and to reassure their subjects that they would persevere in the orderly conduct of the affairs of the Monarchy.

* * *

Among the instruments that the Habsburgs customarily used to achieve such ends, one stands out for its awe-inspiring combination of art, royal spectacle, and solemn religious observance: the celebration of royal exequies (*exequias reales*), also known as funerary honors (*honras fúnebres*). These events, which should not be confused with burial rites, took place several weeks after a royal personage had been entombed. Unlike their French neighbors, the Spanish had not developed a tradition of elaborate state funerals for their kings, and the speed with which a corpse could decompose in the Spanish climate required that royal remains be dealt with swiftly.[5] Under ordinary circumstances, the government would see to the prompt entombment of a Habsburg's remains within a few days of his death. The interval between an entombment and royal exequies permitted the regime to have the church that had been selected as the site for the funerary honors decorated for the occasion. The nature of these decorations, and of the ceremonies that were performed when the decorations were in place, depended upon the status of the deceased. The most elaborate arrangements were reserved for royal exequies in honor of a king, queen, or *príncipe jurado*.

The term *príncipe jurado* ("sworn prince") requires a digression on the political organization of the Monarchy. It was not a unified, homogeneous state in the modern sense, but a confederation of realms in Iberia and abroad that maintained considerable political autonomy from one another. No single system of laws, no single coinage, and no single tradition of political rights united them. Instead, the realms had distinct legal codes, their own coinages, and separate traditions of political privileges that governed their relations with their rulers. It was the person of the king, who had inherited sovereignty over these realms by various lines of descent, that held the empire together.[6] The core of the Monarchy— what is regarded today as a single, unified

Spain—consisted of two distinct entities in the seventeenth century: the Crown of Aragon (comprising the Kingdoms of Aragon and Valencia, and the Principality of Catalonia) and the Crown of Castile and León (comprising those realms occupying the remaining territory of modern Spain; hereafter cited simply as the "Crown of Castile"). The marriage of Ferdinand II of Aragon and Isabella I of Castile had brought these two crowns into close alliance, but it was not until their grandson, the Holy Roman Emperor Charles V, inherited them both as Charles I of Spain (that is, Charles I of Aragon and Charles I of Castile) that they were united under the sovereignty of a single Habsburg. Because Charles's father, Philip I of Castile, never inherited the Crown of Aragon, the numeration of subsequent Philips who ruled both crowns was permanently affected. Thus, the man who is commonly known today as "Philip IV of Spain" was actually Philip III of Aragon and Philip IV of Castile.

That he is known as "Philip IV" underscores the preeminence of the Crown of Castile within the Monarchy. After the accession of Philip II, who fixed upon Madrid as the permanent capital of the Monarchy, the Habsburg kings seldom ventured beyond the territories of that crown. Even when Philip III moved the capital to Valladolid for a few years (1601–1606), the court remained within Castilian borders. One reason for this royal predilection was that of all the king's dominions, the Crown of Castile was most firmly pinned beneath the royal thumb. As a result, it was heavily taxed (eventually to the point of economic ruin), and it provided much of the manpower for the king's armies. Other

5. P. David Lagomarsino, "The Habsburg Way of Death." On the funerals of French kings, see also Ralph E. Giesey, *The Royal Funeral Ceremony in Renaissance France*.

6. The division of the Monarchy into distinct realms had critical consequences for Philip's efforts to govern them. See J. H. Elliott, *The Revolt of the Catalans: A Study in the Decline of Spain (1598–1640)*, esp. 1–21; Elliott, *Count-Duke of Olivares*, esp. 191–202 and 244–77; and Stradling, *Philip IV*, esp. 172–88.

realms, notably the Crown of Aragon, had guarded their political privileges vis-à-vis the king's government more successfully, and they resisted the efforts of the royal councils (most of whose members were Castilians) to exert greater control over their affairs. At its most extreme, this opposition erupted into open revolt. The most prolonged rebellion that the Habsburgs faced was that of the United Provinces, an eighty-year conflict that Philip IV inherited from his father and his grandfather's regimes, and that ended with his recognition of Dutch independence in 1648. Closer to home, both the Principality of Catalonia and the Crown of Portugal (the third of the three great crowns into which Iberia was divided) revolted in 1640. Although Catalonia was eventually subdued by force of arms, Philip's troops never brought Portugal to heel. His regime contended with rebels on several fronts, but the loyalty of the Crown of Castile was a political certainty.

This close identification of the king's interests with the Crown of Castile informed the political importance with which a *príncipe jurado* was regarded. Although a king's eldest son would be regarded as his father's eventual successor from the day of his birth, the mere fact of his birth did not suffice to make him the legally acknowledged heir to the Crown of Castile. He attained that status only after he had received an oath of allegiance from the thirty-six *procuradores* who represented eighteen major cities of the crown in its parliament, the *Cortes*; from the grandees and other titled nobility of the realm; from a representative of the clergy; and from any *infantes* (royal sons who were not heirs apparent) and *infantas* (royal daughters) who were present at

the court. The oaths were given in a ceremony called the *juramento*, which customarily took place during the prince's youth at the church of the royal monastery of San Jerónimo in Madrid, whereupon the prince became a *príncipe jurado*, the heir apparent to the Crown of Castile.[7] Only if a prince had received the *juramento* would the court commemorate his passing with the same kind of royal exequies that were accorded kings and queens of Spain.

Royal exequies of this sort consisted of two days of religious observances in a church that the court went to considerable effort and expense to adorn for the occasion. The centerpiece of the decorative ensemble was an enormous catafalque embellished with paintings, sculptures, banners, coats of arms, and thousands of candles. The rest of the church interior was bedecked with funereal hangings and other adornments, and during Philip IV's reign it became the practice to mount decorations on the entrance facade as well. Once everything was in place, an extraordinary audience lent the splendor of its presence to the occasion: the royal family, the grandees and other high nobility of Spain, the royal councils, distinguished clerics, foreign ambassadors, and other worthies whom the regime invited to attend. Under Philip's rule it also became the practice to plan for the publication of illustrated books

7. The procedures followed in this ceremony are summarized in Christina Hofmann, *Das Spanische Hofzeremoniell von 1500–1700*, 123–28; and Antonio Rodríguez Villa, *Etiquetas de la Casa de Austria*, 79–88. For contemporary accounts of specific *juramentos* and further bibliography, see María C. Sánchez Alonso, "Juramentos de príncipes herederos en Madrid (1561–1598)"; and *Relaciones breves de actos públicos celebrados en Madrid de 1541 a 1650*, ed. José Simón Díaz, xxix–xxx, xxxii–xxxiii, 20–29, 49–69, and 412–13.

that would record the exequies and their decorative ensembles, but such projects were not always brought to fruition. When other members of the royal family or their relations died—foreign sovereigns who were parents of Spanish queens, royal brothers and sisters, and archdukes of Austria—the court also commemorated their passing, but in funerary honors at which the extent of the decorations and the ceremonial pomp were more restrained.

The exequies that the regime organized were by no means the only honors to be paid to a Spanish king, queen, or *príncipe jurado*. As news of a death spread throughout the Monarchy, institutions such as city councils, viceregal administrations, seminaries, and universities organized their own exequies for the deceased.[8] Spaniards living outside the Habsburg dominions—the Spanish community in Rome, for example—might also stage funerary honors.[9] Even in colonial settings as remote as Mexico City and Manila, where news of a royal death arrived months after the fact, exequies were staged in honor of the Habsburgs.[10]

The most prestigious and politically important funerary honors for the Spanish Habsburgs were invariably the royal exequies, which should be understood as "royal" in two senses. Like other exequies, they commemorated royal personages; but unlike other exequies, only they were organized and paid for by the royal government. With the extensive resources at its disposal—not only the revenues in the state treasury, but also the artists, craftsmen, and men of letters in the king's service—the court was able to bring into being temporary decorations for royal exequies that far surpassed in majesty and splendor the ensembles erected by other institutions. Moreover, its direct control of the royal exequies enabled the regime to devise the content of the decorations so as to express its views on the social, political, and theological concerns of the moment. The Habsburgs were masters at using ephemeral art to convey their perceptions of the world and their ideals, and royal exequies provided them with a stage from which to issue the political reassurances that a royal death required in the captivating language of visual imagery. Other institutions that performed funerary honors might incorporate meanings into their decorations that reflected their own concerns, but at royal exequies the regime spoke clearly for itself.[11]

8. Although Jenaro Alenda y Mira, *Relaciones de solemnidades y fiestas públicas de España*, remains the most thorough bibliography of public celebrations in Habsburg Spain (many of which featured ephemeral decorations), it omits coverage of most exequies. María del P. Dávila Fernández, *Los sermones y el arte*, cites numerous Spanish exequies from the mid-sixteenth through the eighteenth centuries; and Ignacio Vicens y Hualde, "Arquitectura efímera barroca: un estudio de las estructuras funerarias españolas del siglo XVII," catalogues numerous seventeenth-century Spanish exequies. At this writing, A. Stephen Arbury is completing a doctoral dissertation for Rutgers University on Spanish catafalques of the Habsburg era that will catalogue Spanish exequies of the sixteenth and seventeenth centuries.

9. For example, the exequies staged for Philip IV at San Giacomo degli Spagnuoli in Rome on December 18, 1665; see Antonio Pérez de la Rua, *Fvneral hecho En Roma en la Yglesia de Santiago de los Españoles à 18. de Diciembre de 1665. . . .*

10. For Habsburg exequies in Mexico City, see Francisco de la Maza, *Las piras funerarias en la historia y en el arte de México: grabados, litografías y documentos del siglo XVI al XIX*, 11–59. For an instance of such exequies in Manila, see *Aparato fvnebre y real pyra de honor . . . A Las memorias del serenissimo Principe de España Don Balthassar Carlos. . . .*

11. For an overview of the use of ephemeral art by the government and by other Spanish institu-

At the royal exequies for Philip IV, the regime spoke with uncommon eloquence and conviction. That was fitting because Philip had been an enthusiastic patron of the visual arts who had appreciated them both for the aesthetic satisfactions they provided and for their capacity to express his concerns and beliefs to a public audience. Over the course of his reign he had created a court at which this appreciation manifested itself in decorative ensembles that deftly combined breathtaking beauty with didactic content, both in the long-term adornment of his residences and in the ephemeral art commissioned for special occasions.[12] The latter had included decorations for royal exequies, for under

his watchful eye, the court had celebrated the most elaborate kind of royal exequies for his father, Philip III (1621), for his first wife, Isabella of Bourbon (1644), and for his son Baltasar Carlos, a *príncipe jurado* (1646). As a result, the court that rendered honors to Philip's memory in 1665 was well schooled in staging royal exequies with the pomp and splendor befitting a great monarch. It did not fail him—for a few days in 1665, extraordinary decorations transformed a simple Madrilenian church into a magnificent temple dedicated to Philip's memory.

That ensemble has long since been dismantled, and the artists who created it and the courtiers who marveled at it have gone to their graves. Nevertheless, sufficient written accounts and visual records of the event have survived so that even after more than three centuries, we can take a seat at the king's exequies. The challenge that confronts us is to view the decorations with understanding. The etiquette and expectations of the society that erected them no longer prevail, and the conventions of symbolism that informed their meaning have lost their familiarity. To appreciate the beauty of the decorations and the power of their content, we must first appreciate the customs and practices that governed their creation. By doing so, we can enjoy the king's exequies more fully, sharing perspectives and insights with the courtiers who were privileged to attend them.

tions, see Antonio Bonet Correa, "La fiesta barroca como práctica del poder," in *El arte efímero en el mundo hispánico*, 43–78; Yves Bottineau, "Architecture éphémère et Baroque espagnole"; Julián Gállego, *Visión y símbolos en la pintura española del Siglo de Oro*, 132–75; and Virginia Tovar Martín, "Juan Gómez de Mora, arquitecto y trazador del rey y maestro mayor de obras de la villa de Madrid," in *Juan Gómez de Mora (1586–1648)*, 145–53.

12. There is no adequate general survey of Philip IV's activities as a patron and collector, but Jonathan Brown and J. H. Elliott, *A Palace for a King: The Buen Retiro and the Court of Philip IV*, provides an indispensable introduction to the subject. See also Svetlana Alpers, *The Decoration of the Torre de la Parada*; Jonathan Brown, *Velázquez: Painter and Courtier*; J. Miguel Morán and Fernando Checa, *El coleccionismo en España: de la cámara de maravillas a la galería de pinturas*, 251–82; Steven N. Orso, *Philip IV and the Decoration of the Alcázar of Madrid*; and Barbara von Barghahn, *Philip IV and the "Golden House" of the Buen Retiro: In the Tradition of Caesar*.

I

ETIQUETTE INTO ART

The Creation of Decorations for Spanish Royal Exequies

1
THE ETIQUETTE OF DEATH

The public lives of the royal family were governed by elaborate rules of etiquette, called *etiquetas*, that accompanied them from the cradle to the grave. Indeed, insofar as they concerned royal exequies, the *etiquetas* pursued the Habsburgs into the afterlife. Charles I had introduced the etiquette of the Burgundian court into the Spanish court in 1548, and from the start it was more complex than the native practice it supplanted. Over the ensuing years it was expanded to meet the growing needs of a court that became obsessed with conforming to custom and with maintaining a strictly defined hierarchy of social precedence. Public ceremonies were a means for the Habsburgs to demonstrate their political authority, and the formal structure that the rules of etiquette imposed upon such events enhanced the compelling impressions of majesty that the royal family sought to inspire. By the reign of Philip IV the concerns of court etiquette encompassed matters ranging from the most mundane to the most extraordinary of royal activities.

On May 22, 1647, Philip appointed a junta to thoroughly review and codify the *etiquetas*, a task it accomplished over the next four years. The resulting etiquette of 1647–1651 addressed two fundamental concerns.[1] One was to describe the orga-

nization of the king's household, which it did simply by setting forth the qualifications, duties, and benefits of each of the significant offices within the hierarchy of royal servants. The other was to define the protocols governing a variety of public ceremonies. Etiquette dictated the order of participants in royal processions, the intricacies with which meals were served to the king in the presence of witnesses, the dignities with which he received diplomatic envoys of different ranks for the first time, and the seating arrangements at theatrical performances in his principal residence, the Alcázar of Madrid. Etiquette informed the ways that the court observed religious holidays, that royal infants were baptized, and that the king witnessed *autos de fe*. Etiquette fitted these and other royal activities to straitjackets of forms, courtesies, and conventions. For some events the etiquette was a simple,

---

1. For an overview of etiquette at the Spanish Habsburg court, see Hofmann, *Hofzeremoniell*. Rodríguez Villa, *Etiquetas*, summarizes much, but not all, of the 1647–1651 etiquette. For lists of extant copies of the *etiquetas* (including versions that predate 1647–1651) and related documents, see Hofmann, *Hofzeremoniell*, 75–82; J. E. Varey,

"L'Auditoire du *Salón Dorado* de l'*Alcázar* de Madrid au XVIIe siècle," in *Dramaturgie et Sociéte: rapports entre l'oeuvre théâtrale, son interprétation et son public aux XVIe et XVIIe siècles*, ed. Jean Jacquot with Élie Konigson and Marcel Oddon, 1:81–83; and Varey, "La mayordomía mayor y los festejos palaciegos del siglo XVII," 165–68.

In addition, various parts of the *etiquetas* are examined in Yves Bottineau, "Aspects de la cour d'Espagne au XVIIe siècle: l'étiquette de la chambre du roi"; Deleito y Piñuela, *El Rey se divierte*, esp. 97–160; Orso, *Alcázar of Madrid*, 16–20, 35–37, 118–21, and 138; J. E. Varey, "Processional Ceremonial of the Spanish Court in the Seventeenth Century," in *Studia Iberica: Festschrift für Hans Flasche*, ed. Karl-Hermann Körner and Klaus Rühl, 643–52; and Varey, "Further Notes on Processional Ceremonial of the Spanish Court in the Seventeenth Century."

step-by-step declaration of the procedures to be followed. For others it consisted of a narrative account of how a ceremony had been performed on a particular occasion, in the expectation that the precedent would govern similar situations in the future.

Of course, etiquette could not anticipate every circumstance. When written rules were not available, the court depended upon its memory of past practice. There was no etiquette, for example, that instructed the royal family on how to go about the actual business of dying; yet successive Habsburg kings spent their last days in remarkably similar fashion, emulating the way that the greatest of their line, Charles I, had prepared for his death in 1558.[2] Each king had the fortune to know that his end was near at least a few days before death claimed him, and each used that time to conclude his worldly affairs and to prepare himself for the afterlife. His last days were a time for issuing a few final decrees, bringing his will up to date, blessing his wife and children, and taking leave of his subjects. It was also a time for him to seek spiritual solace by confessing his sins, devoting himself to prayer, having the Viaticum brought to his death-chamber, and receiving Extreme Unction when the end was imminent. Perhaps the most telling manifestation of the later Habsburgs' desire to imitate their predecessors was that Charles I, Philip II, Philip III, and Philip IV each died clutching the same crucifix.[3] So important did the crucifix become that Philip IV took it with him when he traveled. As a result, when Baltasar Carlos fell mortally ill while visiting Zaragoza

with his father in 1646, the crucifix was available for the prince to adore on his deathbed.[4]

As a king lay dying, his doctors remained in constant attendance, and his private chaplains and confessors sought to provide him with spiritual comfort. Meanwhile, the other clerics of the court and the town sought divine intercession to stay the king's illness. In this, too, the weight of custom made itself felt. In the death-chamber, images of Christ and the Virgin Mary might be mounted on the king's bed for his devotion. Relics of the saints could be brought there to enhance the saints' efficacy as intercessors on the king's behalf by their proximity to his person. In the Royal Chapel the Blessed Sacrament might be exposed to view, and both there and in churches throughout Madrid, prayers would be said for the king's recovery. The remains of Saint Isidro, patron of Madrid, or the miraculous image of the Virgin of Atocha might be carried through the streets in supplicatory processions. Such efforts on behalf of an ailing monarch were by no means limited to Madrid. As news of a royal illness spread, the pattern of prayers, processions, and other invocations of divine aid repeated itself throughout the Monarchy. Nor were such measures confined to the illnesses of kings, for queens and other members of the royal family likewise enjoyed the spiritual efforts of their subjects to rescue them from death.

Although the 1647–1651 *etiquetas* did not set forth how a Habsburg should go

2. Lagomarsino, "Habsburg Way of Death."

3. Rodríguez de Monforte, *Descripcion*, fol. 16ʳ.

4. Juan Martínez, "Relación de la enfermedad del príncipe nuestro señor, escrita por el Padre Fray Juan Martínez, confesor de Su Majestad, para el doctor Andrés. (Año 1656.)," in *Relaciones históricas de los siglos XVI y XVII*, ed. Francisco R. de Uhagón, 344.

about dying, they did describe the ceremonies with which his passing was to be acknowledged once it had occurred. At the time that the etiquette was reviewed, the court's memory of such rituals would have been relatively fresh because the deaths of Isabella of Bourbon (1644) and Baltasar Carlos (1646) had taken place only a few years earlier. Two passages in the etiquette specifically pertained to the deaths of kings, queens, and *príncipes jurados* of Spain.

The first dealt with the events in the immediate aftermath of a royal death: the lying-in-state of the corpse, its transport in a solemn funeral procession to the village of El Escorial, and its entombment there at the royal monastery of San Lorenzo.[5] In brief, the *etiquetas* assumed that the royal death had occurred in or near Madrid, which was usually the case in the seventeenth century. (If the death took place far away, the regime simply adapted the etiquette to meet the special circumstances. When Baltasar Carlos died in Zaragoza, for example, it was arranged for his body to lie in state there rather than in Madrid.)[6] The body of the deceased was cleaned, in most cases embalmed, and dressed for interment. It was then taken to the Great Hall, the largest chamber in the Alcázar of Madrid, where it lay in state for a day or two on a bed of mourning.[7] While it was there, delegations of priests from the Royal Chapel, the cathedral chapter, and the monastic communities of Madrid celebrated Masses for the soul of the deceased at temporary altars that had been erected in the hall for that purpose. Then a funeral cortege composed of high-ranking clerics, religious from four monastic orders, high nobility, senior servants in the royal household, and the royal guards conveyed the body in a casket to El Escorial in a solemn procession that usually marched the distance in the course of a single night. There the Hieronymite monks of San Lorenzo received the body for entombment in the royal burial chamber. The construction of a Royal Pantheon at the monastery was completed in Philip IV's reign by 1654, after which the bodies of the Habsburgs already entombed at San Lorenzo were transferred to its confines.[8] Since then the Royal Pantheon has served as the final resting place for the kings and queens of Spain.

The second pertinent section of the *etiquetas* dealt with the two days of royal exequies that the court celebrated some weeks later. Before we take up the text of the etiquette, some preliminary remarks are in order. To begin with, the seventeenth-century writers who dealt with royal funerary honors used the word *exequias* in two senses. It could refer to both days of solemn observances, or it could signify the events of the second day only. In the latter case, the first day was identified as the "vigil" or the "vespers of

5. These ceremonies lie beyond the immediate concerns of the present study. Hofmann, *Hofzeremoniell*, 108–12, and Rodríguez Villa, *Etiquetas*, 151–53, summarize the pertinent etiquette; for the funeral procession, see also Varey, "Processional Ceremonial," 647–51. For detailed contemporary accounts of such events, see *Pompa Fvneral Honras y Exequias en la muerte De la muy Alta y Catolica Señora Doña Isabel de Borbon . . .* , fols. 6ᵛ–15ᵛ, and Rodríguez de Monforte, *Descripcion*, fols. 25–50.

6. Martínez, "Relación," 345; and "Resumen de la vida del Principe D. Baltasar Carlos." A plan of the lying-in-state is found with the manuscript on which Martínez, "Relación," is based; see BNM, Ms. 18,723³⁵, n.p.

7. For the Great Hall, see Orso, *Alcázar of Madrid*, 118–43.

8. George Kubler, *Building the Escorial*, 115–17.

the exequies." To preserve these distinctions, we can use the term *exequies* when referring to both days of observances, *vigil* and *vespers* when referring to only the first day, and *exequies proper* when referring to only the second.

In its treatment of the royal exequies, the etiquette mentions a daunting array of offices within the hierarchy of the king's household. Hundreds of servants ministered to the sovereign's needs, and to describe their positions and duties fully lies beyond the scope of this study.[9] As it happens, the participation of most of the royal attendants at royal exequies was significant not for the services that they ordinarily performed, but for the overall effect that their being there conveyed to those who witnessed the event. The presence of these servants, who included some of the highest-born noblemen in the land, was itself a demonstration of the greatness and the dignity of the royal family whom they served. It will suffice to note here that the participants included the king's chief majordomo (*mayordomo mayor*), who, assisted by several majordomos under his immediate supervision, directed the affairs of the king's household and its legion of servants.

The customary site where the court assembled to celebrate royal exequies was the church of the royal monastery of San Jerónimo at the eastern edge of Madrid.[10] Like San Lorenzo at El Escorial, this establishment was occupied by a chapter of Hieronymites, a Spanish order that had enjoyed close ties with the kings of Castile since the fourteenth century.[11] One measure of this attachment was that from April 9, 1528, when the future Philip II received the *juramento* of the Crown of Castile there, San Jerónimo had been the customary setting for Habsburg princes to receive the traditional oaths of loyalty. The monastery had been constructed during the reign of Ferdinand and Isabella after an earlier establishment that Henry IV of Castile had founded just outside Madrid had been abandoned because its site near the Manzanares River had proved inhospitable. The new monastery was completed in 1505, and the itinerant Spanish court sometimes used it for lodgings. In 1561 Philip II ordered the architect Juan Bautista de Toledo to construct a royal apartment at the monastery, which was completed by 1563. Among its other uses, this apartment became a customary retreat for the king during periods of mourning. Beginning in 1630, a building campaign undertaken by Philip IV to enlarge the royal apartment grew into a far more ambitious enterprise, the construction of the Palace of the Buen Retiro and its gardens, almost all of which was completed by 1640.[12] Most of the monastery and the palace was later destroyed, but the monastery church has survived. Although it has long since been stripped of its seventeenth-century decoration and has undergone four modern campaigns of restoration, the church of San Jerónimo remains a commanding presence in the heart of Madrid (fig. 1).

The Hieronymites of San Jerónimo first celebrated funerary honors for a Spanish

9. Brown, *Velázquez*, 38–41, outlines the organization of the king's household; see also n. 1 above.

10. For the remarks on the history of San Jerónimo that follow, see Baltasar Cuartero y Huerta, *El Monasterio de San Jerónimo el Real: protección y dádivas de los Reyes de España a dicho Monasterio*; Aurea de la Morena, "El Monasterio de San Jerónimo el Real, de Madrid"; and Elías Tormo [y Monzó], *Las iglesias del antiguo Madrid*, ed. María Elena Gómez Moreno, 199–206.

11. On the royal connection with the Hieronymites, see Jonathan Brown, *Images and Ideas in Seventeenth-Century Spanish Painting*, 112–27.

12. Brown and Elliott, *Buen Retiro*, 55–140.

king at their old establishment near the Manzanares upon the death of their initial patron, Henry IV, in 1474. They first celebrated exequies at their new establishment in honor of Charles I in 1559.[13] These were ordered by his successor, Philip II, but they cannot be considered the "royal exequies" in the sense that this study employs the term because Philip's court was then in Brussels, where he staged lavish funerary honors for his father. Nor did that precedent immediately establish San Jerónimo as the customary site for royal exequies when the court was in Madrid. On August 10 and 11, 1568, Philip II had royal exequies celebrated for his son Don Carlos, a *príncipe jurado*, in the church of the royal convent of Santo Domingo, and two months later, on October 18 and 19, royal exequies for the king's third wife, Isabella of Valois, took place in the church of the convent of the Descalzas Reales.[14] Royal exequies for his fourth wife, Anne of Austria, were held in San Jerónimo on January 26 and 27, 1581; although Philip himself was in Portugal at the time, his sisters Isabella Clara Eugenia and Catalina Micaela were present.[15] Thereafter, San Jerónimo regularly served as the setting for royal exequies for kings, queens, and *príncipes jurados*.

Philip III ordered the royal exequies for Philip II to be staged there on October 18 and 19, 1598; and on November 17 and 18, 1611, he used the church for the royal exequies for his wife, Margarita of Austria.[16] The subsequent observances that Philip IV ordered for Philip III (May 3 and 4, 1621), Isabella of Bourbon (November 17 and 18, 1644), and Baltasar Carlos (November 12 and 13, 1646) likewise took place there.[17]

As a setting for funerary honors, San Jerónimo had much to offer. Its capacious interior readily accommodated the large audiences and elaborate decorations that became traditional at such events. Furthermore, as a Hieronymite institution that enjoyed royal patronage, it was a sis-

13. Morena, "El Monasterio," 53; and APM, SH, Hf, caja 76, Noticias sobre el remanente de cera y madera del Tumulo (1644).

14. For Don Carlos, see APM, SH, Hf, caja 76, Príncipe Don Carlos (1568); and Juan López [de Hoyos], *Relacion de la mverte y honras fvnebres del SS. Principe D. Carlos . . .*, fols. 22ᵛ–39. For Isabella, see APM, SH, Hf, caja 76, Doña Isabel, muger de Felipe II; and Juan López [de Hoyos], *Hystoria y relaciõ verdadera de la enfermedad felicissimo transito, y sumptuosas exequias funebres de . . . Isabel de Valoys . . .*, fols. 38ᵛ–55. For them both, see Dalmiro de la Valgoma y Díaz Varela, "Honras fúnebres regias en tiempo de Felipe II," in *El Escorial 1563–1963*, 1:368–70.

15. Valgoma y Díaz Varela, "Honras fúnebres regias," 391–95.

16. For Philip II, see Antonio Cervera de la Torre, *Testimonio avtentico, y verdadero, de las cosas notables qve passaron en la dichosa muerte del Rey nuestro señor Don Phelipe segundo*, 154–56; "Naçimicnto y successos (Por mayor) Del Rey Don Phelipe Segundo nuestro señor, y su Testamᵗᵒ Muerte y Honrras," fols. 44ᵛ–45ᵛ; and "Relaçion de lo que paso a las honrras que su mag. mando hazer en Som Gerᵐᵒ por el rrey nro Senor su padre que aya gloria domingo 17 de otubre de 1598." For Margarita, see Luis Cabrera de Córdoba, *Relaciones de las cosas sucedidas en la córte de España, desde 1599 hasta 1614*, 455–56; and *Relaciones breves*, 72–80. For them both, see also APM, SH, Hf, caja 76, Felipe II y Margarita de Austria (1598).

17. The most important account of Philip III's royal exequies is Juan Gómez de Mora, "Aparato del tvmulo real que se edifico el Conuēto de S. Geronimo De la Villa de Madrid para celebrar las honras Del Inclito y esclaredico Rey Don Filipe. III"; see also Andrés de Almansa y Mendoza, *Cartas*, 21–25; and *Relacion de las Honras del Rey Felipe Tercero que està en el cielo, y la solene entrada del Rey Felipe Qvarto, que Dios guarde*. An account in *Relaciones breves*, 125–26, is marred by errors and should be used with caution. For Isabella's exequies, *Pompa Fvneral Honras* is the most thorough account; however, one in *Relaciones breves*, 493–97, is shot through with errors that compromise its usefulness. For Baltasar Carlos's funerary honors, see "Epitome de todas las cosas suzedidas en Tiempo del señor Rei don phᵉ quartto," fols. 265–90ᵛ.

ter establishment to San Lorenzo at El Escorial, where the Habsburgs were interred. Because the distance separating Madrid from El Escorial made San Lorenzo an inconvenient setting for royal exequies, using the more conveniently located San Jerónimo enabled the court to conduct funerary honors in a setting that was institutionally linked to the site of the royal tombs.[18]

What had become a custom was confirmed in writing by the junta that composed the 1647–1651 etiquette. Its prescription for royal exequies for kings, queens, and *príncipes jurados* specifically names San Jerónimo as the usual site for such honors. (In considering the following text from the *etiquetas* and the accompanying commentary, the reader may find it helpful to refer to Figure 2, a plan of San Jerónimo as the *etiquetas* called for it to be furnished for royal exequies.)[19]

Honors for the Kings, Queens, and *Príncipes Jurados* of Spain, Which Ordinarily Are Celebrated in the Royal Monastery of San Jerónimo in Madrid

The *capilla mayor* of San Jerónimo is hung with cloths of gold, damask, or black velvet, and the nave of the church as far [back] as the entrance [is hung] with black cloths. The pavements and the benches of the ambassadors, the grandees, and the councils [are covered] with baize.

The high altar is covered with its curtains. The grille of the *capilla mayor* is removed to make room, and in it the superintendent of the royal works has erected a covered catafalque [that is carried] on rich[20] columns and is adorned with arms and trophies. At its corners [are] some spires [*agujas*] that are called [a] *capella ardente*.[21] Beneath it on four or five steps[22] is put the *tumba* covered with an opulent cloth. It being honors for a king, a Cross [is put] on top [of the *tumba*] at its head, and at its feet a cushion, upon which [are put] a crown and scepter, the collar of the [Order of the Golden] Fleece, and the sword that represents Justice. It being honors for a queen, only the crown and scepter are put on the cushion. If they are for a prince, only the crown and sword [are used], and the [collar of the Golden] Fleece if he is a member of the Order.

The curtains of the high altar, hangings of the church, *capella ardente*, *tumba*, tapers, and altar candles are adorned with shields of the royal arms and some banners of different colors with arms and trophies.

Within the catafalque seats are placed in the four corners for the bishops who say the Responsories and for the deacons who assist them.

The *tumba* was an oblong, sepulchral monument aligned with the main axis of the church that symbolized the presence of the deceased, whose body remained in its coffin at El Escorial. Its "head," where the cross stood, was at the end closer to the nave, and its "feet" at the end closer to the high altar. The "opulent cloth" that covered the *tumba* and the cushion

18. *Relaciones breves*, 72; and Rodríguez de Monforte, *Descripcion*, fols. 52–52ᵛ.

19. There is no critical edition of the 1647–1651 *etiquetas*, which survive in several complete and partial manuscripts (see n. 1 above). The text presented here is based on the pertinent sections of the seventeenth- and eighteenth-century manuscripts that follow. From BNM: Ms. 1,014, 1,044, 10,616, 10,666, 10,675, and 10,686. From APM: SH, Etiquetas, cajas 50 [1 copy] and 52 [4 copies]; and SH, Hf, caja 76 [8 partial copies devoted to the etiquette for royal exequies]. From BLL: Ms. Add. 28,459 and Ms. Egerton 2,187.

20. Some *etiquetas* manuscripts corrupt *ricas* (rich) to *dóricas* (Doric). Another variant, *negras* (black), turns up less frequently.

21. *Capella ardente*: The *etiquetas* manuscripts give this Latin phrase in both singular and plural corrupted forms such as *capel ardente* and *capelardentes*.

22. In some manuscripts one reads, "and a platform with steps is put nearby, and the *tumba* is put on top . . ."

that rested upon it had been commissioned by Philip II for use at his own funerary honors and at those of his successors and their families. From contemporary descriptions of the cloth, it seems to have been a black-and-white brocade panel decorated with silver embroidery, silver fringe, and silver plates. Its border featured trophies of death linked with skulls and crossbones. The fabric of the cushion matched that of the cloth. The ensemble that Philip had commissioned also included vestments to be worn by the priests who officiated at the royal exequies. These may be identified tentatively as the "Vestments of the Skulls" in the collection of embroideries at San Lorenzo at El Escorial (for example, fig. 3).[23]

Apparently beginning with the royal exequies for Philip III, it became the practice to place a Latin epitaph identifying and praising the deceased in front of the *tumba* facing the nave.[24] The objects resting upon the *tumba* cushion likewise identified the status of the deceased. Because kings, queens, and princes were all royal, a crown always appeared on the monument. Unlike his parents, a prince did not reign, so only a king or queen merited a scepter, which evidently symbolized actual rule. A sword, on the other hand, was apparently considered too warlike an instrument for a woman; that

would account for its restriction to kings and princes. The collar of the Order of the Golden Fleece was the best known insignia of the order, which was one of the most prestigious confraternities of knights in all Europe. It was Burgundian in origin, and the Spanish Habsburg kings commanded the order in their capacity as counts of Flanders (one of their many dignities). The collar comprised a chain of links in the shape of firestriking steels and sparking flintstones, from which depended an ornament in the shape of a ram's fleece. The steels and flints were traditional devices of the House of Burgundy. The pendant recalled both the pagan myth of Jason's quest for the Golden Fleece and the biblical account of the golden-fleeced ram with which the Lord signaled to Gideon his impending victory over the Midianites. These associations symbolized the order's original dedication to the defeat of Islam and the Christian recovery of the Holy Land.[25] One measure of the importance of the order was that its collar was incorporated into the "full" royal coats of arms scattered so liberally throughout the decorative ensemble. These consisted of an escutcheon bearing the heraldic devices of the principal realms of the Monarchy surrounded by a collar of the Golden Fleece, the whole surmounted by a royal crown signifying that the arms pertained to a royal personage (see fig. 26, top center). The collar had been incorporated into the royal arms from the arms of the counts of Flanders (see fig. 29).

The vestments, the cloth, the cushion, and the objects that rested on the cushion were stored at San Lorenzo at El Es-

23. For seventeenth-century descriptions of the cloths and vestments, see Gómez de Mora, "Aparato del tvmulo real," fols. 13–13^v; "Naçimiento y successos," fol. 45^v; *Pompa Fvneral Honras*, fol. 27; *Relaciones breves*, 75 and 79; and Rodríguez de Monforte, *Descripcion*, fol. 67^v. For the "Skulls" vestments, see Paulina Junquera de Vega, "El obrador de bordados de El Escorial," in *El Escorial 1563–1963*, 2:556 and 558.

24. A comparison of expenses for the royal exequies for Margarita of Austria and Philip III in APM, SH, Hf, caja 76, Felipe II y Margarita de Austria (1598), indicates there was no *tumba* epitaph at Margarita's honors.

25. On the origin and meaning of the collar, see Earl E. Rosenthal, "The Invention of the Columnar Device of Emperor Charles V at the Court of Burgundy in Flanders in 1516," 209.

corial, whence an aide to the keeper of the crown jewels (*ayuda de guardajoyas*) fetched them when they were needed.[26] The sole exception was the collar of the Golden Fleece, which would have been found in the Alcázar of Madrid in the care of the keeper of the crown jewels. The practice of the order dictated that upon the death of a knight of the Golden Fleece, his collar was to be returned to the palace for safekeeping.[27]

To resume with the text of the etiquette:

His Majesty's *cortina* is put on the Gospel side, near the altar to Our Lady of Guadalupe, facing the catafalque.[28]

The nave of the church from the [site of the] grille [that was removed] on back is enclosed by barriers that are set off twenty *pies* [5.60 meters] from the main entrance and three *pies* [0.84 meter] from the walls on both sides. The doorkeepers of the bedchamber man the entrances through these barriers. Covered benches are put within them for the councils, which are seated in their order of precedence on one side and the other, as they are shown here:

Royal Council of Castile	Council of Aragon
Council of the Inquisition	Council of Italy
Council of Flanders	Council of the Indies
Council of the Orders	Council of Finance
Council of the Cruzada	

The choir [*música*] of the Royal Chapel is in one of the chapels of the church.

The guards [are] at the doors, and a majordomo [is there] to regulate the order of the people who are to enter.

A *cortina*, also called a *cortina oratorio*, was a portable oratory that set the king's seat apart from the rest of the church in which it was erected. A ceiling canopy and hanging curtains defined its space, which only a royal personage could enter. It was furnished with a chair and a prie-dieu with cushions on its two rails on which the king could kneel and rest his arms. A broad, floor-length, taffeta bolt covered the prie-dieu.[29]

The councils were some of the king's principal instruments of governance. Owing to the far-flung extent of the Monarchy, the Habsburgs had developed an elaborate administrative bureaucracy within which various councils were assigned major areas of responsibility.[30] In brief, the councils of Castile, Aragon, Italy, Flanders, and the Indies directed the affairs of the principal geographic divisions of the empire. The Council of the Inquisition supervised the workings of the Holy Office, the Council of the Orders oversaw the Spanish military orders, the Council of Finance had responsibility for the royal exchequer, and the Council of the Cruzada administered a tax, the *cruzada*, from which it took its name. Al-

26. APM, SH, Hf, caja 76, Noticia de lo que se sirve por el oficio de Guardajoyas en las Honras de Personas Reales, and Honras: Disposiciones que deben preceder á la celebracion de las mismas (14 setiembre 1746).

27. Rodríguez de Monforte, *Descripcion*, fols. 35ᵛ–36.

28. *Púlpito* (pulpit) is occasionally given for *túmulo* (catafalque).

29. These remarks are based on a description of the *cortina* used by the king in the Royal Chapel of the Alcázar of Madrid in "Tratado de las ceremonias," 1:fols. 9–9ᵛ.

30. On the conciliar system, see Elliott, *Revolt of the Catalans*, 9–10, and *Imperial Spain 1469–1716*, 160–72; J. M. Batista i Roca's foreword to Helmut Koenigsberger, *The Government of Sicily under Philip II of Spain: A Study in the Practice of Empire*, 15–35; and Stradling, *Philip IV*, 22–32.

THE CREATION OF DECORATIONS

though other councils and juntas participated in the governance of the Monarchy, only these nine were seated within the nave enclosure.

The councils contributed to the spectacle of the funerary honors by arriving ostentatiously at the church on both days of the observances. Whereas many other dignitaries entered San Jerónimo by less public side entrances, the councils arrived at its main entrance in full view of the crowds of spectators who gathered outside the church.[31] The members of each council arrived together in coaches preceded by their respective subordinates, who rode on horseback. Thus, the members of the Council of Castile (also known as the Royal Council) rode in coaches with justices of the royal household and court (*alcaldes de casa y corte*), and they were preceded by constables (*alguaciles*) of the court, ushers, and scribes. Familiars and notaries preceded the coaches occupied by the Council of the Inquisition, whereas knights of the three great Spanish military orders (Alcántara, Calatrava, and Santiago) signaled the arrival of the Council of the Orders. In such manner, each council arrived with its appropriate accompaniment. When the counselors entered the church, they took their seats at the benches that had been reserved for them in the center of the nave. The space assigned to each council was marked by its respective coat of arms, which was mounted on the railing that separated the benches from the rest of the church. The Council of Castile enjoyed pride of place nearest the catafalque on the Gospel side, and the Council of Aragon sat opposite it in the second most prestigious seats on the Epistle side.

31. For example, see Rodríguez de Monforte, *Descripcion*, fols. 71^v–81.

The seven other councils likewise sat in order of precedence in a sequence that alternated back and forth across the nave: Inquisition, Italy, Flanders, Indies, Orders, Finance, and Cruzada.

Everything being prepared and the councils in their places, His Majesty comes down to vespers on the afternoon prior [to the exequies proper] by the staircase that has been built from the Palace of the Buen Retiro [and] that ends in the first chapel on the Gospel side. The justices [are] in front. Then [follow] the pages with their governor, ordinary captains, gentlemen of the household, titled nobility, gentlemen of the table, macebearers with their maces, majordomos, grandees, kings-at-arms with the royal coats of arms (sometimes full ones, other times distributed among those of the [deceased's] four grandparents), and the chief majordomo with his staff held diagonally on his shoulder. His Majesty [enters] with a long mourning gown and cowl, and on it the collar of the [Order of the Golden] Fleece. The groom of the stole carries his train. Behind [the king come] cardinals, ambassadors, the captain of the Guard of Archers, gentlemen of the bedchamber, and the [gentlemen] of the Council of State. The guards are in two files, and from His Majesty's place on back that of the Archers encloses the procession.

Upon His Majesty's seating himself, all take their places in the same manner as in the [Royal] Chapel, and the office begins.

When there is no *cortina* because the royal personage is in the tribune of the high altar on the Epistle side, the bench of the grandees is moved to that side, and the seats of the cardinals and the benches of the ambassadors and the chaplains [are moved] to the Gospel side,[32] without making any change in the benches of the councils and the disposition of the nave of the church.

32. Some *etiquetas* manuscripts specify the Epistle side, but that would render the passage meaningless.

The staircase and the entrance by which the king was to descend from his apartments in the Buen Retiro into San Jerónimo (fig 2, Z) had been constructed in 1644 so that Baltasar Carlos could use it to enter the church for the royal exequies for Isabella of Bourbon. Its construction resolved an old problem of providing royal access to the *cortina* when it stood in the north transept (the Gospel side of the church). At the royal exequies for Philip II in 1598, Philip III had entered the nave of San Jerónimo from the cloister on the south side of the church (fig. 2, FF). From there he had had to make his way to his *cortina* in the north transept along a roundabout route requiring him to squeeze between the catafalque and the presbytery steps while the grandees who accompanied him had walked around the nave side of the monument.[33] At the royal exequies for Philip III in 1621, the problem had been alleviated by putting Philip IV's *cortina* in the south transept (the Epistle side).[34] Building the new entry into the north side of the church in 1644 made it possible to return the *cortina* to the Gospel side.

The royal entourage specified here is comparable to those that the *etiquetas* prescribed to accompany the king in royal processions on other public occasions. On the basis of what is known of such processions, the guards who were to be arranged in two files must have been members of the Spanish and German Guards, which together with the Guard of Archers (also called the Flemish Guard) were the three companies that ordinarily protected the king's person.[35]

The explicit reference to the king's wearing a long mourning gown with a cowl is the only description of costume found in the etiquette for royal exequies other than references to priests' vestments. In fact, the entire court would have dressed in mourning following a death in the royal family, and it would have remained in official mourning for whatever period the king decreed. (Apparently that was such an obvious action that the junta that revised the *etiquetas* saw no need to mention it.) On the day that Isabella of Bourbon died, for example, the members of the royal councils adopted mourning dress of gowns (*lobas*) and cowls. What is more, each council had the walls, floors, and furnishings of its principal chambers covered in black, as well as the furnishings and floors of its less important rooms. When the councils subsequently met to conduct business, they did so with their heads covered, and their subordinates also adopted solemn dress. After the completion of the queen's royal exequies the counselors ceased wearing cowls, but they wore the remaining mourning garb for a year.[36]

When the king took his place, whether in a *cortina* or a tribune, four kings-at-arms (*reyes de armas*) and four mace-bearers took up positions on the catafalque.[37] The kings-at-arms were heralds who stood at the four corners of the *tumba*, and each wore a garment bearing

33. *Pompa Fvneral Honras*, fols. 21–21[v].

34. See Gómez de Mora, "Aparato del tvmulo real," fols. 13 and 15–15[v], with an accompanying engraving by Pedro Perret that shows the plan of the exequies. The plan is reproduced in Virginia Tovar Martín, *Arquitectura madrileña del siglo XVII (datos para su estudio)*, fig. 23b, and in her "Juan Gómez de Mora, arquitecto y trazador del rey y maestro mayor de obras de la villa de Madrid," in *Juan Gómez de Mora (1586–1648)*, 86.

35. For example, see Varey, "Processional Ceremonial," 644–47. For the guard companies, see Deleito y Piñuela, *El Rey se divierte*, 109–11; and Rodríguez Villa, *Etiquetas*, 53–63.

36. *Pompa Fvneral Honras*, fol. 39.

37. Gómez de Mora, "Aparato," fols. 16[v]–17; and *Relaciones breves*, 76.

a coat of arms. Either each displayed the arms of one of the four grandparents of the deceased, or all four displayed the full royal arms of Spain.[38] The macebearers stood at a lower level on one of the steps, two on the Gospel side and two on the Epistle side, each resting his ceremonial mace on his shoulder. Neither the kings-at-arms nor the macebearers moved from their posts during the offices.

The candles of the catafalque were lighted in advance of the king's arrival so that when he and his entourage took their places, all was ready for the vigil to begin. Royal exequies fused two great traditions of ceremonial pomp: the secular etiquette of royal comportment and the sacred rituals of the Catholic liturgy. The sumptuous decorations of the church and the carefully planned movements of the priests as they proceeded through the rites captivated the assembled spectators, who sat in hushed silence as the harmonies of the choir and the mellifluous voices of the priests penetrated to the farthest recesses of the church. Over the course of the two-day observance the anguish of grief yielded to spiritual joy as the mysteries of the Faith and the consolations of a learned preacher offered solace to the court.

In brief, the vigil service consisted of the Vespers of the Dead, matins, and lauds. The office was performed by a high-ranking cleric—at least a bishop, of-

ten a cardinal—who was to figure prominently in the exequies proper as well. Then the audience withdrew, and overnight the stumps of wax left on the catafalque were replaced with fresh candles. The exequies proper began the following morning, before the courtiers returned to the church, when two other senior clerics celebrated two Pontifical Masses. The first was a Mass of the Holy Spirit, for which the priests wore red vestments, and the second was a Mass of the Virgin, for which they donned white ones.[39] Because each was a festal Mass, the mourning curtains that covered the high altar for the exequies were drawn back while these rites were performed. Then the spectators who had attended the vigil returned to the church in the same order as the day before, and while they made their way to their seats, the candles on the catafalque were lighted. The king and his entourage were the last to enter, and when they had taken their places, the prelate who had presided at the vigil celebrated a Pontifical High Mass of the Dead in black vestments (the set that Philip II had commissioned for such occasions). For this Requiem Mass the curtains on the high altar were again drawn shut. In the course of the rite one of the king's preachers delivered a learned sermon that praised the deceased and celebrated the Christian salvation of his soul. Owing to the royal status of the deceased, the ceremony concluded with not one, but five Absolutions. Four bishops attended by eight deacons took their places in the corner seats of the catafalque, and each

38. An untitled book of ceremonies compiled in the sixteenth century by Juan de España, a king-at-arms to Philip II, includes a drawing showing the design of such garments—see RAH, Col. Salazar y Castro, Ms. K-53, fol. 81ᵛ (reproduced in Valgoma y Díaz Varela, "Honras fúnebres regias," 366). España's text, which is the principal source for Valgoma y Díaz Varela's article, describes important ceremonies at the courts of Burgundy and Spain from 1383 to 1584, especially funerary honors, with particular attention to the roles played by the kings-at-arms.

39. As will be seen, the *etiquetas* specify "colored" vestments for the Mass of the Holy Ghost. Red vestments would have been appropriate for that, and it is recorded that red vestments were used at the royal exequies for Isabella of Bourbon (*Pompa Fvneral Honras*, fol. 50ᵛ) and Philip IV (Rodríguez de Monforte, *Descripcion*, fol. 88ᵛ).

bishop conducted a responsory. The prelate who had presided over the Requiem Mass led the fifth responsory, and with that, the royal exequies concluded.

In describing this order of worship, the *etiquetas* devote particular attention to the role of the king:[40]

Upon completing the vespers, matins, and lauds, His Majesty returns to his quarters with the same accompaniment.

The next day, after the Pontifical Masses of Our Lady (with white vestments) and of the Holy Spirit (with colored ones) have been said (the lights of the catafalque are meanwhile lighted), His Majesty comes down in the manner of the day before, and the Requiem Mass with black vestments begins. His Majesty comes out from the *cortina* and goes to [participate in] the offertory. The chief majordomo (or, in his absence, the majordomo of the week) puts the cushion [for the king] on a cloth that the keeper of tapestries and carpets spreads from the *cortina* to the altar. The ambassadors, grandees, and majordomos accompany him [the king] from the *cortina* to the altar by way of the steps, the senior majordomo taking precedence over the last ambassador. The almoner and head chaplain gives His Majesty a yellow candle with a gold coin, and His Majesty offers it to the prelate, giving it to one of the deacons, who puts it on a tray.[41] He returns to the *cortina*. But if the almoner has not been consecrated, he gives it

[the yellow candle with the gold coin] to the grandee whom His Majesty indicates, from whose hand His Majesty takes it.[42]

Upon the conclusion of the Mass, the chief almoner gives a yellow candle to His Majesty; the master of ceremonies [gives yellow candles] to the chaplains and the preachers who are on the bench; and the chandler [gives them] to the ambassadors, grandees, and majordomos.

The bishops who are in the catafalque say the Responsories, and then the prelate who said the Requiem Mass [says a Responsory], and if he is a cardinal, he has a seat in the catafalque between the two bishops who are on the nave side of the church.

When the [last] Responsory is finished, the prelate returns to divest himself at the altar, and His Majesty [returns] to his quarters accompanied in the manner that he came down [into the church].

The banners, ceremonial pieces, and other spoils [from the decorations] belong to the kings-at-arms.

The ceremonial pieces (*piezas de honor*) to be given to the kings-at-arms at the conclusion of the exequies traditionally consisted of some of the coats of arms and other symbolic objects from the catafalque. By the time the *etiquetas* of 1647–1651 were compiled, however, it had become customary to pay each king-at-arms a cash sum instead.[43]

The etiquette concludes with a key to a plan showing how San Jerónimo was to be arranged for royal exequies. Most of the surviving *etiquetas* manuscripts lack

40. As will be seen, the *etiquetas* do not provide a detailed account of the liturgy. For example, they do not indicate that on such occasions, some of the king's pages took the role of torchbearers who entered the sanctuary during the first two Masses of the exequies proper at the Gospel and at the consecration and elevation of the Host, and during the Requiem Mass at the five Absolutions—see *Pompa Fvneral Honras*, fols. 51–51[v], and *Relaciones breves*, 79–80. The most detailed account of the order of worship for royal exequies in this period is found in Díaz de Ylarraza, *Relacion diaria*, n.p. The author was a master of ceremonies in the Royal Chapel.

41. Some manuscripts give *bufete* (table) for *fuente* (tray).

42. Some manuscripts insert the precedent for this: "In the honors for the lord King D. Philip II, D. Alvaro Carbajal, the chief almoner, gave the candle with a *doblón de a cuatro* in it to the Admiral [of Castile], from whose hand the King D. Philip III took it."

43. The concerns of a sixteenth-century king-at-arms for maintaining his perquisites are well documented in España, untitled book of ceremonies, passim.

such plans, but at least one, drawn by Juan Gómez de Mora, has survived (fig. 2).[44] It is based upon an engraved plan that illustrates the official chronicle of the royal exequies for Isabella of Bourbon, which took place three years before the *etiquetas* review of 1647–1651 began.[45] In the etiquette text that follows, the letters signifying the corresponding items in the legend to Gómez de Mora's plan are inserted in brackets at the end of each numbered entry:

Plan of the Church of San Jerónimo in Madrid for Honors for Kings, Queens, and Princes

1. Tribune for His Majesty when he is in retirement, and opposite the *infantas* and the ladies, in the tribunes on the sides of the *capilla mayor*. [A]
2. *Cortina* for the prince, if there is one. [B]
3. Chair for the prelate who performs the office. [C]
4. Chaplains in vestments. [D]
5. Bench for the prelates. [E]
6. The pulpit. [F]
7. Stool [*silla rasa*] for the chief majordomo. [G]
8. Bench for the grandees. [H]
9. Bench for the ambassadors. [Y]
10. Bench for the king's private chaplains. [K]
11. Place for the majordomos. [L]
12. Royal Council. [M]
13. Council of Aragon. [N]
14. Council of the Inquisition. [O]
15. Council of Italy. [P]
16. Council of Flanders. [Q]
17. Council of the Indies. [R]
18. Council of the Orders. [S]
19. Council of Finance. [T]

20. Council of the Cruzada. [V]
21. Place for the gentlemen who accompany the prince. [X]
22. Chapel through which His Highness enters. [Z]
23. Catafalque. [+]
24. Place for the choir. [AA]
25. Barriers four *pies* [1.12 meters] in height. [BB]
26. Candlesticks around the catafalque. [CC]
27. Chapels where the ladies customarily are. [DD]
28. Entrance to the church. [EE]
29. Cloister where they customarily say Masses. [FF]
30. Two justices of the court and the others of the council. [HH]
31. Antesacristy. [YY]

Item 29 draws attention to aspects of the royal exequies that the *etiquetas* do not describe.[46] The commemorative activities at San Jerónimo were not confined to the monastery church, but extended into the adjacent cloister, where both clergy and laity contributed to the observances. On the morning of the exequies proper, while the Masses of the Virgin and of the Holy Spirit were celebrated in the church, delegations of forty religious from the cathedral chapter and from each of the monastic establishments of Madrid celebrated additional Sung Masses and Low Masses for the soul of the deceased at temporary altars that had been erected in the cloister.[47] The number of altars varied from one occasion to the next. After each delegation had com-

44. APM, SH, Etiquetas, caja 51; first cited in Carmen Sáenz de Miera Santos, "Túmulos madrileños del siglo XVII," 38. See also Tovar Martín, "Juan Gómez de Mora," 16–17 and 147.
45. *Pompa Fvneral Honras*, between fols. 20ᵛ and 21.

46. The following remarks draw on ibid., fols. 37ᵛ–38; Gómez de Mora, "Aparato," fols. 14ᵛ and 17–17ᵛ; "Epitome," fols. 268ᵛ–69; and *Relaciones breves*, 77.
47. A document in APM, SH, Hf, caja 76, Isabel de Borbón (1644), indicates that twenty-three delegations, each of forty religious, celebrated such Masses at the royal exequies for Isabella of Bourbon.

pleted its Masses, one of its members entered the church to perform a responsory at the catafalque. There he found a priest from the Royal Chapel tending a basin of holy water and an aspergillum for his use in the rite.

Furthermore, court literati hung their own tributes to the deceased on the walls of the cloister in the spaces between the temporary altars. At the royal exequies for Isabella of Bourbon the four walls were filled with "Poems, Hieroglyphs, Emblems, Symbols, Dirges, Elegies, and Epitaphs; of which a large number were seen in Latin, Greek, Italian, French, Portuguese, and Castilian. [They were] on papers, shields, and pictures—printed works and manuscripts, in illumination and in painting. There were heroic, lyric, and elegiac works of the highest elegance, erudition, and subtle wit [agudeza]."[48] Such private tributes were kept in the cloister out of custom and out of concern that they might otherwise detract from the greater majesty of the decorative ensemble that the regime had erected in the church. Guards stood on duty there during the royal exequies, but unlike their counterparts who controlled access to the church, their presence was purely ceremonial. At Baltasar Carlos's royal exequies they "only served there for royal os-

tentation" and did not prohibit anyone from entering.[49]

Two other passages in the 1647–1651 etiquetas prescribe how the court was to stage royal exequies for other members of the royal family and for the parents of the queens of Spain (see Appendix A). The comparative brevity of these texts and the simpler observances that they describe underscore the greater importance that the court attributed to the royal exequies for kings, queens, and príncipes jurados of Spain. Because the most frequent sites for the lesser royal exequies were the church of the convent of the Descalzas Reales and the Royal Chapel of the Alcázar, neither of which was as large as San Jerónimo, the decorations for these funerary honors were necessarily more modest as well.[50] In this, too, the etiquetas reveal the court's obsession for observing a strict sense of hierarchy in the social order.

48. *Pompa Fvneral Honras*, fol. 38.

49. "Epitome," fol. 269.
50. Detailed accounts of the decorations for such events in both the sixteenth and seventeenth centuries are rare. See, however, Francisco de Benavides, *Aparato, y Pompa Fvnebre a las devidas Honras en la Muerte de la Cesarea Magestad la Señora Emperatriz Doña Margarita de Austria Infanta de España . . .*; España, untitled book of ceremonies, passim [cited extensively in Valgoma y Díaz Varela, "Honras fúnebres regias," 367–91 passim]; and "Tratado de las ceremonias," 1:fols. 117–21*v*.

2
ENDS AND MEANS

The etiquette governing royal exequies devotes far more attention to the seating arrangements in San Jerónimo than to its decoration. At no point is this imbalance more striking than in the abbreviated description of the necessary characteristics of the catafalque. Royal catafalques were essentially small, elaborate buildings that required teams of artists and craftsmen for their construction. Nevertheless, the *etiquetas* say little more than that a catafalque is to be carried on steps and columns, that it is to contain seats for the clerics who give the Absolutions, and that it is to be adorned with arms, trophies, and candles. Only the *tumba*, the symbolic representation of the deceased, is described in any detail, and that betrays a concern for the eminence of the deceased, rather than an interest in architectural design. In like fashion, the etiquette describes the other decorations tersely, if at all. One would never know from the text that it had become customary to decorate the entrance to San Jerónimo as well as its interior.

The goals that the designers of the decorations sought to achieve can be inferred from contemporary accounts of their works. Their fundamental concern was to produce ensembles that displayed *majestad* and *grandeza*—majesty and greatness. As visual expressions of the splendor of the royal family—both the deceased and his survivors—the decorations were intended to inspire awe. The simplest way to accomplish this was to overwhelm the spectators with the towering bulk of the catafalque and the profusion of adornments on its fabric. Indeed, the capacity of San Jerónimo to house a large catafalque was one reason that it became the usual setting for royal exequies.

Of course, size alone did not guarantee majesty and greatness, which depended as much upon tasteful design and skillful craftsmanship. The court expected the decorations for royal exequies to accord with the gravity of the occasion and to display refinement as well as richness. The catafalque was usually designed by the king's chief architect, who presumably had attained his position by being the best talent available to the court. The praise that the official account of the royal exequies for Isabella of Bourbon lavishes upon the decorations that Juan Gómez de Mora created on that occasion (figs. 4 and 5) reveals many of the desired traits. The finished works featured "such ostentation, propriety, orderliness [*aseo*], richness, and gravity"; the church interior displayed "richness in its ornament, majesty in its disposition, sadness in the general, and rarity [*curiosidad*] and orderliness in the particular"; the ensemble "was altogether majestic, sad, grave, and doleful"; and the centerpiece of it all was "the most ostentatious, splendid, and well constructed Catafalque that art knew how to design and talent to adorn."[1]

1. *Pompa Fvneral Honras*, fols. 17^v, 20–20^v, and 22.

27

Table 2
THE TIMING OF ROYAL EXEQUIES

Name	Death	Royal Exequies	Interval
Margarita of Austria	October 3	November 17–18	45 days
Philip III	March 31	May 3–4	33 days
Isabella of Bourbon	October 6	November 17–18	42 days
Baltasar Carlos	October 9	November 12–13	34 days
Philip IV	September 17	October 30–31	43 days

This artful display was achieved in no small part by means of skillful illusionism. Catafalques were made of wood, but they were painted, gilded, and silvered to simulate colored marbles and precious metals. It was an adept compromise between ostentation and efficiency. The time-consuming effort required to build a catafalque from stone and metal was not justified for a temporary monument that was to be dismantled as soon as the exequies were completed. Furthermore, constructing it from wood and then painting it facilitated the swift completion of the work. Speed of execution was an overriding concern because after a Habsburg died, his survivors sought to celebrate his funerary honors promptly. An interval of about five or six weeks between a death and the subsequent royal exequies was typical (see Table 2).

Another advantage to building a catafalque from wood and painting it to resemble stone and metal was that doing so cost less. However desirable majesty and greatness might have been, the court had to pay for them, and staging royal exequies was expensive. In 1644, for example, the government originally budgeted 176,000 reales to pay for the decorations for the royal exequies for Isabella of Bourbon, but the known costs exceeded that figure by about 30 percent.[2] That could not have been welcome news

to the king's ministers because Spain was fighting wars on several fronts, and the cost of defending the Monarchy was propelling the regime toward bankruptcy. In fact, just two years later the court's growing financial difficulties constrained the celebration of royal exequies for Baltasar Carlos.[3] When Gómez de Mora submitted a proposed design for a catafalque in the prince's honor, the Count of Montalbán (who, in his capacity as the king's senior majordomo, was one of the officials in charge of the exequies) objected to it. The design has not survived, but if it was like his catafalque for Isabella of Bourbon's royal exequies two years earlier, it would have been several stories tall. Montalbán wanted Gómez de Mora to create a simpler, two-story monument based upon an example in a book of designs, and to that end, he sent the book to the architect. The superintendent of the royal works, the Marquis of Malpica, concurred in Montalbán's judgment and reported to the king that the simpler design would be easier to construct, could be ready by the day that the king wanted, and would cost less than any other design to build. In reply, Philip explicitly stated that he wanted the catafalque "to be of the most moderate cost possible" so long as it was appropriate to the dignity of the deceased and could be ready on time.

2. See Chapter 4.

3. See APM, SH, Hf, caja 76, Baltasar Carlos (1646), for documentation of the remarks that follow.

THE CREATION OF DECORATIONS

With those restrictions, he left the selection of the design to the marquis. As it was built, the catafalque comprised two columniated stories surmounted by a dome.[4]

Beyond achieving the speedy construction of affordable decorations infused with majesty and greatness, the architects who designed royal exequies were concerned with the programmatic content of their ensembles. It was not enough that decorations impress spectators by virtue of their scale, richness, and harmony of design. They also had to proclaim the virtues and qualities of the deceased, and to declare the values and beliefs that the royal family sought to promote. To that end, the architects conceived the decorations with their symbolic meaning as much in mind as their surface appearance. Describing the ensemble that he had created for the royal exequies for Philip III, Gómez de Mora related that Philip IV had ordered him to raise "a catafalque that would reflect in part the piety and the merits of the deceased."[5] To meet that requirement, he had the artists working under his direction create eight sculptures and eight paintings of over-lifesized figures personifying the late king's virtues with which to adorn the catafalque (among other decorations).[6] Written statements that explicitly declare the meaning of such ensembles are rare, but the programs that informed them can be deduced from contemporary descriptions and from illustrations of the works.

To make their statements, the designers drew upon a body of familiar architectural types and symbolic devices that grew more sophisticated with the experience of successive royal exequies. This repertory of images constituted the vocabulary with which they wrote their panegyrics to Habsburg glory.

A catafalque was the centerpiece of an exequies ensemble. The exact circumstances that led to the emergence of Renaissance catafalques in the sixteenth century as a type of funerary monument distinct from the late medieval *capella ardente* and *castrum doloris* are still being debated. Although the importance of Italian contributions to the development of early catafalques has often been emphasized, the most recent review of the evidence argues that the first catafalques appeared in southern Spain in the 1530s and 1540s.[7] Whatever the outcome of this debate, it seems clear that it was the death of a Habsburg that popularized the use of such structures across Europe. When Charles I died in 1558, his former dominions, foreign courts, and Spanish institutions in foreign lands celebrated exequies in his memory. A few of these observances—the royal exequies staged by Philip II in Brussels and other exequies held in Bologna, Piacenza, and Rome—were watershed events at which catafalques figured prominently. The impact of these monuments was considerable, and the admiration that they aroused led to the widespread adoption of catafalques for the funerary rites of heads of state and other notables.[8] The Spanish

4. The catafalque is described in "Epitome," fols. 265^v–67.

5. Gómez de Mora, "Aparato," fols. 5^v–6.

6. Ibid., fols. 8–9 and 10^v–11^v; and Almansa y Mendoza, *Cartas*, 22. The sculptures represented Glory, Fame, Faith, Prudence, Continence, Gentleness, Liberality, and Religion; the paintings represented Peace, Benignity, Truth, Piety, Justice, Victory, Clemency, and Honor.

7. Vicens y Hualde, "Arquitectura efímera barroca," 1:43–62.

8. See ibid., 1:62–78; Jaynie Anderson, "'Le roi ne meurt jamais': Charles V's Obsequies in Italy"; Olga Berendsen, "The Italian Sixteenth and Seventeenth Century Catafalques," esp. 1–28; and

Habsburgs were as committed to their use as any regime, and their example was emulated by institutions throughout the Monarchy.[9]

Of the manifold associations that a catafalque could evoke, the most fundamental was its resemblance to a baldachin, the honorific canopy over the seat occupied by a royal or imperial personage at a public occasion.[10] In essence, the catafalque was a baldachin sheltering the *tumba* that symbolized the deceased. Its other functions—as a seating area for the clerics who led the responsories, and an armature for paintings, sculptures, banners, and thousands of candles—were secondary to its role as a canopy. One feature of the seventeenth-century catafalques confirms this reading: The ceiling directly above a *tumba* was decorated with a painting. To the sophisticated observer, these ceilings called to mind the embroidered patterns that often adorned the dossals of more conventional, fabric canopies. That is how the financial records for Isabella of Bourbon's royal exequies describe the painting in her catafalque (fig. 6): "the ceiling that is to serve as the dossal in the upper part of the vault of the catafalque."[11] The emphasis that

the *etiquetas* of 1647–1651 put upon the presence of the *tumba* within the catafalque, rather than upon the design of the catafalque itself, implicitly attests to the subordinate role of the catafalque as a housing for the *tumba*. It was a colossal canopy, to be sure, but a canopy nonetheless.

The resemblance of catafalques to baldachins by no means exhausted the symbolic associations that the monuments evoked as architectural types. Because they were designed in the vocabulary of classical architecture, catafalques also called to mind the traditions of antique structures with funerary associations. Implicit in the Spanish court's erection of catafalques and celebration of royal exequies was its belief that doing so emulated the honors with which ancient civilizations—Christian and pagan—had paid tribute to their dead. This was a legacy of Charles I. In his capacity as the Holy Roman Emperor Charles V, he had revived ceremonies and practices of the ancient Roman emperors as a means to demonstrate his standing as the worthy successor to the illustrious caesars of antiquity. In the sphere of artistic patronage this had led him to commission permanent and ephemeral works of art *all' antica* that glorified him and his house.[12] His innovations were a master stroke of political propaganda, and other royal houses of Europe soon followed suit. By the time that Philip IV ascended the throne, the desirability of emulating an-

Eve Borsook, "Art and Politics at the Medici Court I: The Funeral of Cosimo I de Medici."

9. Vicens y Hualde, "Arquitectura efímera barroca," vols. 2–3, catalogues Spanish seventeenth-century catafalques. Dávila Fernández, *Los sermones y el arte*, 93–285 passim, quotes contemporary descriptions of Spanish catafalques erected from the mid-sixteenth through the eighteenth centuries. In addition, the Spanish catafalques of the Habsburg era are the subject of a forthcoming doctoral dissertation by A. Stephen Arbury. For an overview of catafalques erected in seventeenth-century Madrid, see also Tovar Martín, *Arquitectura madrileña*, 431–38.

10. Berendsen, "Catafalques," 73–75.

11. APM, SH, Hf, caja 76, Isabel de Borbón (1644).

12. For Charles and the imperial theme, see Jean Jacquot, ed., *Les Fêtes de la Renaissance, II. Fêtes et cérémonies au temps de Charles Quint*; Roy Strong, *Art and Power: Renaissance Festivals 1450–1650*, 75–97; Hugh Trevor-Roper, *Princes and Artists: Patronage and Ideology at Four Habsburg Courts 1517–1633*, 11–45; and Frances A. Yates, *Astraea: The Imperial Theme in the Sixteenth Century*, 1–28.

tique precedents in royal ceremonies was considered indisputable.

This conviction often manifested itself in books that were published throughout the Monarchy as documentary records of particular exequies. The more ambitious authors of such texts discoursed on the history of funeral practices and commemorative rites as a prelude to describing the particular exequies that were their nominal subjects. These writers ransacked the classics of Greco-Roman antiquity, the Bible, and the writings of the Church Fathers in search of pagan and Christian precedents with which to justify modern practice. A passage on the nature of funerary honors from the official account of Philip IV's royal exequies typifies the approach:

This reverent solemnity is composed of Pyres, of Lights, of Cults, and of praises. This was the mode of celebrating the memories of the Deceased [that is recorded] in profane and Divine letters, whence, by the one as by the other, this custom is made illustrious and pious. Among the Ancients this practice was not only an act of piety, but an obligation—thus [it was] among the Lycians, Macedonians, Carthaginians, Greeks, Egyptians, Lacedaemonians, Thracians, Massilians, and Romans. And among the Faithful are found so many testimonies, like the notices that the writings of the Saints give us. Pontius the Deacon relates the honors that were paid to Saint Cyprian, Bishop of Carthage, by his family. Aurelius Prudentius makes mention of the solemnity with which exequies were performed for the dead in his time (being a very ancient Writer). Saint Gregory of Nyssa relates those of Meletius, and [Saint Gregory] of Nazianzus, those of his brother Caesarius and those of Constantius; Eusebius of Caeserea, those of the Emperor Constantine; Saint Jerome, those of the Roman Matrons Paula and Sapia [sic]; and Saint Augustine wrote an entire book on

the obligation that one has to celebrate this memorial.[13]

This attitude informed the design of exequies decorations. The same author felt compelled to explain the presence of an epitaph on Philip IV's catafalque, even though it was obvious for whom the monument had been raised, by invoking antique precedent: "On the front of the *Tumba*, which faced toward the nave of the Church, there was a Latin epitaph, for although there were many such things in this solemnity that declared the person for whom it was made, the want of an Inscription that stated his virtues would be a remarkable deficiency according to the ceremony of the ancients."[14]

The desire to legitimize royal exequies by relating them to ancient practices accounts in part for the recurrent use of centralized plans in the catafalques built by the Spanish court. Such plans recalled the designs of early Christian martyriums and mausoleums, two building types with funerary connotations.[15] What is more, the simple geometric shapes on which such plans were based—circles, squares, and octagons—were charged with symbolic associations that lent themselves to royal exequies. Circles, which were endless, could signify eternity, and octagons gained significance from a venerable tradition that associated the number eight with resurrection.[16] Allusions to eternity

13. Rodríguez de Monforte, *Descripcion*, fols. 51–51*v*. "Sapia" may be a corruption of "Fabiola;" see Jerome, *Epistles* 77.

14. Rodríguez de Monforte, *Descripcion*, fol. 69*v*.

15. Berendsen, "Catafalques," 18–22 and 100–104; see also Vicens y Hualde, "Arquitectura efímera barroca," 1:110–17, for a consideration of catafalques as expressions of the Christian tradition of the *mons sanctus*.

16. Richard Krautheimer, "Introduction to an

and resurrection were perfectly in keeping with observances that celebrated the Christian salvation of a Habsburg soul. However, centralized plans also had practical advantages: A square or octagonal ground story easily accommodated the seats in four corners around the *tumba* for the four bishops who gave the first four Absolutions at the exequies proper.

The thousands of candles mounted on royal catafalques likewise evoked an antique precedent. To be sure, the Renaissance catafalque was derived in part from the late medieval *capella ardente* (literally, "burning chapel")—an arrangement in which a deceased personage (or a representation of him) lay in state in a chapel where banks of candles mounted on a scaffolding burned in his memory. Unlike the medieval scaffolding, however, the catafalque was designed in the classical vocabulary, bringing to mind another structure, the funeral pyre of a Roman emperor.[17] In imperial practice the lighting of such a pyre followed by the release of an eagle signified the apotheosis of an emperor to immortality. To an audience that regarded a catafalque as a successor to a Roman pyre, the allusion to imperial apotheosis suggested a Christian analogy, the eternal salvation of the soul of the deceased. For a seventeenth-century conception of what such a pyre looked like, we can refer to Domenichino's painting of the *Exequies of a Roman Emperor* (fig. 7), which was commissioned from him and shipped to Madrid in the 1630s for the decoration of the Buen Retiro. It depicts an emperor's funeral pyre as a tall,

multistoried structure built to a centralized plan—a description that applies as well to the catafalques for royal exequies (compare fig. 5).[18]

The number of candles that could be incorporated in a catafalque was an important consideration in its design. At the royal exequies for Philip III and Isabella of Bourbon, some 3,400 candles adorned each catafalque.[19] As a practical matter, their glow made it possible to see the other decorations.[20] Symbolically, the profusion of candles signified the merits of the deceased and the esteem in which he was held. The resulting desire to maximize the number of candles accounts for the use of freestanding *agujas* around the four corners of royal catafalques, a practice evidently begun in 1611 when Gómez de Mora set four *agujas* about the catafalque he had designed for the royal exequies for Margarita of Austria.[21] In a typical *aguja* a tall central shaft was planted in a pedestal and crowned by a single, large candle. Mounted on the shaft were tiers of candle-pans that diminished in width the higher they were placed, like the branches of a tree. By referring to *agujas*, albeit incorrectly, as a *capella ardente*, the 1647–1651 etiquette tacitly acknowledges their derivation from the scaffoldings of the medieval "burning chapels."

Supplying the candles was a major undertaking for the royal chandler. Depending upon the requirements of the archi-

'Iconography of Mediaeval Architecture,'" 9–11 and 29.

17. See Anderson, "'Le roi ne meurt jamais,'" 390–92; Berendsen, "Catafalques," 10–18, 139, and 156–57; and Vicens y Hualde, "Arquitectura efímera barroca," 1:99–110.

18. For this picture, see Brown and Elliott, *Buen Retiro*, 123; and Richard E. Spear, *Domenichino*, 1:303–6, no. 112.

19. Gómez de Mora, "Aparato," fol. 16^v; and *Pompa Fvneral Honras*, fol. 36^v.

20. As noted in *Pompa Fvneral Honras*, fol. 35^v.

21. The catafalque at the royal exequies for Philip II in 1598 lacked such a feature; see APM, SH, Hf, caja 76, Felipe II y Margarita de Austria (1598), for a document comparing the decorations for the two events.

THE CREATION OF DECORATIONS

tect who designed the catafalque, several kinds of candles were needed. The financial accounts for royal exequies distinguish among *velas* (ordinary candles); *cirios* (round tapers that were longer and thicker than *velas*); *hachas* (each consisting of four long *velas* joined together and covered with wax to form a straight, giant, four-wicked candle); *antorchas* (each consisting of three or four *velas* joined together like an *hacha*, but twisted rather than straight); and *ambleos* (short, thick candles). Custom dictated that candles for funerary rites be made from yellow wax, but in practice candles with shells of yellow wax coating cores of white were often used instead. White wax produced more light and less smoke, an advantage in churches with little fenestration.[22]

This last is not to say that smoke from candles was not a problem, for it was. What is more, the proximity of so many candles to the wooden fabric of a catafalque constituted a serious fire hazard. As a result, staging royal exequies entailed special precautions. For the royal exequies for Isabella of Bourbon some window panes at San Jerónimo were temporarily removed to allow smoke to escape, and men with water and firefighting gear were concealed within the catafalque while its candles burned.[23]

The repertory of painted, sculpted, and woven adornments at the disposal of architects who designed catafalques was considerable, and it was through their use that the subtleties of programmatic

meanings were conveyed to the audience. Such decorations could also be mounted independently from the catafalque on the interior and exterior walls of the church. Deciding what kinds of embellishments to use, how many to employ, and where to put them was part of the challenge that royal exequies posed to their designers.

Coats of arms were the most familiar of the symbolic devices that appeared at royal exequies. They were often featured amid displays of ephemeral art at the Spanish court because they asserted the greatness of the Habsburgs by signifying their identities, their illustrious lineage, their institutional authority, and the global extent of their dominions.[24] The royal exequies featured the coats of arms of individuals, royal councils, and the realms of the Monarchy. The individual arms to be seen were the full royal arms, which were identified with the king, and, at royal exequies for queens and *príncipes jurados*, the personal arms of the deceased. In addition, the four kings-at-arms often wore the arms of the four grandparents of the deceased, which demonstrated his distinguished ancestry as another sign of his greatness. As has been noted, the arms of the royal councils marked their respective benches in the nave. At least two decorative ensembles for royal exequies—those of Baltasar Carlos and Philip IV—featured a series of escutcheons representing the principal realms of the Monarchy.[25] In each case,

22. *Pompa Fvneral Honras*, fols. 36ᵛ–37.

23. Ibid., fol. 37; AGS, CM3, leg. 756, Extraordinario, fol. 15bis, no. 52; and APM, SH, Hf, caja 76, Isabel de Borbón (1644). Payments for glazing and leadsmith's work at San Jerónimo for the royal exequies for Philip III may also refer to the removal of windows to allow smoke to escape; see APM, SH, Libro de pagos, fol. 141bisᵛ.

24. Orso, *Alcázar of Madrid*, 124. España, untitled ceremonies book, fol. 82, lists quantities of coats of arms that were required for parts of the catafalque and church in the sixteenth century; however, it is not certain that all his prescriptions applied in the seventeenth century, when exequies decorations became more profuse.

25. For Baltasar Carlos's exequies, see "Epitome," fols. 273ᵛ–90ᵛ; and for Philip IV's exequies, see below, Chapter 6.

their sequence was keyed to the recitation of titles that began the text of each of Philip's royal decrees: "Don Philip by the grace of God King of Castile, of León, of Aragon, of the two Sicilies, of Jerusalem, of Portugal, of Navarre, of Granada, of Toledo, of Valencia, of Galicia, of Mallorca, of Seville, of Sardinia, of Córdoba, of Corsica, of Murcia, of Jaén, of the Algarves, of Algeciras, of Gibraltar, of the Canary Islands, of the East and West Indies, and of Tierra Firme of the Ocean Sea; Archduke of Austria; Duke of Burgundy, of Brabant, and of Milan; Count of Habsburg, of Flanders, of Tirol, and of Barcelona; Lord of Vizcaya and of Molina; etc."

The etiquette of 1647–1651 makes a passing reference to adorning the catafalque with trophies. In fact, the display of trophies at the royal exequies for Habsburg kings and *príncipes jurados* was not an option left casually to an architect's whim; rather, it conformed to a well-defined, traditional practice.[26] Three trophies were erected in stands on the nave side of the catafalque along the longitudinal axis of the church. The trophy closest to the catafalque featured four taffeta flags suspended from lances—from left to right, as viewed from the nave, a gonfalon (*guión*), a square banner of the

full royal arms (*bandera cuadrada de plenas armas*), a pennon (*pendón*), and a great standard (*gran estandarte*). All four were painted with the full royal coat of arms. The second trophy comprised three lances on which three taffeta flags were mounted—from left to right, a gonfalon, a great standard, and a cornet (*corneta*). Each was one of the three colors of the deceased. The third trophy, farthest from the catafalque, consisted of two sculptures supported on two shorter lances. To the left one lance carried an open helmet guarded by seven semicircular bars (*estrilli*) with lambrequins of gold, silver, and ermine. Its crest was a golden castle with blue doors and windows, from the top of which emerged a purple lion rampant with a naked sword in its paw. The castle and lion were the heraldic devices of Castile and León, and the fierce aspect of the armed beast surely alluded to Spanish royal might. To the right, the other shaft carried a three-dimensional shield bearing the full royal arms on both faces, complete with a surmounting royal crown and a surrounding collar of the Order of the Golden Fleece.[27]

In addition to these trophies, four more flags known as the "banners of the four quarters" (*banderas de los cuatro cuartos*) were mounted on the four corners of the catafalques for kings and *príncipes jurados*. Each was decorated with the arms of one of the grandparents of the deceased, and each had its assigned place. Viewing the catafalque from the nave, one saw the arms of the paternal grandfather at the front right corner; those of the paternal grandmother at the rear

26. España, untitled ceremonies book, fols. 81–83, provides a detailed description of the catafalque trophies and how they were to be arranged. His remarks are accompanied by illustrations showing the design of the different flags; these are reproduced in Valgoma y Díaz Varela, "Honras fúnebres regias," 366. It should be noted that the later accounts of royal exequies do not always describe the freestanding trophies in the precise arrangement specified by España; it is not clear whether such departures reflect variations in practice or a lack of precision on the part of the later writers. See also "Epitome," fol. 266ᵛ; Gómez de Mora, "Aparato," fols. 12–12ᵛ; López [de Hoyos], *Relacion*, fols. 29–31; "Naçimiento y successos," fol. 45ᵛ; and "Relaçion de lo que paso," n.p.

27. None of these trophies is illustrated in the known views of catafalques for royal exequies, but their presence at Philip III's funerary honors is indicated on Pedro Perret's engraved plan of the event, for which see chap. 1, n. 34.

right; those of the maternal grandfather at the front left; and those of the maternal grandmother at the rear left.

The freestanding trophies facing the nave and the four banners with the arms of the grandparents did not appear on the catafalques for Habsburg queens. The reason for this is easily deduced: Trophies and banners suggested combat, and such martial associations were deemed inappropriate to women. (The same attitude manifested itself in the way the *etiquetas* restricted the sword of justice to the *tumbas* of kings and *príncipes jurados*.) Prior to the royal exequies for Isabella of Bourbon, architects had used ten sculpted angels to incorporate the coats of arms of a deceased queen, her husband, and her four grandparents into the queen's catafalque. Two angels would be suspended from the ceiling over the *tumba*, one bearing the late queen's arms and the other those of her husband. The other eight angels would be mounted in pairs elsewhere on the catafalque, and each pair would display the arms of one of the queen's grandparents. Such was the case at the royal exequies for Isabella of Valois, Anne of Austria, and Margarita of Austria.[28] As Gómez de Mora wrote of the catafalque he designed for the latter's exequies, "Standards and banners are always put on Catafalques of Kings, some with the full Royal arms, others with the arms of individuals. But on Catafalques of Queens, these angels are used in place of banners and standards for the decoration and accompaniment of the Cata-

falque."[29] Although Gómez de Mora refrained from using such angels on his catafalque for Isabella of Bourbon's royal exequies, he did not replace them with trophies and banners.[30]

Regardless of the sex of the deceased, painted and sculpted personifications appeared regularly among the decorations at royal exequies. The most frequently seen was Death in her traditional, skeletal aspect.[31] Although she sometimes took the form of a full-length skeleton, Death appeared more often as a skull or a skull-and-crossbones. These skulls were often crowned, thereby evoking the tradition of *mors imperator*—Death as the empress under whose unyielding sovereignty all must die. Many personifications represented the virtues and qualities that the deceased had displayed while living, as in the case of the sixteen virtues on Philip III's catafalque mentioned above. They were usually accompanied by attributes that facilitated their recognition, and Latin inscriptions often identified them and commented upon their pertinence to the deceased. Personifications also signified the different realms that the deceased had ruled, and these might be accompanied by explanatory inscriptions, by symbolic attributes, or by the arms of the territories in question. Philip III's catafalque, for example, also incorporated sixteen paintings of crowned figures personifying realms of the Monarchy, each identified by an appropriate coat of

---

28. For Isabella of Valois: España, untitled ceremonies book, fol. 88^v; López [de Hoyos], *Hystoria*, fols. 48^v–49; and APM, SH, caja 76, Isabel, muger de Felipe II (1568). For Anne of Austria: España, untitled ceremonies book, fols. 132–32^v. For Margarita of Austria: *Relaciones breves*, 74 and 79; and APM, SH, Hf, caja 76, Felipe II y Margarita de Austria (1598).

29. *Relaciones breves*, 74.

30. I intend to analyze the decorations for Isabella's royal exequies, including this departure from traditional practice in her catafalque, in a future study.

31. Cesare Ripa, *Iconologia, o vero descrittione d'imagini delle Virtv', Vitij, Affetti, Passioni humane, Corpi celesti, Mondo e sue parti*, 362; and Guy de Tervarent, *Attributs et symboles dans l'art profane 1450–1600: dictionnaire d'un language perdu*, cols. 365–66.

arms.[32] Attributes of royal dignity and human mortality might also be on hand independent of personifications—lions signifying royal greatness, the scythe with which Death mowed down the living, or a sandglass measuring the duration of a human life, for example.[33]

By far the most sophisticated decorations to be found at royal exequies were paintings known as "hieroglyphs" (*jeroglíficos*). Their name was a misnomer reflecting a Renaissance misunderstanding of how ancient Egyptian hieroglyphs were meant to be interpreted. This misunderstanding, which had been popularized by such influential books as Piero Valeriano's *Hieroglyphica*, had given rise to the Renaissance enthusiasm for devising emblems, which is what *jeroglíficos* really were.[34] Owing to their presumed origin in antiquity, hieroglyphs contributed to the welter of classical associations that royal exequies were meant to evoke.

As emblems, hieroglyphs were intellectual puzzles that had to be deciphered. A typical hieroglyph (for example, fig. 10) consisted of a symbolic image and two inscriptions—a Latin motto and a Spanish verse. Only by relating the visual and verbal references to one another could a viewer penetrate the meaning of the work as a whole. This piqued the interest of spectators at the exequies by challenging their wits. It is telling that in the official accounts of royal exequies published by the Habsburg court, hieroglyphs are described and illustrated, but not explained. Instead, the intellectual pleasure of the task is left to the reader.

The striking appearance of a catafalque was further enhanced by the contrast of its thousands of candles against the enormous black hangings that lined the church interior. These were not left entirely unadorned, however, for that would have been too plain for the degree of pomp expected for a royal personage. Gold trim accented the broad expanses of fabric, and paintings (hieroglyphs, coats of arms, or skulls-and-crossbones) embellished the fields of black. When these were painted on paper, their light weight facilitated mounting them on the hangings. Candles lining the nave at regular intervals supplemented the glow from the catafalque in the crossing. (Their candlesticks were probably attached to the permanent masonry that stood behind the temporary hangings.) The black expanses of material concealed much of the church from view, but the high altar had to be accessible for celebrating the Masses that

32. Gómez de Mora, "Aparato del tvmulo real," fols. 6–6ᵛ; see also Chapter 3, below.

33. For the scythe and sandglass, see Tervarent, *Attributs*, cols. 165 and 330–31; and for leonine imagery, see below, Chapter 9, Hieroglyph 1.

34. Mario Praz, *Studies in Seventeenth-Century Imagery*, rev. ed., 23–25. For an introduction to Spanish emblematic literature, see Aquilino Sánchez Pérez, *La literatura emblemática española (Siglos XVI y XVII)*; and Giuseppina Ledda, *Contributo allo studio della letteratura emblematica in Spagna (1549–1613)*. Typical of Spanish perceptions of the origins of hieroglyphs are Luis Hurtado, *La Philipica oracion, historico fvneral, en la mverte de la Catolica Magestad del Rey Nuestro Señor D. Phelipe Qvarto . . .*, 55–58; and Pedro de Quiroş, *Parentacion real qve en la mverte de Felipe IV. el Grande . . . Celebro la . . . Civdad de Salamanca*, 328–29. Some writers of the time regarded hieroglyphs as different from emblems—for example, Juan de Vera Tassis y Villarroel, *Noticias historiales de la enfermedad, mverte y exsequias de . . . Doña María Lvisa de Orleans . . .*, 171–80, differentiates hieroglyphs from other symbolic constructions, including emblems, chiefly by virtue of their greater subtlety. Because such distinctions seem to have been honored more in theory than in practice, it will suffice to regard a hieroglyph as a kind of emblem. See Fernando R. de la Flor, "El jeroglífico y su función dentro de la arquitectura efímera barroca . . . ," for a review of this matter with further literature.

THE CREATION OF DECORATIONS

were essential to the exequies. For that reason the altar was left exposed, although a curtain hid its retable for much of the time as a sign of mourning. The altar itself was furnished with an opulent frontal, six candles in gold or silver candlesticks, and a cross. The curtain concealing the retable might be decorated with coats of arms, as specified by the *etiquetas*.

Beginning with the royal exequies for Isabella of Bourbon, the entrance facade of the church where royal exequies were to be celebrated was decorated as well (fig. 4). To those who came to attend the honors, the exterior decorations heralded the ostentatious display they would find within the church. The designers of royal exequies drew upon the same repertory of decorative embellishments for these ensembles as they did for those inside. Sometimes augmenting the existing facade with temporary architecture, they adorned the entrance with imaginative combinations of hangings, hieroglyphs, personifications, coats of arms, and epitaphs.

When an architect planned such decorations for the interior and exterior of a church, he had to compromise between the ideal of royal splendor and the practical restrictions of time and expense, just as he did when designing the fabric of the catafalque. This led him to rely again upon illusionism. Sculptures were made of wood or paste, painted or gilded to resemble more precious materials. Some "statues" in "niches" on catafalques were nothing more than illusionistic paintings. At the royal exequies for Isabella of Bour-

bon and Baltasar Carlos, the coats of arms on the catafalques were painted on nothing more substantial than paper.[35] (On the other hand, the coats of arms that marked the seats for the royal councils at the royal exequies for Baltasar Carlos were painted on wood.[36] Evidently when the decorations were within easy reach of the spectators, durability became a greater concern.) The materials from which hieroglyphs were made were seldom recorded, but records of payments to artists who worked on the royal exequies for Isabella of Bourbon indicate that eight hieroglyphs for the facade of San Jerónimo were painted in tempera on canvas, whereas other hieroglyphs, which were shown inside the church, were painted on paper.[37] (Perhaps those displayed outdoors were made of stronger material in order to withstand the elements.) So long as the decorations had the ostentatious look and the panegyric content to meet the court's demand for pomp and propaganda, the materials from which they were constructed mattered little.

35. APM, SH, Hf, caja 76, Isabel de Borbón (1644); AGS, CM3, leg. 756, Destajos, fol. 8ᵛ, no. 26, and Extraordinario, fols. 23bis–23bisᵛ, no. 77, fols. 29bisᵛ–30, no. 97, and fols. 31bis–32, nos. 103 and 105.

36. AGS, CM3, leg. 756, Extraordinario, fol. 32bisᵛ, no. 108.

37. Ibid., fols. 21bisᵛ–22ᵛ, no. 73; AGS, CM3, leg. 1,461, Destajos, fols. 108–8ᵛ, no. 486, and fols. 115bisᵛ–16, no.519; and APM, SH, Hf, caja 76, Isabel de Borbón (1644). Although *Pompa Fvneral Honras*, fol. 18ᵛ, states that the facade hieroglyphs were painted in oil, that could be either a mistake or an exaggeration to impress the reader.

3
ASSEMBLING THE IDEAS

Designing ostentatious exequies decorations that could be erected within a few weeks required considerable ability, but the official who was most often entrusted to make such arrangements, the superintendent general of the royal works, was not an architect. Instead, he was a nobleman whose talent lay in administration. For that reason, he would assign the job of designing the ensemble to the king's chief architect, whose professional qualifications fitted the task. This practice persisted until 1689, when the court held a competition for the commission to build the catafalque for the royal exequies for Charles II's first wife, María Luisa of Orleans. The Constable of Castile, who had charge of the arrangements, ordered the leading painters and architects of Madrid to submit designs for the monument, and José Benito de Churriguera emerged the winner.[1] Following the death of Charles II in 1700, the king's chief majordomo, the Duke of Medina Sidonia, submitted five possible designs for a catafalque for the king's funerary honors exequies to his widow, Mariana of Neuberg. It is not recorded whether these were the work of one architect or more.[2]

An architect who undertook to design such decorations would not have ignored

past practice at the court. The royal exequies for each Habsburg became a precedent for his descendants' honors, and records of the ensembles erected in the past were readily available to the king's servants. One room in the king's quarters in the Alcázar of Madrid was a library of plans, views, and accounts of royal residences and ceremonies, among them the "designs and their accounts of the Catafalques that were made on different occasions of honors for Kings, Queens, Emperors, and Empresses, of Princes, Infantes, and Archdukes."[3] Under Philip IV the regime began to publish illustrated accounts of royal exequies, and these provided lasting records of the funerary ensembles. In addition, an architect like Gómez de Mora had his own experience to draw upon. Over the course of his career he designed the decorations for the royal exequies for Margarita of Austria, and for both the royal exequies and the town of Madrid's exequies for Philip III, Isabella of Bourbon, and Baltasar Carlos.[4]

Gómez de Mora was Philip IV's chief designer (*trazador mayor*) and master-in-chief of the royal works (*maestro mayor de las obras reales*), offices that attested to his aptitude in both design and construction. Practical experience was important to an architect who planned exequies en-

---

1. Vera Tassis y Villarroel, *Noticias historiales*, 140–41.

2. APM, SH, Hf, caja 76, Carlos II (1700), and Ceremonial para la celebracion de Honras en sufragio de Señores Reyes, Reinas, Príncipes Jurados, y Soberanos y Principes extrangeros, "Noticias que se han podido adquirir para el Reximen de las Ordenes y Disposiciones."

3. Vicente Carducho, *Diálogos de la pintura: su defensa, origen, esencia, definición, modos y diferencias*, ed. Francisco Calvo Serraller, 432; see also Orso, *Alcázar of Madrid*, 21.

4. For an overview of Gómez de Mora's work as an exequies designer, see Tovar Martín, "Juan Gómez de Mora," 85–88.

sembles because he had to oversee the artists and craftsmen who brought his plans to fruition. Evidence of how much guidance Gómez de Mora provided his subordinates is fragmentary, but indications of his role are found in the financial accounts for the royal exequies for Isabella of Bourbon. These records state that the three carpenters who made the catafalque for that event did so "according to the design made by Juan Gómez de Mora, *maestro mayor* of the said [royal] works."[5] In addition, he provided other artisans with studies for decorative motifs on the monument. The painter and gilder Miguel Pueyo, for example, made the ceiling painting over Isabella's *tumba* "according to the design that Juan Gómez de Mora made and gave [him]."[6]

Another such reference is more ambiguous in its implications. The sculptor Antonio de Herrera executed sixteen figures for the catafalque—eight personifications of Spanish realms and eight personifications of the queen's virtues. The accounts repeat the formula that he carried out his work "according to the design that was given to him by Juan Gómez de Mora, *maestro mayor*,"[7] but there is no way to tell whether the "design" was a general view or diagram of the catafalque (thereby leaving it to Herrera to design the figures himself), a sketch of one virtue and one realm to serve as prototypes, or a sheet with studies for all sixteen figures. It is even possible that the "design" Gómez de Mora provided was not by his own hand. When Gómez de Mora had overseen construction of the catafalque for the royal exequies for Philip III, Herrera had carved four pairs of personified

virtues for it. Preparatory drawings for three of the four pairs are known, and they are the work of the painter Eugenio Cajés.[8] The same catafalque had also required sixteen paintings of personifications of Spanish realms, and thirteen studies for them by the painter Vicente Carducho have survived.[9] The presence of corrections and color notes on the studies of the realms suggests that Carducho himself devised each figure. Carducho and Cajés were the preeminent painters at the court in 1621—both held the office of *pintor del rey* (painter to the king)—and it is conceivable that Gómez de Mora would have entrusted the design of the figures to them, subject to his review. Although this does not resolve the question of who drew the "design" that Gómez de Mora provided Herrera in 1644, the precedent raises the possibility that he delegated responsibility for such figures to an assistant or collaborator.

It was another architect, Sebastián de Herrera Barnuevo, who had charge of the decorations for the royal exequies for Philip IV. Among his surviving preparatory drawings for the ensemble is one that features studies for coats of arms with color notes (fig. 70). In addition, studies for two swans and a harp occupy the

5. AGS, CM3, leg. 1,461, Destajos, fols. 108bis–8bis[v], no. 488.

6. Ibid., fol. 117bis[v], no. 528.

7. Ibid., fols. 106bis[v]–7, no. 480.

8. See Diego Angulo [Íñiguez] and Alfonso E. Pérez Sánchez, *A Corpus of Spanish Drawings, II. Madrid 1600–1650*, 24, nos. 84–86. The subjects of the drawings correspond to descriptions of the sculptures in Gómez de Mora, "Aparato del tvmulo real," fols. 8–9.

9. See Angulo [Íñiguez] and Pérez Sánchez, *Spanish Drawings, II*, 42–43, nos. 212–24; and Alfonso E. Pérez Sánchez, *Historia del dibujo en España de la Edad Media a Goya*, 159. The subjects of the drawings correspond to descriptions of the paintings in Gómez de Mora, "Aparato del tvmulo real," fols. 6–6[v], on the basis of which a drawing in New York (Metropolitan Museum of Art, Sperling Bequest, inv. no. 1975.131.210) can be re-identified as representing *Naples* and a drawing in Florence (Uffizi, inv. no. 14,394) as *Sardinia*.

lower right corner of the sheet along with a Spanish verse, and they correspond to the swans, harp, and verse found in a hieroglyph from the king's exequies (fig. 12).[10] This suggests that Herrera Barnuevo provided detailed guidance to the painters who worked under his direction.

Inventing the figurative decorations for royal exequies was no easy task. Designing a personification, for example, entailed more than determining its pose. Its sex, age, costume, and attributes had to conform to allegorical convention so that an educated viewer could recognize what the figure represented. The planners of seventeenth-century royal exequies must have referred to Cesare Ripa's *Iconologia* frequently because personifications on royal catafalques from that period often matched its formulations.[11] Recognizing that a popular handbook like Ripa's was relied upon, however, leaves unanswered the question of who consulted it. It might have been the architect who was responsible for the entire ensemble, a painter or sculptor who was assigned to design the individual figures, or a man of letters brought in to advise the artists. Moreover, personifications often appeared on the catafalques with accompanying Latin inscriptions, many of them taken from the Vulgate. Someone had to assemble such quotations, but who? Devising hieroglyphs required both artistic and literary talents: an ability to design symbolic images, a knowledge of texts that could serve as mottoes, a knack for composing verses, and the capacity to blend the three elements harmoniously.[12]

Some clues to this creative process as it worked in 1665 are found among papers that have survived from the preparations for Philip IV's royal exequies.[13] Among them are two worksheets bearing notes for three of the hieroglyphs (figs. 12, 20, and 42) that were displayed on that occasion. One sheet contains short, written descriptions of their images and the texts of their verses, although the text for one (fig. 12) lacks the first two lines seen in the finished work. Each description and its verse are accompanied by the notation, "It lacks a Latin motto." At the bottom of the sheet is a reminder, "Four mottoes are also lacking from the four virtues Faith, Hope, Charity, and Justice," which refers to four gilded statues that occupied niches in Philip's catafalque. The second worksheet consists of Latin quotations from the Vulgate to accompany the statues and to complete the hieroglyphs. There is one text each for Faith, Hope, and Justice, and a pair (from which to choose?) for Charity. Because the inscriptions that actually accompanied the statues are not recorded, it cannot be confirmed whether these texts

10. Fernando Marías and Agustín Bustamante, "Apuntes arquitectónicos madrileños de hacia 1660," 36–38, first noted this; the drawing is in AHN, Códices 228b, fol. 27[v].

11. I base this assertion on comparisons of the *Iconologia* with descriptions of the personifications on the catafalques at the royal exequies for Margarita of Austria (*Relaciones breves*, 73); Philip III (Gómez de Mora, "Aparato del tvmulo real," fols. 8–9 and 10[v]–11[v]); Isabella of Bourbon (*Pompa Fvneral Honras*, fols. 30–31[v] and 32–35); Baltasar Carlos ("Epitome," fols. 265[v]–66); and Philip IV (Rodríguez de Monforte, *Descripcion*, fol. 66[v]).

12. Even seemingly straightforward decorations like coats of arms required expertise, for someone with a knowledge of heraldry had to ensure that arms were rendered correctly. At the royal exequies for María Luisa of Orleans in 1689, the coats of arms were overseen by Juan de Mendoza, a king-at-arms and a royal historian (*coronista general*)—see Vera Tassis y Villarroel, *Noticias historiales*, 167.

13. APM, SH, Hf, caja 76, Felipe IV (1665), for the worksheets cited in the remarks that follow.

appeared on the catafalque.[14] The list continues with suggested mottoes for the three hieroglyphs, each of which was used, two in slightly abridged form. Together the two worksheets suggest that these decorations may have been invented in a collaborative effort. Whoever found the Latin texts need not have been the same person who selected the virtues to be personified or who conceived the hieroglyphs in the first place.

Two lines written on the back of a worksheet bearing an epitaph for Philip IV also suggest that ideas for the decorations may have been assembled piecemeal:

de lo q alcanço en la vida
a lo q alcanço en la muerte

(from that which he attained in life to that which he attained in death)

This couplet expresses an idea resembling one found in the verse of another hieroglyph from Philip's exequies (fig. 15). Perhaps using the verb *alcanzar* in the couplet was a first thought that was later revised to *dar* in the finished hieroglyph; on the other hand, it might have been the germ of an idea that its author abandoned.

In a similar vein, another worksheet carries this proposal for a hieroglyph: "Paint some pinkish clouds darkened with some black-and-white shadows; a small sun opposite whose rays pierce the clouds; and from a large sun below no more is seen than its last rays as at sunset." For its verse, the following is suggested:

consuelete Aurora Vella
lo que tu fineça siente
aquel ocaso; este Oriente

14. For the figures and their proposed inscriptions, see Chapter 7.

(May the Beautiful Dawn console you [for] what your sensitivity suffers; that one [is] a sunset; this one [is] a Sunrise.)

The description of the image recalls that of another hieroglyph from the king's exequies (fig. 37), but the latter features two suns of equal size and a different verse. Perhaps the worksheet suggestion evolved into the finished hieroglyph, but it is also possible that the idea was rejected because it too closely resembled the hieroglyph that was used.

Among the more revealing papers to have survived is a letter that was sent to one of the officials in charge of the preparations for the king's exequies:

Most Excellent Sir
I have known that the catafalque for the honors of the King our lord (whom God keeps) proceeds in Your Excellency's care and that inscriptions or epitaphs for it are being sought. If the anagram mentioned hereafter is useful, I entreat you to order it put up, first examining whether any letter is used overmuch or is missing. God keep Your Excellency.

Soy Felipe quarto el grande
[I am Philip IV the Great]
Anagram
y Logrè ser quanto pide la Fe
[and I succeeded at being whatever
Faith requests]

The anagram was not used, but the manner in which it was submitted to its unnamed recipient suggests that the search for literary inscriptions was a broad one and that suggestions from interested courtiers were welcome.

Epitaphs, too, seem to have been selected from ideas submitted to the administrators in charge of the exequies. Among the working papers are several sheets of epitaphs, some of which duplicate in full or in part the texts of four of seven epitaphs that were displayed at Philip's exequies. Because some of these texts only partly match the epitaphs that were finally displayed, it would seem that epitaphs were put through more than one draft before they were accepted. Other worksheets bear epitaphs that are unrelated to those that appeared at the king's exequies, which indicates that, as with other decorations, not every proposal was adopted.

4
CONSTRUCTING THE DECORATIONS

Translating the inventions of the king's architect and the court literati into finished decorations required the concerted efforts of a team of artists and craftsmen. Working under the immediate supervision of the architect, a paymaster, and a foreman, they raced to meet the deadline of five or six weeks that had been imposed upon them. As soon as the architect had worked out his designs, the chiefs of the royal chandlery and the office of tapestries and carpets had to be advised how much wax would be required for candles and how much fabric would be needed for hangings to dress the church in mourning.[1] Meanwhile artisans had to be hired to construct the catafalque and the rest of the ensemble. During the preparations for the royal exequies for Philip III, the cloister adjacent to the church of San Jerónimo became an on-site workshop: "Three divisions were made in the first courtyard of San Jerónimo, and dividers [were put] between the columns of the said courtyard so that the sculptor who made the sculpture and worked the figures was accommodated in the one part and the painters and gilders in the other two parts."[2]

As the catafalque rose in place, the government issued advance payments to the craftsmen, whose total compensation usually was not determined until their finished works could be appraised. All this activity left a trail of paper—estimates, contracts, purchase records, memoranda, appraisals, payment authorizations, receipts, and itemized entries in the financial accounts of the royal works—that provides invaluable insights into aspects of royal exequies that go unmentioned in the *etiquetas* and the official chronicles of such events. Without such documentation, little would be known of the costs of decorative ensembles, the materials from which they were made, and the identities of the men who carried them out.[3]

The exceptional documentation on the construction of decorations for the royal exequies for Isabella of Bourbon (figs. 4 and 5) illustrates the extent to which creating such ensembles was a collaborative effort.[4] The Count of Castrillo, who had

---

1. For example, see APM, SH, Hf, caja 76, Felipe III (1621), for a memorandum prepared by Gómez de Mora and Sebastián Hurtado, an overseer in the royal works, listing the candles that would be needed for Philip III's royal exequies.

2. APM, SH, Hf, caja 76, Felipe II y Margarita de Austria (1598) [*sic*].

3. José María de Azcárate: "Datos sobre túmulos de la época de Felipe IV," first drew art historians' attention to the extensive documentation in the Archivo General de Simancas of funerary honors that the court celebrated between 1612 (for Holy Roman Emperor Rudolf II) and 1665 (for Philip IV). The archive is rich in detailed records of payments to the artists and craftsmen who created decorations for these events. Also noteworthy for the Habsburg era is the material preserved in Madrid, Archivo del Palacio Real, Sección Histórica, Honras fúnebres, caja 76.

4. See the following archival sources: (1) APM, SH, Hf, caja 76, Isabel de Borbón (1644). (2) AGS, CM3, leg. 756, Destajos, fols. 1bis–1bis^v, no. 3; fols. 12–12^v, no. 41; fol. 24, no. 82; and fols. 55–55^v, no. 192. (3) AGS, CM3, leg. 756, Extraordinario, fols. 4bis–5bis, nos. 13–15; fols. 14bis^v–18, nos. 50, 52–53, 55, and 60; fols. 21bis–29,

overall charge of the event, was ultimately responsible for the decorations, but the day-to-day responsibility for assembling them lay with three officials of the royal works: the master-in-chief of the works, Juan Gómez de Mora, who as chief designer had planned the decorations; a paymaster (*pagador*), Francisco de Villanueva; and a foreman (*sobrestante*) and procurement officer (*tenedor de materiales*), Francisco de Arce. It is a measure of their feverish rush to complete the decorations on time that the regime paid for their midday meals for the forty days "that they were present all day at the arranging and execution of the work" on the ensemble. (The interval between the queen's death and her funerary honors lasted forty-two days.) Five other employees of the royal works were likewise on hand for forty days—an assistant architect (*aparejador*), a senior officer (*oficial mayor*) of the controller's office (*veeduría y contaduría*), a constable (*alguacil*), a constable's assistant (*ayuda de alguacil*), and an attendant (*peón*). Two other officials—one of unspecified office, the other both a judge (*juez*) of the royal works and a justice (*alcalde*) of the royal household and court—were present long enough to have six midday meals paid for.

This administrative team supervised the artists and craftsmen who built and installed the decorations at San Jerónimo. The royal accounts name three master carpenters and one joiner who erected the catafalque. One sculptor provided its sculptural ornamentation, as well as another figure and temporary architecture for the church entrance. Ten men variously identified as painters and gilders carried out those tasks, from the illusionistic stonework of the catafalque to sixteen hieroglyphs inside the church and eight others on its entrance facade. The latter eight were mounted in frames constructed by a frame-maker especially for the occasion. Two drapery-hangers (*colgadores*) had charge of installing huge expanses of black velvet and baize in the church and the adjacent cloister. (The bolts of fabric were variously rented or purchased for the occasion.) A master of the works (*maestro de obras*) repaired the pavement of the cloister, and a printer produced twenty-nine paper sheets bearing different poetical works in Latin and Spanish that were displayed there on the day of the exequies proper. Eight altars were erected in the cloister for monastic delegations to say Masses for the queen's soul.[5]

The royal chandler saw to the provision of the enormous quantities of wax that were required for the candles: 4,583 *libras* (2,108 kilograms) of white wax and 537 *libras* (247 kilograms) of yellow. A "servant of His Majesty" provided 3,000 tin-plate sockets for mounting candles on the catafalque; it is not recorded whether he was a tinsmith or an intermediary who procured the sockets from one. Another carpenter constructed wooden candlesticks with tin sockets for more candles, and an ironworker provided eight iron candlesticks with points

nos. 72–77, 85–86, and 94; and fols. 31bis–31bis[v], no. 103. (4) AGS, CM3, leg. 1,461, Destajos, fols. 101–18[v], nos. 453, 458, 475, 477–90, 509–10, 512–20, and 524–30. (5) AGS, CM3, leg. 1,461, Compras, fols. 50bis–59, nos. 182–83, 194–95, 207, and 219. (6) AGS, CM3, leg. 1,461, Conventos y Iglesias, fols. 3bis[v]–4, no. 17.

5. A document in APM, SH, Hf, caja 76, Isabel de Borbón (1644), records that the carpenter Jusepe Gutiérrez was owed 136 *reales* for making four of the altars. No payment record has survived for the other four, but the government surely paid for them, too.

for mounting the *hachas* that crowned eight *agujas* that were incorporated in the catafalque. A silversmith had to silver twenty large candlesticks that had been borrowed from the convents of La Encarnación and the Descalzas Reales so that their color would match other candlesticks that had been brought from the royal monastery of San Lorenzo at El Escorial. In anticipation of the smoke that so many candles would produce, a glazier removed the panes from the church windows. He replaced them after the exequies had ended.

Isabella's royal exequies also prompted the construction of the staircase descending from the Palace of the Buen Retiro into a side chapel at San Jerónimo so that Baltasar Carlos could take his place in his *cortina* conveniently.[6] This project entailed the efforts of two masters of the works, a stonecutter, a paving-master, a locksmith, and a master carpenter. Miscellaneous expenses included payments to another stonecutter for removing a stone pulpit from the church, and to assistants to the keeper of the crown jewels for unrecorded tasks. Other minor expenses were incurred for purchasing miscellaneous items; for the services of carters (*chirrioneros*), unskilled laborers (*peones*), and porters (*portilleros*); for providing refreshments that the Count of Castrillo ordered to be distributed; and for other things that were apparently too trivial to record in detail.

Additional expenses were incurred during the performance of the exequies. The corporals of the Spanish and the German Guards received payments to distribute among those of their respective companies who had assisted in controlling the crowds that gathered at San Jerónimo.

6. See Chapter 1.

Eight carpenters were recompensed for dressing in cassocks [*sotanas*] and going into the catafalque during the Vespers of the Dead and the Requiem Mass— that is, when the candles were burning. (These would have been the men with fire-fighting equipment who were concealed within the dome of the catafalque as a precaution. Perhaps they wore cassocks to disguise themselves as priests and thereby avoid alarming the spectators.) The four kings-at-arms collected a payment in accordance with a traditional right that they asserted was due them owing to the presence of the crown on the *tumba*. As the 1647–1651 *etiquetas* declare, the ceremonial pieces from the catafalque became the property of the kings-at-arms, but by custom they were paid 400 *reales* instead so that the objects remained in the king's possession.[7] The court also provided funds for the celebration of Masses in the monastery cloister. In accordance with a memorial submitted by the king's head chaplain, the court made payments to the twenty-three monastic communities that sent delegations to San Jerónimo, and to six youths who assisted at the Masses.

Because no master document has survived that lists every expenditure for Isabella's royal exequies, it is not possible to give a precise figure for their total cost. Table 3 summarizes the expenses that can be determined from the available documents, and they amount to 227,522 *reales*.[8] That exceeds the 176,000 *reales*

7. See APM, SH, Hf, caja 76, Informe sobre instancia de los Reyes de Armas exponiendo tocarles las coronas que se ponen en las tumbas, en ocasion de Exequias Reales (1711).
8. Table 3 is based on a "Relaçion de como se an distribuido los çiento y setenta y seis mil Reales que su magestad, Dios le guarde mando probeher para el Tumulo que se hiço en el combento Real de san geronimo desta Villa de madrid, Para las hon-

that were originally budgeted for the event by 51,522 *reales*, almost 30 percent of the original estimate. Like many another government enterprise, the queen's exequies fell victim to cost overruns.

Furthermore, a few expenses for other events related to the queen's death were paid out of funds designated for her royal exequies. A wood merchant received 525 *reales* for the lumber from which a platform was made for displaying Isabella's body at the lying-in-state in the Great Hall, and a leadsmith received 406 *reales* for making the lead coffin in which her corpse was placed. The queen's glazier collected 40 *reales* for installing a window in the coffin and 1,200 *reales* for making four lanterns for the litter on which the coffin was conveyed to El Escorial. Another 400 *reales* were paid to the Capuchins of the royal monastery of La Paciencia for the offices they performed in honors for the queen that the king ordered to be celebrated at their establishment.

The artists and craftsmen who are named in the financial accounts need not have been the only persons to have made the decorations for the queen's honors; more likely, they are only the persons whom the government paid directly. The three carpenters and the joiner who built the catafalque, for example, may have employed assistants from their respective shops whom they would have paid from the sums they received from the paymaster. Because the officials of the royal works would have had no reason to record such payments, the number of such assistants and what they did remains open to speculation.

Although the government paid directly for some materials that were used at the exequies—the wax for the candles and the paper on which the hieroglyphs were painted, for example—many of the artists and craftsmen were expected to provide their own. They knew their expenses would be taken into account when they were paid for their efforts. When an artist completed a royal commission, the price was usually set by two experts—one named by the regime and the other by the artist—who appraised the finished work. In the intervening time the artist would receive advance payments toward his final compensation that enabled him to purchase his materials, pay his assistants' wages, and cover any other costs that he incurred in the course of his labors.

The sculptor Antonio de Herrera's participation in the preparations for the royal exequies for Philip III and for Isabella of Bourbon is well documented, and his experiences typify the dealings that took place between artists and administrators. On April 3, 1621, three days after Philip III died, Herrera signed an agreement to create sculptures for the catafalque for the king's royal exequies.[9] In it he committed himself to provide "the sculpture and carving that may be ordered of me by the *señor* Juan Gómez de Mora, His Majesty's master-in-chief, for the said catafalque, [to be priced] by appraisal or by agreement with the senior

rras de La Reyna nuestra señora que este en gloria en esta manera" in APM, SH, Hf, caja 76, Isabel de Borbón (1644). This *relación* does not record adjustments for "extras" carried out by the artists and craftsmen beyond the work they had originally agreed to undertake for the exequies. The most notable such adjustment (to be discussed below) brought the sculptor Antonio de Herrera an additional 3,600 *reales*; this payment has been included in Table 3's figures.

9. The following account is based on APM, SH, Hf, caja 76, Felipe III (1621); and APM, SH, Libro de pagos, fols. 133bis*v*, 134*v*, 137bis, and 309bis*v*.

Table 3

INCOMPLETE LIST OF EXPENSES FOR THE ROYAL EXEQUIES FOR ISABELLA OF BOURBON
(1644)

	Cost (reales)
Carpentry for the catafalque	18,608
Joinery for the catafalque	10,900
Sixteen sculpted figures for the catafalque	9,700
Figure of Spain and temporary architecture for the church exterior; figure of Fame for the catafalque	3,600
Frames for the hieroglyphs on the church exterior	324
Painting and gilding (including hieroglyphs)	47,874 and 22 mrs.*
Paper for the hieroglyphs and other works	72
Wax for candles	35,550
3,000 tin plate candle sockets	1,500
Wooden candlesticks with sockets	732
Eight iron candlesticks for hachas	96
Twenty-four baskets for bringing candlesticks from El Escorial	146
Silvering of candlesticks from La Encarnación and the Descalzas Reales	3,500
Removing and replacing window panes in the church	300
Hangings for the church and cloister	72,226
Installing the hangings in the church and cloister	2,200
Repairs to the cloister pavement	100
Printed poetical works for the cloister	352
Construction of the staircase from the Buen Retiro into the church and related works	10,624 and 12 mrs.*
Removal of a stone pulpit from the church	240
Assistants to the keeper of the crown jewels	201
Forty meals for persons from the royal works:	
Master-in-chief, paymaster, and foreman-procurement officer	1,280
Assistant architect	240
Senior officer of the controller's office	160
Constable	200
Constable's assistant	120
Attendant	80
Six meals for two other administrators	192
Payment to the four kings-at-arms	400
Payment to the corporal of the Spanish Guard	140
Payment to the corporal of the German Guard	60
Payment to eight carpenters who were in the catafalque while its candles burned	1,600
Payment to twenty-three monastic communities that sent delegations to celebrate Masses in the cloister	2,600
Payment to six youths who assisted at the Masses in the cloister	60
Miscellany	1,544
TOTAL	227,522 reales

* 1 real = 34 maravedís

officials of the said [royal] works, without abandoning it until [it is] finished for the day that is commanded of me." This contract provided that Herrera would receive an advance payment to begin his work (the sum was not specified), and that he would be paid the balance due upon its completion.

Sometime on or before April 7 a *libranza* (payment authorization) was issued that enabled Herrera to collect an initial advance of 800 *reales*, and subsequent authorizations for identical amounts were issued on April 15 and 24. He must have completed his task before May 3, the day of the vigil, but it was not until May 13 that two sculptors signed the official appraisal of his work. Alonso Carbonel, who represented the king, and Antonio Riera, who represented Herrera, concurred that the eight figures with attributes and four Corinthian capitals that Herrera had made for the catafalque were worth 4,300 *reales*. Eleven days later, in compliance with the appraisal, a *libranza* was issued authorizing the payment of the 1,900 *reales* that were still due the sculptor. However, authorization was one thing and payment another. Apparently the funds to cover the *libranza* were unavailable, for like many an artist in the Habsburg service, Herrera had to wait. Not until July 2, 1625, did Philip IV order that 1,900 *reales* be issued from the treasury of the royal mint in Valladolid to the paymaster Juan Gómez Mangas so that Herrera could be paid.

The formal appraisals of finished works did not always result in immediate agreement because it was in the government's interest for its representative to quote a low price, whereas the artist's representative was inclined to quote a higher figure. Herrera's work in 1621 was the fortunate object of prompt agreement, but some of his work for the royal exequies for Isabella of Bourbon in 1644 met a different fate.[10] Herrera initially agreed to make capitals, festoons, and sixteen figures with attributes for the queen's catafalque. At some point it was determined that he would receive 9,700 *reales* for the work, and he collected the final installment of that sum on November 14, 1644, three days before Isabella's exequies began. By that time Herrera had agreed to carry out additional works for the ensemble: a personification of Fame to surmount the catafalque and a personification of Spain seated atop temporary architecture at the entrance to San Jerónimo. These "extras" (*demasías*) had to be appraised, but the two experts who undertook to do so failed to agree. The court's appraiser, Pedro de la Peña, an assistant architect in the royal works, set their worth at 3,300 *reales*, whereas Herrera's representative, the sculptor Miguel Pereira, appraised them at 5,200 *reales*, a difference of 1,900 *reales*. Herrera, who had used his own money to cover his expenses while making the sculptures, protested the lower valuation as an "affront" and "a great injustice" to the care and punctuality with which he had worked, and the matter had to be submitted to the Count of Castrillo for resolution. In the light of the speed with which Herrera had completed his tasks and the greater costs that he had had to bear as a result of the additions to his original commission, Castrillo ordered that Herrera be paid

10. The following account is based on APM, SH, Hf, caja 76, Isabel de Borbón (1644); AGS, CM3, leg. 1,461, Destajos, fols. 106bis[v]–7, no. 480, fols. 114bis[v]–15, no. 516, and fols. 118–18[v], no. 530; and AGS, CM3, leg. 756, Extraordinario, fols. 17bis[v]–18, no. 60.

3,600 *reales* for the extra works. That was an increase of 300 *reales* over Peña's estimate, but still 1,600 *reales* short of Pereira's. What Herrera thought of the decision is not recorded, but he did not press his case any further. The necessary *libranza* was issued on November 10, and Herrera signed a receipt for the 3,600 *reales* on November 17, the day of the vigil.

5
DENOUEMENT

The decorations for royal exequies, events that acknowledged the transience of earthly life, were themselves ephemeral. After funerary honors were concluded, the ensembles that had been the products of so much effort and expense stood in place for at most a few days so that the general public might see them, albeit in diminished grandeur. Following the royal exequies for Isabella of Bourbon, "The Catafalque remained lit all the rest of the afternoon, so that the infinite crowd that was awaiting this hour could see it; and it entered immediately, admiring the magnificence, praising the beauty, and venerating the gravity of such a Royal and funereal decoration. And because the numerousness of the Court could not be accommodated in so short a time, it [the catafalque] was there for some days without being dismantled, although without lights it lost much of its greatness. As a result, there was no one in Madrid, nor in its vicinity, who did not come to see that marvel."[1] The catafalque was respected, but the decorations that had been mounted in the cloister fell victim to souvenir hunters: "The crowd that was present was such that, it being impossible to avoid it, the greater part of that decoration was lost and usurped."[2]

In due course all the decorations had to come down so that the monks of San Jerónimo could return their church to ordinary use. Sometimes it was discovered that the church had been damaged. After the royal exequies for Philip III, the monastery was paid 360 ducats to repair damage that the weight of the catafalque had inflicted on the church pavement.[3] Following the royal exequies for Baltasar Carlos, the monastery received 3,000 reales "in order to repair what was ill treated by the catafalque."[4] Apparently the pavement had suffered again.

Some decorations would have been preserved as a matter of course. Candlesticks borrowed from royal convents were returned to their owners, any collar of the Golden Fleece from the tumba was returned to the Alcázar of Madrid, and the other tumba instruments (cloth, cushion, and royal insignia) and the vestments for the Requiem Mass were sent back to El Escorial. Hangings with which the church had been draped that had been borrowed or rented were restored to their owners. On the other hand, many of the decorations were not meant to last. Souvenir hunters could have carried off paper hieroglyphs and coats of arms, but such objects were not meant to be preserved—and none has survived. The wood from the catafalque and the wax from candle stumps remained useful, and the right to salvage them sometimes became a matter of contention. By custom the government gave such remnants to the establishment where the royal exequies had been celebrated, but it was a

1. *Pompa Fvneral Honras*, fol. 53.
2. Ibid., fol. 38.

3. Brown and Elliott, *Buen Retiro*, 9.
4. AGS, CM3, leg. 756, Destajos, fols. 7bis–7bis^v, no. 24.

privilege that the religious had to protect.

In 1644, for example, the architect Jusepe de la Torre had contracted to carry out the joinery for the catafalque for Isabella of Bourbon with the understanding that his work would revert to him upon the completion of the exequies. When he went to San Jerónimo to dismantle his work, however, the Hieronymites refused to give him access to the catafalque on the grounds that the king had made a gift of it to them. On November 17, the day of the vigil, the king had instructed the *furriera* (the office of the royal quartermaster) to give the wood from the catafalque to the monks, and the following day he had instructed the royal chandlery to give them the leftover wax. More than a month later the catafalque had been reduced to pieces, many of which had been taken away, and Torre was petitioning the government to reimburse him for more than 2,000 *reales* in losses. The disposition of his case is not known.[5]

Two years later a similar problem arose in the wake of the royal exequies for Baltasar Carlos. The government had contracted with one of the men who made the catafalque (the surviving documents do not name him) either to return the wood to him or to give him 4,000 *reales*. Evidently the regime elected to return the wood, because the king's administrators recommended that the Hieronymites be paid 3,000 *reales* in order to satisfy their traditional claim on it. Philip approved the payment, and, as was customary, the monastery received the leftover wax as well.[6]

After the decorations for funerary honors were dismantled, some ensembles enjoyed a second life of sorts in documentary books that recounted the pomp and solemnity of the observances to a wider audience. Such books conveyed to their readers the same declarations of royal grandeur and purpose that the actual events had expressed to those who had attended. As further demonstrations of royal splendor, the texts and illustrations of these books became increasingly lavish over the course of Philip's reign. In a sense, publishing an official chronicle of the event became the final step in staging royal funerary honors. The commemorative books reduced the sumptuous decorations to illustrations that measured only a few square inches, but they possessed a permanence that the originals had lacked.

Although unillustrated books describing royal funerary rites in Madrid had appeared in the sixteenth century, the practice of publishing illustrated accounts of these events was slow to take hold at the Spanish court. In fact, the first book to illustrate decorations for exequies that had been celebrated in Madrid recorded an event that had been staged by a monastic establishment. The exequies with which the Jesuit College in Madrid honored its patron, the Empress María of Austria, in 1603 are documented in an anonymous book that the college published, the *Libro de las Honras qve hizo el Colegio de la Cõpañia de Iesvs de Madrid, à la M. C. de la Emperatriz doña Maria de Austria, fundadora del dicho Colegio, que se celebraron a 21. de Abril de 1603* (Madrid, 1603). It begins with a general account of the decoration of the college church and a more detailed description of the catafalque that was erected there (fols. 1–11ᵛ). There follows a Latin funerary oration in honor of the

5. See APM, SH, Hf, caja 76, Isabel de Borbón (1644), and Noticias sobre el remanente de cera y madera del túmulo (1644).

6. APM, SH, Hf, caja 76, Baltasar Carlos (1646).

empress that Padre Juan Ludovico de la Cerda delivered after the office of the vespers had been performed (fols. 12–20^v), as well as the sermon that Padre Jerónimo de Florencia preached at the exequies proper (fols. 21–42^v). The remainder of the book consists of the "Hieroglyphs, and various Hebrew, Greek, Latin, and Spanish poetical works" that were displayed for the occasion (fols. 37–138^v). Of particular interest in this last section are thirty-six double-page spreads (fols. 37^v–73) that illustrate hieroglyphs from the exequies and explain their meanings.

The court did not immediately adopt the Jesuits' commemorative book as a model for its own chronicles of royal exequies. The first royal honors at San Jerónimo after 1603 were those that Philip III celebrated for his wife, Margarita of Austria, in 1611, and no illustrated book records that event. However, Juan Gómez de Mora, who designed the decorations for the occasion, did publish a description of the event in an unillustrated pamphlet entitled *Relacion de las honras fvnerales qve se hizieron para la Reyna doña Margarita de Austria nuestra senora, en esta villa de Madrid por su Magestad del Rey don Felipe nuestro senor* (n.p., n.d.).[7]

Gómez de Mora begins his text with a detailed account of the decorations, with particular emphasis on the catafalque. Next he describes the arrival of the celebrants and spectators at the vigil, using that as a vehicle for relating where the different personages sat or stood within the church. Many of the notables are identified by their offices or titles, and a few by name. He reduces the vespers service itself to a single sentence, but he pro-

vides a more detailed account of the exequies proper and the principals who conducted them. The Mass of the Holy Ghost, the Mass of the Virgin, the celebration of additional Masses by the monastic delegations in the adjacent cloister, the Requiem Mass, the sermon, the four Responses led by four bishops, and the final Response led by the prelate are each reduced to a single paragraph. With that, the architect concludes his account.

This *relación* became an important precedent for later exequies books that were published by the regime. On the occasion of the royal exequies for Philip III in 1621, Philip IV ordered the creation of a documentary book describing the honors "so that a record would remain of what would have to be done in the future on other occasions."[8] That was yet another manifestation of the Habsburg obsession with conforming to the past. The engraver Pedro Perret was commissioned to make three plates to illustrate the work—a title page, a view of the catafalque from the church nave, and a plan of San Jerónimo as it was furnished for the rites. For that he received 600 *reales* in accordance with two *libranzas* for 200 and 400 *reales* issued respectively on April 13 and May 29, 1621.[9] Because the initial payment was authorized three weeks before the exequies, the book must have been conceived along with the decorations that it was intended to describe. Gómez de Mora again prepared a text describing the decorations and the ceremonies, but for reasons that remain to be determined, the book was never published. It survives only as a manuscript illus-

7. Rpt. in *Relaciones breves*, 72–78.

8. APM, SH, Hf, caja 76, Felipe II y Margarita de Austria (1598) [*sic*].

9. APM, SH, Hf, caja 76, Felipe III (1621); and APM, SH, Libro de pagos, fols. 133bis and 140bis.

THE CREATION OF DECORATIONS

trated with unique impressions of Perret's engravings.[10] Neatly printed by hand in regularly spaced lines, the manuscript fills twenty small pages that provide the most detailed account of the exequies by a contemporary witness. The presence of a few lacunae in the text suggests that plans to publish it were broken off abruptly, before Gómez de Mora had the chance to fill in the remaining details.

Perret's frontispiece gives the intended title of the book: "Aparato del tvmulo real que se edifico en el Conuēto de S. Geronimo De la Villa de Madrid para celebrar las honras Del Inclito y esclarecido Rey Don Filipe. III." That title page, a dedication to Philip IV, the view of the catafalque, and the plan of the church stand at the head of the manuscript (fols. 1–4). Gómez de Mora's text commences with a brief account of Philip III's death, his lying-in-state, and the funeral procession that conveyed his body to El Escorial (fols. 5–5^v). A mention of Philip IV retiring to the monastery of San Jerónimo and ordering royal exequies introduces a description of the decorations that were erected within its church (fols. 6–14^v). The catafalque is described in greatest detail, but other adornments receive attention as well. One page is given to a transcription of the *tumba* epitaph. The architect next describes the arrival of the celebrants and spectators for the vespers service and the seating arrangements (fols. 14^v–17), and he again reduces the vigil itself to a single sentence. The exequies proper are described at greater length (fols. 17–18^v). The manuscript concludes with two Latin epitaphs from the many peripheral decorations at the

exequies that were not provided by the government (fols. 18^v–19). (These were probably displayed in the cloister adjoining the church.) All in all, the organization of the text parallels Gómez de Mora's earlier account of the royal exequies for Margarita of Austria. The principal change is that he introduces additional subjects at the beginning (the events preceding the exequies) and the end (the two peripheral epitaphs) of his account.

Although the commemorative book that was intended to record Philip III's funerary honors was stillborn, the unpublished manuscript and its engravings became the model for a more ambitious work that Philip IV ordered to be printed twenty-three years later to document the royal exequies for Isabella of Bourbon: the anonymous *Pompa Fvneral Honras y Exequias en la muerte De la muy Alta y Catolica Señora Doña Isabel de Borbon Reyna de las Españas y del Nuevo Mundo Que se celebraron en el Real Convento de S. Geronimo de la villa de Madrid* (Madrid, 1645). Following the plan of the "Aparato del tvmulo real," its text presents comparable material at greater length. The book opens with a narrative of Isabella's last days and demise (fols. 1–8^v), her lying-in-state (fols. 9–11^v), and the funeral procession that conveyed her body to San Lorenzo at El Escorial for entombment (fols. 11^v–15^v). An account of how the king ordered royal exequies in her honor (fols. 15^v–18) introduces descriptions of the decorations that were mounted at the entrance to San Jerónimo (fols. 18–20) and within the church and the adjacent cloister (fols. 20–38). A lengthy review of the arrival of the celebrants and spectators at the vigil (fols. 38^v–49^v) and a brief summary

10. Salamanca, Biblioteca Universitaria, Ms. 1,973; a photographic copy of the manuscript and its plates is in BPM, II–739.

of the service (fols. 49^v–50) precede a short account of the exequies proper (fols. 50 –52). The author then interjects his own tribute to the queen (fols. 52–52^v) before reporting the aftermath of the exequies (fols. 53–53^v). The text of the sermon that was preached after the Requiem Mass follows (fols. 54–70^v).[11] The remainder of the book, which is longer than all that precedes it, describes many of the decorations in honor of the queen that courtiers posted in the monastery cloister (fols. 71–171).

As opposed to the concise summaries of the funerary honors for Margarita of Austria and Philip III with which Gómez de Mora contents himself, the author of the *Pompa Fvneral Honras* chronicles Isabella's royal exequies with encyclopedic thoroughness. Time and again his narrative bogs down in lists of persons who attended the queen's exequies and performed the solemn rites. Gómez de Mora acknowledges the presence of the royal councils at the exequies in 1611 and 1621, but he mentions only their presidents by name, if that; in contrast, the *Pompa Fvneral Honras* lists the entire membership of each council. Similarly, the *Pompa Fvneral Honras* includes the complete text of the exequies sermon; whereas each of Gómez de Mora's accounts provides little more than the preacher's name and, for Philip III's exequies, the biblical verse that he took for his theme.[12] Including the sermon in the *Pompa Fvneral Honras* looked back not

to Gómez de Mora's example, but to the Jesuit College's *Libro de las Honras* of 1603.

The same desire to document the exequies with exhaustive coverage informs the number of illustrations that were commissioned for the *Pompa Fvneral Honras*. In addition to three engravings that correspond to the trio that Perret had provided in 1621—a title page, a view of the catafalque (fig. 5), and a plan of the church—the later volume contains ten other plates. These include an allegorical portrait of Isabella, a view of the decorations at the entrance to San Jerónimo (fig. 4), six plates illustrating twenty-four hieroglyphs that were part of the ensemble, a cartouche bearing the Latin epitaph that adorned the *tumba*, and a view of the cciling painting that hung above the *tumba* (fig. 6). One plate is signed by Pedro de Villafranca y Malagón, and two by Juan de Noort. On the basis of their style, the other engravings may be attributed to Noort as well.

The *Pompa Fvneral Honras* documents Isabella's honors better than any previous royal exequies to have been celebrated in Madrid. Inasmuch as the court's prior attempt at such a book had been abandoned, its publication is all the more striking. The renewed enthusiasm for such an undertaking may have sprung from Philip IV's greater sophistication at the time of his wife's death. When he ascended the throne in 1621, Philip was a sixteen-year-old with little experience as a patron of the arts. By 1644 his tastes were well defined, and he had acquired considerable expertise at collecting art and staging ceremonies and entertain-

---

11. Some writers have identified Gregorio de Pedrosa, who preached the sermon, as the author of the *Pompa Fvneral Honras*. There is no evidence that he wrote the rest of the book, and it is unlikely that he did so.

12. The two earlier sermons were published elsewhere: Jerónimo de Florencia, *Sermon qve predico . . . en las Honras que su Magestad hizo a la serenissima Reyna D. Margarita . . .* , and *Sermon qve*

predico a la magestad Catolica del Rey Don Felipe Quarto . . . en las Honras que su Magestad hizo al Rey Felipe III. . . .

THE CREATION OF DECORATIONS

ments in specially decorated settings.[13] With his greater experience, he may have been more disposed to publish an exequies book of unprecedented length and quality of illustration for the Spanish court.

Two years later plans were laid for another illustrated book to chronicle the royal exequies for Baltasar Carlos. Payment records indicate that three engravers—Noort, Villafranca, and Herman Panneels—received 3,094 *reales* "for twenty-two copper plates that they engraved for the book that was to be printed of the account of the honors for the Prince our lord (may he be in glory) that were celebrated in the royal monastery of San Jerónimo"[14] and an additional 800 *reales* for engraving five copper plates with "the arms of the realms and the councils, which were for the book that was printed of the honors for the Prince our lord, may he be in glory."[15] No such book is known, and it seems likely that it was never printed. Owing to its lack of funds, the regime had designed the prince's exequies with a conscious effort to hold down costs. The same fiscal constraints may have forced it to abandon the book sometime after the three engravers had completed its illustrations. As we shall see later in this study, there is circumstantial evidence that five plates were salvaged for use in another book, but the remainder have been lost.[16]

In the aftermath of the funerary honors for Philip IV, the Spanish court published its most ambitious exequies book yet: Pedro Rodríguez de Monforte's *Descripcion de las honras qve se hicieron a la Catholica Mag.ᵈ de D. Phelippe quarto Rey de las Españas y del nuevo Mundo en el Real Conuento de la Encarnacion qve de horden de la Reyna nῆa Señora como svperintendente de las reales obras dispvso D. Baltasar Barroso de Ribera, Marques de Malpica Mayordomo y Gentilhombre de Camara de su Mag.ᵈ que Dios aya y Gouernador de la guarda Alemana* (Madrid, 1666). As its publication followed rather than preceded the king's exequies, a consideration of the efforts that brought the book into being is better deferred until we have completed our examination of the exequies that it recounts. Suffice it to say here that the author was a private chaplain to the king who had witnessed firsthand many of the events that his book reports, and that his extensive text is generously illustrated with fifty-nine plates and vignettes, most of which were engraved by Villafranca. (Figures 8 through 66 reproduce these illustrations in the order in which they appear in the book.) In effect, the *Descripcion* provides its readers with an excellent view of the royal exequies for Philip IV.

13. On Philip IV as a patron, see Introduction, n. 12.

14. AGS, CM3, leg. 756, Destajos, fols. 36bis–36bisᵛ, no. 125. See also fols. 45bis–45bisᵛ, no. 157; AGS, CM3, leg. 756, Extraordinario, fols. 109–9ᵛ, no. 303; and APM, SH, Hf, caja 76, Baltasar Carlos (1646). The three engravers also received 300 *reales* "for the books that they were to illuminate" (APM, SH, Hf, caja 76, Baltasar Carlos [1646]), but there is no indication whether those books were part of the same project.

15. AGS, CM3, leg. 756, Destajos, fols. 29bis–29bisᵛ, no. 101.

16. See Chapter 10.

II
THE ROYAL EXEQUIES FOR PHILIP IV OF SPAIN

6
STAGING THE EXEQUIES

In his last will and testament, Philip IV named his son Charles heir to the Monarchy, but because the royal successor was still a child, Philip also named his widow Mariana to serve as "governor" (regent) of his realms and as Charles's "tutor" until he reached the age of fourteen.[1] To assist her in administering the government, Philip constituted a junta consisting of the President of the Council of Castile, the Vice-Chancellor of Aragon, the Archbishop of Toledo, the Inquisitor General, a member of the Council of State, and a grandee. He directed Mariana to follow the advice of the junta, but it was she, not they, in whom he vested the authority to rule during Charles's minority.

One of Mariana's first responsibilities as queen governor was to stage royal exequies in Philip's memory. These she commanded Baltasar Barroso de Ribera, Marquis of Malpica, to arrange in his capacity as superintendent general of the royal works. Her written charge to the marquis made her sense of urgency plain: "Although I well credit the care of your zeal and application that you will apply to the necessary arrangements for the honors of the King my lord (whom Holy Glory keep), which are to be made in the place and form that are accustomed and which are in your charge, it being fit to perform this function with all possible speed, I command that you endeavor to

hasten the preparations as much as might be possible. Thus, I entrust it to you."[2] As her reference to the "place and form that are accustomed" suggests, she initially designated the church of San Jerónimo as the site for the exequies, but she soon changed her mind.[3] Charles, a sickly child just approaching his fourth birthday (November 6), had not withdrawn in mourning to the Buen Retiro upon his father's death, as was customary. Instead, he had remained with his mother and his sister Margarita María in the Alcázar, which was situated on the western edge of Madrid. To attend royal exequies at San Jerónimo, he would have had to cross to the eastern edge of town. Winter was already threatening, and Mariana was unwilling to risk her son's delicate health on the unpredictability of the weather.

Accordingly, she looked for a suitable location for the exequies that was closer to hand. On September 23 she instructed Malpica that the exequies were to take place in the Royal Chapel of the Alcázar, where Charles could attend them without exposing himself to the elements.[4] At first Mariana believed the greater safety that this arrangement afforded the new king would compensate for the reduction in pomp that the smaller capacity of the Royal Chapel would require. However, once work had begun on designing decorations that would fit the space, it became

---

1. For Philip's will, see *Testamento de Felipe IV: edición facsimil*, ed. Antonio Domínguez Ortiz.

2. Rodríguez de Monforte, *Descripcion*, fols. 51[v]–52.
3. Ibid., fols. 52–54.
4. APM, SH, Hf, caja 76, Felipe IV (1665).

clear that the chapel was simply too small to accommodate the ostentatious display deemed necessary to honor Philip's memory. Mariana then shifted the exequies to the nearby church of the royal convent of La Encarnación. Although it was not part of the Alcázar, it was linked to the palace by an enclosed passageway that would permit Charles to attend the services without venturing outdoors (fig. 67). The convent church was not as capacious as San Jerónimo, but it was large enough to accommodate decorations worthy of the late king. La Encarnación was also appropriate because it, too, was an establishment that enjoyed royal patronage.[5] In due course the exequies were scheduled for October 30 and 31.

Mariana's decision had long-term consequences for Habsburg royal exequies. Although the *etiquetas* of 1647–1651, which continued to be used during Charles's reign, specified that funerary honors for kings, queens, and *príncipes jurados* ordinarily would take place at San Jerónimo, in practice La Encarnación became their setting. After María Luisa of Orleans died in 1689, initial preparations to celebrate her royal exequies at San Jerónimo were halted when it was determined that its interior dimensions

posed difficulties. (The nature of those difficulties remains unknown.) Moreover, the nuns of La Encarnación petitioned the king to stage the honors in their church, asserting that they had acquired that right by virtue of the special favor Mariana had granted them in celebrating Philip IV's royal exequies there, and Charles acceded to the nuns' request.[6] He went on to hold his mother's royal exequies there in 1696, and his second wife and widow, Mariana of Neuberg, likewise staged royal exequies in his honor there in 1700.[7] The proximity of the church to the Alcázar was convenient, to be sure, but what may have proved decisive was that as a smaller church, La Encarnación was cheaper to decorate than San Jerónimo. That was the reasoning of the Duke of Medina Sidonia when he arranged Charles's royal exequies: On November 14, 1700, he wrote to Antonio de Ubilla y Medina, secretary of the Universal Dispatch, that the royal honors for Philip IV "were carried out in the church of La Encarnación, which example it appears can be followed; in respect of which, the costs of having them in San Jerónimo would be much greater."[8]

Once La Encarnación had been settled upon as the site of Philip's exequies, Malpica undertook to adapt the customary arrangements that were made in San Jerónimo to the smaller confines of the convent church. To that end he assigned the design of the exequies decorations to the architect Sebastián de Herrera Barnuevo, master-in-chief of the royal works for the royal dwellings (*maestro mayor de las*

---

5. Philip III had the convent built in fulfillment of a vow that Margarita of Austria had made for the success of the Expulsion of the Moriscos; the order of Augustinian nuns cloistered there formally occupied it in 1616. For its history and architecture, see Antonio Bonet Correa, *Iglesias madrileñas del siglo XVII*, 2d ed., 25–28 and 53; Agustín Bustamante García, "Los artífices del Real Convento de la Encarnación, de Madrid"; José del Corral, "Felipe IV y el Real Monasterio de la Encarnación"; Jerónimo de Quintana, *A la mvy antigva, noble y coronada villa de Madrid. Historia de sv antigvedad, nobleza y grandeza*, fols. 437–38; *Relaciones breves*, 101–3; Tormo, *Las iglesias del antiguo Madrid*, 33–36; Tovar Martín, *Arquitectura madrileña*, 241–42, and "Juan Gómez de Mora," 103–5.

6. Vera Tassis y Villarroel, *Noticias historiales*, 141.

7. APM, SH, Hf, caja 76, Mariana de Austria (1696), and Carlos II (1700). Apparently the court did not publish commemorative books describing these events.

8. APM, SH, Hf, caja 76, Carlos II (1700).

obras de las casas reales) and a steward in the quartermaster's office (*ayuda de la furriera*). Herrera Barnuevo concerned himself with readying both the interior and exterior of the church. Among his surviving preparatory studies for the event is a simple plan of La Encarnación which he may have sketched for convenient reference (fig. 68).[9]

Rodríguez de Monforte's *Descripcion de las honras* describes the decorations that were displayed outside the church but provides no illustration of them, most likely because their disposition did not lend itself to a single perspective view.[10] Those who attended the exequies approached La Encarnación by way of a small courtyard defined by two walls that projected from the ends of the church facade (fig. 69). Herrera Barnuevo had these walls draped with black-and-silver hangings that ran from the giant pilasters framing the entrance portico to the stone pilasters in which the walls ended. (To Rodríguez de Monforte, the silver represented opulence and the black signified melancholy.)[11] Six hieroglyphs measuring 6 x 4 1/2 *pies* (1.68 x 1.26 meters) hung at regular intervals on each side wall. Two large dossals made from the same black-and-silver fabric stood in the corners where the walls met the church facade, and each carried a Latin epitaph that was 3 *varas* (2.52 meters) tall and mounted in a black frame. Herrera Barnuevo also had two canvases in black frames fitted to the pilasters that flanked the central entrance portal, and five more Latin epitaphs were inscribed upon them.

(See Appendix B for the seven texts.) In the church atrium behind the portal, each of two small chapels was decorated with two hieroglyphs whose size is not recorded.

The church proper had been built to a simple cruciform plan that joined a nave to a *capilla mayor*.[12] As usual, the catafalque dominated the interior (fig. 57). It was set back from the center of the crossing as close to the presbytery as was possible so that it could be seen better within the limited confines of the church and so that the glare and smoke from its candles would not bother Charles, who was to witness the exequies from a tribune in the left transept (fig. 55, A). Four large *agujas* flanked the central structure, which was embellished with paintings, trophies, banners, coats of arms, and candles. (To simplify his composition, Villafranca includes only the two front *agujas* in his view of the monument, but his plan of the church shows the disposition of all four.)

The high altar and the two collateral altars in the transepts were each set off by a small step, and each was adorned with a black frontal with gold brocade, six gilded candlesticks with small *hachas*, and a cross. This use of black and gold was reiterated elsewhere in the decoration of the church, for from the edges of the high altar retable all the way back to the atrium door, the walls were decked with black velvet hangings trimmed with gold fringe. These depended from the corona of the highest cornice to a point 3 *pies* (0.84 meter) from the floor. To Rodríguez de Monforte, the black repre-

9. AHN, Códices 288b, fol. 28[v]. Marías and Bustamante, "Apuntes arquitectónicos," 36, first reported the existence of this plan.

10. Rodríguez de Monforte, *Descripcion*, fols. 54–54[v].

11. Ibid., fol. 54.

12. The church interior was transformed markedly in the eighteenth century. For the disposition of the interior decorations, see ibid., fols. 61–64 and 67[v]. For the dignitaries who attended and the events of the two-day observance, see ibid., fols. 71–113, and Díaz de Ylarraza, *Relacion diaria*, n.p.

sented the mourning of the king's subjects and the gold the perfection of their loyalty.[13]

Two rows of paintings were mounted along the lateral sides of the nave just below the fringe at the top of the hangings. The first consisted of thirty-four coats of arms of the realms of the Monarchy painted on rectangular fields. Each escutcheon was surmounted by a golden crown appropriate to the title associated with its realm. From the point of view of a spectator in the nave, the series began with the combined arms of Castile and León, which had been placed on the left-hand pier bearing the arch that separated the nave from the *capilla mayor*. Next came the arms of Aragon, directly across the nave on the right-hand pier. The arms of twenty-two more kingdoms, one archduchy, three duchies, four counties, and two seigniories followed in their customary order of precedence, in a sequence that alternated back and forth across the nave. Thus, the greater the status of a realm, the closer its arms were to the catafalque. Four engravings in Rodríguez de Monforte's book illustrate the arms in sequence (figs. 26–29). Among Herrera Barnuevo's surviving drawings for the exequies is a sheet of studies for these devices with color notes (fig. 70), which he probably made as a guide for the artists who carried out the paintings.[14]

The coats of arms were spaced at regular intervals, each one's bottom corners touching the upper corners of two adjacent paintings in a second row of pictures of the same size. This lower row consisted of identical paintings of a death's-head

wearing a gold crown. The arrangement created an undulating band of images whose juxtaposition signified to Rodríguez de Monforte either that all realms had to end in death or that all the realms mourned the late king.[15] Herrera Barnuevo might have intended either or both of those readings; however, coats of arms were often incorporated into ephemeral decorations at the Spanish court to express the greatness of the empire, and death's-heads routinely appeared at royal exequies as reminders of the nature of such events.

Far below the coats of arms and the death's-heads, twenty-four hieroglyphs hung along the two sides of the nave at regular intervals 12 *pies* (3.36 meters) above the floor. Each measured 2 x 1 1/3 *varas* (1.68 x 1.12 meters), which almost matched the dimensions of the courtyard hieroglyphs. In addition, one colossal hieroglyph that measured 4 x 3 *varas* (3.36 x 2.52 meters) was mounted on the grille of the convent tribune overlooking the rear of the nave (fig. 55, Y).

Seating arrangements for the dignitaries attending the exequies were adapted from the prescriptions of the 1647–1651 etiquette for San Jerónimo (compare fig. 2). Instead of a royal *cortina*, Charles and Margarita María occupied an L-shaped tribune with a projecting balcony in the left transept (fig. 55, A), accompanied by their governess and a few ladies of honor (*señoras de honor*), ladies in waiting (*damas*), and maids of honor (*meninas*). This kept them on the preferred Gospel side of the church. Other royal attendants who could not be accommodated there occupied the convent tribune at the back of the nave. Ordinarily a blue lattice with blue taffeta curtains and a valance con-

---

13. Rodríguez de Monforte, *Descripcion*, fol. 61.

14. AHN, Códices 288b, fol. 27ᵛ; the identification was made by Marías and Bustamante, "Apuntes arquitectónicos," 36–38.

15. Rodríguez de Monforte, *Descripcion*, fol. 61ᵛ.

cealed those seated in the royal tribune from view, but for the exequies these were replaced with black taffeta curtains with gold stripes and fringe.

The presbytery and its steps were covered with opulent carpets. To the right of the high altar a black velvet chair and prie-dieu (B) were provided for Cardinal Geronimo Colonna, Bishop of Tusculum, the prelate who conducted the vespers service and the Requiem Mass. Nearby were small, flat benches for the king's private chaplains who were to assist him (C). A bench for the other bishops in attendance (D) occupied the opposite side of the presbytery. The Patriarch of the Indies (who was Archbishop of Tyre) took first place there, as was customary, followed by five others who sat in the order of their consecration: the Archbishop of Amasia, and the Bishops of Avila, Segovia, Cuenca, and Oviedo.

In the right transept a bench covered with black velvet and a prayer stool covered with baize were provided for ambassadors to the court (G). The papal nuncio and the envoys from the Holy Roman Empire and Venice sat there, but the French ambassador was ill and did not attend. The pulpit stood to their left (E), and three benches for the king's other private chaplains, his confessors, and his preachers occupied the space between the ambassadors and the sacristy door (H). The queen governor's majordomos took their places near the right-hand collateral altar and the presbytery steps (I).

All the grandees who were in Madrid attended the exequies, and twenty-three who were not members of the royal councils sat on a baize-covered bench (F) that extended from the presbytery steps across the left transept beneath the king's tribune. In order to accommodate them all, the bench was bent into a three-sided

crescent. Other gentlemen in the king's service stood behind it. The choir, which usually occupied the space beneath the king's balcony, was moved to the opposite tribune (T), where the church organ was located.

Barriers 4 *pies* (1.12 meters) high were erected in the nave 6 *pies* (1.68 meters) from the walls in order to set apart space for double rows of benches for the royal councils (K–S) while leaving room outside the enclosure for other spectators (Z). The barriers, benches, and floor within the enclosure were covered with black baize, and the councils' places were marked by their respective coats of arms (figs. 58–66).

All was ready by October 30, the day of the vigil. At 3:30 P.M., after all the other dignitaries had taken their places with the customary pomp and all the candles had been lighted, the curtains of the royal tribune were drawn and the upper shutters of its lattice were opened to reveal the king and his sister. The queen governor was indisposed and did not attend. Cardinal Colonna celebrated the Vespers service, which ended at 6:00 P.M. The assembled company then withdrew, and overnight workmen replaced all the candle stumps in the church with fresh candles.

At 8:00 A.M. the next day the chaplains who were to assist at the first Mass of the exequies proper donned their vestments in the sacristy, and at 8:15 the papal nuncio, Vitaliano Visconti Borromeo, Archbishop of Ephesus, entered the church to celebrate the Mass of the Holy Ghost. At 9:00 A.M. Francisco de Zárate, Bishop of Cuenca, celebrated the Mass of the Virgin. He was a substitute for the French ambassador, Georges Dubesen, Archbishop of Embrun, whose illness prevented him from performing the office.

After the second Mass, the congregation that had attended the vigil returned to La Encarnación, and the fresh candles on the catafalque were lighted. At 10:45 the curtain and lattice on the royal tribune opened once more to reveal Charles and Margarita María taking their places, but Mariana remained indisposed. Cardinal Colonna celebrated the Requiem Mass, and Padre Maestro Fray Miguel de Cárdenas, a Shod Carmelite and a king's preacher, delivered the sermon. Cárdenas took as his text a variation on I Maccabees 6:14–15, *Et vocavit ad se, Philippum, unum de Principibus suis. Et preposuit super universum Regnum suum, et dedit ei Diadema, et Stolam suam, et Annullam* ("And he called to himself Philip, one of his Princes, and put him over all his Kingdom. And he gave him the Crown, and his Robe, and the Ring"). The sermon was received with considerable applause. As usual, the clerics ended the rites with five Absolutions. These responsories were led in succession by Ambrosio Ignacio de Espínola y Guzmán, Bishop of Oviedo; the Bishop of Cuenca, who had earlier celebrated the Mass of the Virgin; Diego Escolano, Bishop of Segovia; Francisco de Rojas, Bishop of Avila; and Cardinal Colonna. The royal exequies ended at 2:30 P.M.

7
THE CATAFALQUE

Measuring almost 20 *pies* (5.60 meters) square in plan and rising to a height of 59 *pies* (16.52 meters), the catafalque that Herrera Barnuevo designed as a monument to Philip IV dominated the interior of the convent church (fig. 57).[1] Nevertheless, by the standards of earlier royal exequies for Spanish monarchs, it was small. The catafalques that Juan Gómez de Mora had erected in San Jerónimo for Margarita of Austria, Philip III, and Isabella of Bourbon (fig. 5) had all been 27 *pies* (7.56 meters) square in plan and 71 *pies* (19.88 meters) tall.[2] The diminished scale of Philip IV's catafalque was the most obvious consequence of moving his exequies to La Encarnación. Herrera Barnuevo had entrusted the execution of his design[3] to two men in particular: Pedro de la Torre, a master builder (*maestro arquitecto*) who received 33,198 *reales* for constructing and assembling the monument, and Clemente de Avila, who collected 28,637 *reales* for painting and

gilding it.[4] Such large sums must have included both the costs of their materials and the wages of their assistants, whose names have gone unrecorded.

The main body of the catafalque rested on an octagonal base 5 *pies* (1.40 meters) tall. It was not a regular octagon; rather, the four axial faces were wider than the non-axial ones (fig. 55). Doubtless owing to the limited space available, the trophies that usually stood on the nave side of catafalques for Habsburg men were omitted from the ensemble. Herrera Barnuevo retained the customary four *agujas* surrounding the central structure, but because the catafalque had been set as close to the presbytery as was possible, the *agujas* were not disposed at its four corners in perfect symmetry. All four were mounted on rectilinear pedestals 8 *pies* (2.24 meters) tall painted in imitation of black-and-white jasper with gilded moldings. Rising an additional 30 *pies* (8.4 meters) in height, each *aguja* carried six gilded, octagonal socket-pans that were connected by spokes to its central shaft. An ornamental pedestal bearing a single candle crowned each spire.

The first story of the central structure was built in the composite order. On each non-axial side of the base, a socle 1.5 *pies* (0.42 meter) high carried a pedestal 3.5 *pies* (0.98 meter) tall. Atop the ends of these pedestals stood eight columns that rose another 11 *pies* (3.08 meters). Each

1. The following account of the catafalque is based on Villafranca's engravings and Rodríguez de Monforte, *Descripcion*, fols. 64–69ᵛ. Antonio Bonet Correa, "El túmulo de Felipe IV, de Herrera Barnuevo y los retablos-baldaquinos del barroco español," relates the design of the catafalque to contemporary developments in Spanish architecture.

2. *Relaciones breves*, 72; Gómez de Mora, "Aparato del tvmulo real," fol. 6; and *Pompa Fvneral Honras*, fols. 22–22ᵛ.

3. Figure 71 is Herrera Barnuevo's only known preparatory drawing for the catafalque (AHN, Códices 288b, fol. 27). For the differences between the drawing and the catafalque as Villafranca engraved it, see Marías and Bustamante, "Apuntes arquitectónicos," 38.

4. AGS, CM3, leg. 1,810(2), Gastos del Alcázar, fols. 168–72.

had a gilded base, plinth, and capital, and its shaft was painted black and white in imitation of San Pablo jasper. The bottom third of each shaft was covered with ivy leaves that climbed to a crowned skull-and-crossbones. Rodríguez de Monforte characterizes the death's-head as the symbolic fruit of the ivy. Citing Pliny as his authority, he explains that the natural property of ivy is for its roots to penetrate the wall that it climbs and to tear it down. He compares this to the passage of days with which Time overturns the most constant column "and makes it the feeble plunder of Death's scythe."[5] This combination of ivy and death's-heads was one of several symbolic reminders of earthly mortality incorporated into the structure. The upper two-thirds of the shafts were dressed with golden sashes that depended from the capitals. All eight columns carried a continuous, gilded entablature with a frieze incorporating more skulls-and-crossbones on its metopes. Four full, royal coats of arms were mounted on the axial faces of the entablature, and four pairs of crowned, golden lions acted as their heraldic supporters. The king of beasts thereby signaled the royal status of the deceased. In addition, a scythe emerged from behind each of these devices to signify that Death had claimed the person in whose honor the catafalque had been erected.

The interior of the first story could be entered directly from the elevated presbytery or by ascending five steps facing the nave. Seats for the four bishops who gave the first four Absolutions and the eight chaplains who assisted them were arranged along the narrow sides of the octagon. The *tumba*, which stood in the center, was 7 *pies* (1.96 meters) tall and

covered with the traditional brocade funeral cloth that had been brought from El Escorial. The matching cushion sat atop it, and on that rested a gold crown and a gold-and-crystal scepter. Rodríguez de Monforte does not specify that the sword of justice and the late king's collar of the Order of the Golden Fleece were on the cushion, but they must have been there to conform with the 1647–1651 etiquette. In fact, the sword is visible in Villafranca's engraving of the catafalque. Furthermore, it is recorded that after Philip's body had lain in state, his collar of the Golden Fleece was removed before his coffin was locked for the funeral procession to El Escorial.[6] Accordingly, the keeper of the crown jewels would have had it on hand in the Alcázar for use at the king's exequies. As usual, a Latin epitaph praising the deceased stood in front of the *tumba* facing the nave.[7] (See Appendix B for its text.)

Above the *tumba* was a flat, painted

5. Rodríguez de Monforte, *Descripcion*, fol. 65.

6. Ibid., fol. 35[v].

7. A *libranza* of May 10, 1666, authorized payment of 300 *reales* to the merchant Marcos Junio for "the price of a print [*lámina*] that was bought in order to present to Father Antonio Rosende of the Minorite Clerics and his provincial, a preacher of His Majesty, in appreciation of having composed an epitaph for the *tumba* for the honors of the King our lord, who is in glory" (AGS, CM3, Leg. 1,362, Cosas extraordinarias, fols. 6–6[v]). That same day another *libranza* authorized payment of 200 *reales* to Juan de Burgos, a *maestro de niños*, "for having written an epitaph that was made for the *tumba* of the catafalque for the honors of the King our lord who is in glory" (ibid., fol. 5bis[v]). Among the worksheets for these exequies is one bearing all but nineteen of the seventy-one lines of the *tumba* epitaph, to which another hand has added the name *Rosende* (APM, SH, Hf, caja 76, Felipe IV [1665]). That confirms that Rosende composed most of the epitaph, but the seeming contradiction between the two payments remains unresolved. One possibility is that Burgos contributed the other nineteen lines. Another is that the epitaph Burgos composed was one of those displayed in the courtyard of La Encarnación.

ceiling surrounded by a gilded interior cornice (fig. 56). At its center was a medallion containing a Cross of Jerusalem with castles and lions, the heraldic symbols of Castile and León, set in its interstices. The phrase *PHILIPVS .IV. HISPANIARVM REX.* ("Philip IV, King of the Spains"—that is, Old Spain and New Spain), encircled this image, and each of its letters began an inscription emitted in a golden ray set against a field of blue. These texts, most of which were taken from the Vulgate, variously praised the dead king, declared that he had gone to his just reward, and asserted that he had left a worthy successor to the crown. (All are transcribed in Appendix C.) This was surely inspired by the ceiling painting that had hung over the *tumba* at the royal exequies for Isabella of Bourbon (fig. 6). In it a golden sun inscribed *ELISABETH REGINA* ("Isabella, the Queen") had emitted rays of light bearing simple adjectives proclaiming her virtues and eminence.[8]

Eight pyramidal *agujas* mounted on pedestals stood atop the first story of the catafalque aligned with the composite columns below. Each was 8 *pies* (2.24 meters) tall, carried tiers of socket-pans of diminishing widths, and culminated in a golden ball into which an *hacha* was set. The spaces between these *agujas* on the narrower sides of the octagon were occupied by galleries behind balustrades. Within this perimeter of *agujas* and balustrades rose the second story. Recessed 3 *pies* (0.84 meter) from the edge of the first, it, too, was octagonal in plan. Its base was a pedestal 2 *pies* (0.56 meter) tall, on which each axial face carried a rectangular window defined by jambs

8. *Pompa Fvneral Honras*, fols. 27–28.

and a lintel. These, in turn, were framed by a rectilinear trim and two volutes from which golden fruit hung. Each window was surmounted by a cornice and a triangular pediment set against leaf-ornaments (*cartones*) and shields in which a skull nestled. A sandglass resting atop the skull served as a candlestick for an *hacha*.[9] This *memento mori* was completed by a scythe (the instrument of Death) and a scepter (more likely indicative of Death's sovereignty over earthly life than of Philip's sovereignty over the Monarchy).

On each non-axial face of the octagon, two pilasters carried a continuous cornice in which the second story culminated. Between each pair of pilasters was an arched niche occupied by a gilded statue of a woman who personified one of Philip's virtues: Faith, Hope, Charity, and Justice. Faith, blindfolded and holding a chalice and Host, occupied the front, left-hand niche (as seen from the nave). Her companion to the right, Hope, had an anchor and fixed her attention upon Heaven. Charity, who nursed children at her breasts, and Justice, whose attributes are not recorded, occupied the niches that faced the corners of the presbytery. Faith, Hope, and Charity's attributes were all conventional.[10] It is not known who sculpted these virtues.

At the center of the base on which each virtue stood lay putti holding a garland

9. Rodríguez de Monforte, *Descripcion*, fol. 66, interprets the sandglass as measuring the total of the instants of time during which the candle consumes itself—an unlikely reading that strays too far from the fundamental concern of the royal exequies, the death of Philip IV.

10. For example, Ripa, *Iconologia*, 72–73, 161–62, and 497, accounts for all but Faith's blindfold. The blindfold may be taken as an indication of her trusting nature—that is, "blind faith." See also below, Chapter 9, Hieroglyph 32.

that surrounded an oval bearing an inscription. Rodríguez de Monforte does not provide these inscriptions, but the handling of similar personifications at the royal exequies for Philip III and Isabella of Bourbon suggests that each oval bore the virtue's Latin name and a Latin phrase (possibly taken from the Vulgate) commenting upon her pertinence to the deceased.[11] In fact, one of the surviving worksheets from the exequies preparations lists citations from the Vulgate corresponding to the four virtues.[12] Even if they did not appear on the catafalque, they convey the spirit in which the virtues were meant to be understood. Faith's inscription may have been, *Fide grandis factus est. ad Heb. 11* ("He is made great by faith" [a variation on Hebrews 11:24]). *Felix, qui non exidit a spe sua. ecclessiastisi 14* ("Happy is he who has not fallen from his hope" [Ecclesiasticus 14:2]), was put down for Hope. Two inscriptions were considered for Charity: *Perfecta charitas fixas mitit timorem. Epist. 1. Joann cp. 4* ("Perfect charity casts out [*foras*] fear" [I John 4:18]); and *Qui autem seruat verbum christi vitios charitas dei perfecta est. epist. 1. Joan. cp. 2* ("But the man who keeps the word of Christ, truly in him [reading *vitios* as a corruption of *vere in hoc*] the love of God is brought to fulfillment" [a variation on I John 2:5]). The proposed quotation for Justice was, *Iusticia veró liberabit a morte. Prou. 10* ("But justice will deliver from death" [Proverbs 10:2]). All expressed an optimistic message: Because Philip had demonstrated these virtues in life, he was to be rewarded in death. Thus, the mourners were assured that

when the king was called before his Maker for judgment, he was admitted to eternal glory.

Faith, Hope, and Charity were the three Theological Virtues, and of the four Cardinal Virtues, Justice was selected for the catafalque rather than Prudence, Temperance, or Fortitude. Rodríguez de Monforte remarks that the equity of Justice fortifies Faith, Hope, and Charity, which may or may not have been Herrera Barnuevo's reason for including it.[13] Whatever the case, asserting that Philip had ruled justly was a recurrent theme in the decorations. It was declared by the presence of the sword of justice on the *tumba*, by two hieroglyphs (figs. 33 and 54), and by two inscriptions on the ceiling painting above the *tumba* (Appendix C, 3 and 9).[14]

On the third story an octagonal socle 2 *pies* (0.56 meter) tall supported an octagonal cupola that reached 10 *pies* (2.80 meters) in height. Its voussoirs and fillets were aligned with the pilasters on the second story, and each of its faces incorporated two oval windows that were bordered by decorative moldings, shields, and golden fruit. Rodríguez de Monforte fails to mention the flags with coats of arms that emerge from two cupola windows in Villafranca's view of the catafalque, but there is no reason to doubt their inclusion is accurate. They were probably two of the four *banderas de los cuatro cuartos*, which would have displayed the arms of Philip's four grandpar-

---

11. See Gómez de Mora, "Aparato del tvmulo real," fols. 8–9 and 10ᵛ–11ᵛ; and *Pompa Fvneral Honras*, fols. 30–34.

12. APM, SH, Hf, caja 76, Felipe IV (1665).

13. Rodríguez de Monforte, *Descripcion*, fol. 66ᵛ.

14. Similarly, in a panegyric published after Philip's death, Mauricio de Lezana, *Memorial de las virtudes con que el Rey N. S. Filipo IV. (que está en gloria) mereció el renombre de Grande . . .*, fols. 5–6ᵛ, discusses the importance of justice for good kingship and praises Philip IV for having been just.

ents. Atop the cupola a large torus molding, a fillet, and a cavetto molding carried an octagonal pedestal that measured 5 *pies* (1.40 meters) from its base to its cornice. The pedestal supported a plinth 1 *pie* (0.28 meter) tall, on which a mound of trophies, palms, crowns, banners, trumpets, and instruments of war rested. A globe 3 *pies* (0.84 meter) in diameter surmounted this pile, which to Rodríguez de Monforte signified the world astride its spoils.[15] Capping the whole was the crown of the Monarchy. Its presence atop the globe declared that as king of Spain, Philip had exercised triumphant dominion over a worldwide empire.

The main body of the catafalque and the freestanding *agujas* supported a forest of candles that consisted of white wax cores with yellow wax coatings.[16] Their distribution within the ensemble is documented by a memorandum that the Count of Montalbán, the king's senior majordomo (*mayordomo más antiguo*), prepared for Roque de Alcántara, the chief of the royal chandlery, listing the numbers of candles and estimating the corresponding weights of wax that were needed for the exequies, and by a second memorandum that records the quantities of white wax that were actually purchased to make the candles.[17] Although these documents make it possible to determine the numbers of candles on the different parts of the catafalque with precision, they are more important as indications of features of the catafalque that

Rodríguez de Monforte's text and Villafranca's engravings do not account for. The disposition of *cirios* and *ambleos* broke down as follows:

—80 *cirios* 3 *pies* (0.84 meter) tall for the eight voussoirs of the cupola.

—80 *cirios* 3 *pies* (0.84 meter) tall for the cornice of the second story.

—288 *cirios* 2 1/4 *pies* (0.63 meter) tall for the eight pyramidal *agujas* above the columns of the first story.

—20 *cirios* 3 *pies* (0.84 meter) tall for the galleries on the cornice of the first story. (Perhaps these were the candles shown on the balustrades atop the first story in Villafranca's engraving.)

—46 *cirios* 3 *pies* (0.84 meter) tall for the projections of the corona of the cornice of the first story. (Perhaps these included the single tapers shown on pedestals in front of the pyramidal *agujas* in Villafranca's engraving and other tapers that he omitted from his print.)

—96 *cirios* 2 *pies* (0.56 meter) tall "for the eight columns, which have been in the four cornucopias of each column [*para las ocho colunas que han estado en las quatro cornucopias de cada coluna*]." (Neither Rodríguez de Monforte nor Villafranca indicates that there were cornucopia-shaped candle fixtures on the columns.)

—60 *cirios* 3 1/2 *pies* (0.98 meter) tall for the crowns of the pedestals on which the columns stood.

—28 *ambleos* "of ordinary size" for the pinnacles of the *agujas* and their buttresses (*arbotantes*). (The reference to buttresses cannot be explained adequately on the basis of Villafranca's engraving. The view also crowns each *aguja* with a long taper rather than with a short, thick *ambleo*.)[18]

—600 *cirios* 2 *pies* (0.56 meter) tall for the *agujas*. (These would have been for the four *agujas* surrounding the central structure.)

---

15. Rodríguez de Monforte, *Descripcion*, fol. 67[v].

16. It will be recalled that although white wax burned more brightly with less smoke, yellow candles were considered the appropriate color for funerary honors; see *Pompa Fvneral Honras*, fols. 36[v]–37.

17. APM, SH, Hf, caja 76, Felipe IV (1665).

18. What is more, Rodríguez de Monforte, *Descripcion*, fol. 69, states that each of the four freestanding *agujas* was crowned by an *hacha*.

That amounts to 1,298 candles for each day of the rites. (Small wonder that Villafranca reduced their numbers when he engraved the catafalque!) As a precaution against the hazard that so many candles posed, men with water and fire-fighting gear were concealed within the cupola of the catafalque while the candles burned.

Owing to the lack of space in La Encarnación, another 60 *cirios* were distributed "away from the catafalque in lieu of *blandones* [large candlesticks with *hachas*] all around the catafalque." Perhaps some of these were mounted in the nave in order to illuminate the coats of arms, death's-heads, and hieroglyphs. If so, then Villafranca omitted them from his view of the ensemble. Another possibility is that they were installed on the walls of the transepts and presbytery to better illuminate the *capilla mayor*.[19]

Brilliant as the glare from so many candles must have seemed, the display was small by royal standards. At the royal exequies in San Jerónimo for both Philip III and Isabella of Bourbon, 3,400 candles had burned each day in honor of the deceased.[20] In his account of the decorations, Rodríguez de Monforte seeks to excuse the reduced number of candles:

It seems a small number [of candles] for the greatness of the one [Mariana] who erected it, as [it seems] little light by which to see the [now] obscured merits of him who has gone to the grave. But his posterity [Charles II] will reveal the latter in more sovereign splendor, and the former did not need such ostentation of numbers, as that of which other Pyres raised to this Royal memory will be composed. For if the site were more capacious, how could it be doubted that the power and affection of the one who staged the Honors would not exceed all numbers with the lights, and would not move to rival the Egyptian pyramids?[21]

With a politician's knack for transforming adversity into advantage, Rodríguez de Monforte turns the constraints that La Encarnación imposed upon the exequies into grounds for praising Mariana's devotion to her husband and her son's promise of greatness.

19. Taking into account the additional candles needed for use on the altars and during the services brought Montalbán's estimate of the number required each day to 1,692—APM, SH, Hf, caja 76, Felipe IV (1665). It was probably that figure that prompted Rodríguez de Monforte, *Descripcion*, fol. 69, to assert that the catafalque had 1,700 candles, which overestimates the actual number by about 400.

20. Gómez de Mora, "Aparato del tvmulo real," fol. 16*v*; and *Pompa Fvneral Honras*, fol 36*v*.

21. Rodríguez de Monforte, *Descripcion*, fol. 69.

8
HIEROGLYPHS OF DEATH AND SUCCESSION

Although the forty-one hieroglyphs at Philip's exequies were sufficiently important to justify Villafranca's engraving a separate illustration of each for the *Descripcion de las honras*, Rodríguez de Monforte says nothing more about their meanings than that they combined beauty and sadness.[1] He is hardly more forthcoming about the authors who devised the emblems, saying only that their names do not appear on their works because of their modesty or because the contents of the hieroglyphs, while noteworthy when judged by what is possible in that genre, are of little consequence in relation to their authors' talents.[2] Just as the surviving worksheets from the exequies preparations suggest that several persons proposed ideas for the hieroglyphs, so, too, does the internal evidence of the finished works. Their verses address the viewer in different persons, tenses, and voices, and the sophistication of their meanings ranges from the obvious to the arcane. The identities of the artists who painted them likewise remain to be discovered.[3]

It is not even possible to determine the exact positions that forty of the forty-one hieroglyphs occupied within the ensemble. The sixteen that hung in the courtyard and atrium (figs. 10–25) can be distinguished from the twenty-five in the nave (figs. 30–54) because Rodríguez de Monforte's book illustrates them in separate groups. The internal evidence of the hieroglyphs offers no clue to their specific placement, and the sketchily rendered hieroglyphs in Villafranca's view of the catafalque cannot be matched convincingly to his engravings of the individual works. Furthermore, no apparent thematic pattern governs the sequence of hieroglyphs within the groups of sixteen and twenty-five. The sole hieroglyph whose precise location can be deduced is one that is illustrated by a larger engraving than the other forty (fig. 54). The last in the sequence of illustrations, it must reproduce the colossal hieroglyph that was mounted on the tribune at the rear of the nave.

The hieroglyphs conform to a standard design from which there are only occasional, minor departures. The upper four-fifths of each is occupied by the symbolic image and the Latin motto, which is inscribed in a banderole. Although the ban-

1. Rodríguez de Monforte, *Descripcion*, fol. 54[v].
2. Ibid., fol. 62.
3. Bonet Correa, "El túmulo de Felipe IV," 286, speculates that Herrera Barnuevo, Juan Carreño de Miranda, and Francisco Rizi might have painted the hieroglyphs; however, the question is best left open. Past practice is an inconclusive guide to the matter. In 1621 two of the leading painters at the court, Vicente Carducho and Eugenio Cajés, made significant contributions to the royal exequies for Philip III. See APM, SH, Hf, caja 76, Felipe II y Margarita de Austria (1598), and Felipe III (1621); and APM, Libro de pagos, fols. 134[v], 134bis, 137bis[v]–38, and 309bis[v]–10. On the other hand,

at Isabella of Bourbon's royal exequies in 1644, the most important paintings were the work of such lesser figures as Félix Castelo, Gabriel Félix, Giulio Cesare Semini, and Domingo de Yanguas. For documentation of the queen's exequies, see chap. 4, n. 4; much of the AGS documentation is summarized in Azcárate, "Datos sobre túmulos," 292–94.

derole usually floats near the top of the image, in one instance it is placed near the bottom (fig. 49), and in three others the composition has to accommodate two banderoles (figs. 14, 35, and 50). When the motto is a quotation (usually from the Vulgate), its source is cited in abbreviated form. The bottom fifth of each hieroglyph is a *trompe l'oeil* rendering of a bolt of cloth tacked onto a plain, dark background. The cloth bears a Spanish verse of three to five lines that, together with the Latin motto, provides the key to interpreting the symbolic image.

Each hieroglyph is a distinct invention that must be deciphered individually, but a few symbols recur among them. Most prominent is the sun, which represents Philip IV in several images. This may come as a surprise to those who associate seventeenth-century solar imagery with Louis XIV of France, the "Sun King" of Versailles, but identifying the king with the sun was a common panegyric image at the Spanish court.[4] As the brightest of the heavenly bodies, it was a fitting symbol of royal splendor—"the king of the planets," as one writer put it.[5] Its capacity to warm and nurture could signify the king's benevolence toward his subjects. When Philip ascended the throne in 1621, the sculptor Rutilio Gaci struck a portrait medal of him, and on its verso Apollo drove the solar quadriga beneath the inscription *LVSTRAT. ET. FOVET.*

("He shines and nurtures").[6] In a similar vein, one posthumous tribute to Philip declared,

The Sun is the symbol of a perfect King . . . and Saint Gregory of Nazianzus says of the Sun, that it does not burn, but rather that with its temperate warmth, it fructifies, rules, and governs; that burning is [the property] of fire; that destruction and ruination [are the properties] of cruel tyrants; and that temperance, the warmth of justice, and dominion with grace and clemency [are the properties] of great Kings. God wishes the perfect Prince to be like the Sun—such was the King our Lord. Who complained of his asperity? Who did not proclaim aloud his supreme humanity? Gentleness of disposition? Peaceful gravity of his person? Affability of his countenance? Gentleness of his words? Goodness of his heart, and the inestimable clemency of his heart?[7]

Identification with the sun especially suited Philip because one of his epithets was *el rey planeta*, "the Planet King." This recognized his dominion over an empire that stretched around the world, but there was more to it than that. He was Philip the *Fourth*, and in the Ptolemaic system of the universe, the sun was the *fourth* planet. The numerical coincidence was not lost upon his flatterers.[8] In a sonnet composed in honor of the newly constructed Palace of the Buen Retiro, Luis Vélez de Guevara wrote in part, "This is the house of the Sun: Philip IV / Planet of Austria."[9] More explicit is a passage from an account of the exequies that the city of Valencia staged in Philip's honor on October 31, 1665. A hiero-

---

4. Louis's adoption of solar imagery may have been inspired in part by a desire to rival his Spanish counterparts. With a Spanish mother and a Spanish wife, he surely had opportunity to learn how solar imagery was used at Madrid. Of course, using the sun to symbolize royal glory had a long tradition that he could have known without benefit of a Spanish example; see Ernst H. Kantorowicz, "*Oriens Augusti—Lever du Roi.*"

5. *Relaciones breves*, 385.

6. Adolfo Herrera, "Rutilio Gaci," 61.

7. Lezana, *Memorial*, fol. 16.

8. Elliott, *Count-Duke of Olivares*, 177–78.

9. "Al Buen Retiro," in *Elogios al Palacio Real del Bven Retiro*, ed. Diego de Covarrubias y Leiva, n.p.

glyph displayed on that occasion used the sun to represent the king and was explained as follows: "The Sun is the fourth Planet, the King is Philip the Fourth. The influence of the Sun reaches the four parts of the world, the Empire of Philip [does] too. And finally, Philip is the one who merited renown as 'the Great,' and holy Scripture attributed it [the epithet] to the Sun: *Fecit Deus duo luminaria magna* ['God created two great lights'—Genesis 1 : 16]."[10]

The sun's daily course across the sky became a metaphor for the lives of the royal family. Sunrises were appropriate images for beginnings such as royal births. Thus, Rodríguez de Monforte could remark of Philip's birthplace, "Valladolid was the East of this Sun."[11] When Baltasar Carlos was born at sunrise in 1629, one poet wrote,

Tierno sol, en cuyo oriente
nace el sol cuasi celoso
de ver que un sol más hermoso
presta rayos a tu frente.[12]

(Tender sun, in whose East the sun rises, almost jealous to see that a more beautiful sun lends rays to your countenance.)

Similarly, Pedro Calderón de la Barca celebrated the birth of Prince Felipe Próspero in 1657 by writing *El laurel de Apolo*, in which it is declared, "Today with prosperous dawn for all a sun is born."[13] Another sort of beginning was

the *juramento* of Castile, whereby a Spanish prince became a *príncipe jurado*. Philip IV's *juramento* on January 13, 1608, prompted one writer to describe Castile as saying, "*Surge illuminare* [Rise up to shine] Castile, seeing and consider-. ing the new Sun that gives you light, before whose rays tremble the enemies and the Princes of the earth, envying those of Castile and similar triumphs!"[14]

Sunsets and eclipses, when the sun disappeared from view, were appropriate to endings, especially the deaths of kings. When Philip III died, various writers observed that "the Majesty of God . . . eclipsed from us the Sun of all Christendom," that "The Sun of Spain and of Christendom, the bright star of justice, the thunderbolt against the heretics has vanished from the earth," and that the king's death was a "doleful eclipse / to our Spanish Hemisphere."[15] When Philip IV died, one commemoration began, "The Sun of Spain has vanished."[16] As far away as Mexico City, the author of a book recording the exequies that were staged there for Philip IV entitled his work, *Llanto del Occidente en el Ocaso del mas claro Sol de las Españas . . .* ("The Weeping of the West on the Setting of the Brightest Sun of the Spains . . .").[17]

The daily cycle of sunrise and sunset lent itself to extended imagery. One writer who compared Philip III's death to the sun disappearing from view went on to describe his successor as "a new Sun, the Prince our lord Philip IV, whose res-

10. Antonio L. de Velasco, *Funesto geroglifico, enigma del mayor dolor, qve en reresentaciones mvdas manifesto . . . Valencia, en las honras de su Rey Felipe el Grande . . .* , 131.

11. Rodríguez de Monforte, *Descripcion,* fol. 113ᵛ.

12. Manuel Izquierdo Hernández, "Bosquejo histórico del Príncipe Baltasar Carlos de Austria," 2.

13. Cited by Carl Justi, *Diego Velazquez and His Times,* rev. ed., trans. A. H. Keane, 411.

14. *Relaciones breves,* 60.

15. *Relacion de la mverte de nuestro catolicissimo y bienaventvrado Rey y Señor Don Felipe Tercero . . . ,* n.p.; *Relacion breve de la muerte del Rey N. S..* n.p.; and *Relaciones breves,* 122, respectively.

16. Untitled *gaceta,* BNM, Ms. 2,392, fol. 237.

17. Isidro Sarinaña, *Llanto del Occidente en el Ocaso del mas claro Sol de las Españas. . . .*

plendencies and reflections begin to dispel the present shadows."[18] When the new king had the celebrated Trinitarian friar Hortensio Félix Paravicino Arteaga deliver a sermon in the Royal Chapel to honor Philip III's memory, the preacher introduced his remarks on the late king's life with a solar metaphor: "Let us begin to consider, then, the rising of his light at his birth, the passage of his light in his life, and the shadows about it at his death."[19] The birth of the Infante Fernando Tomás on December 21, 1658, inspired the king's chief chronicler, Rodrigo Méndez Silva, to write, "It is also worth pondering that this fortunate birth took place on the autumnal Solstice, when the night reaches its greatest augmentation, and day begins to lengthen its splendors—indicating that with the nocturnal banishment of adversities, Spain will return to enjoying the refulgent light of her glories."[20]

Yet another attraction of solar imagery was that by increasing the number of heavenly bodies in a hieroglyph, it became possible to allude symbolically to other members of the royal family. When the king was the sun, the queen could be the moon. Mariana of Austria had been symbolized by a lunar metaphor as early as her arrival in Spain in 1649. Before she made her formal entry into Madrid, she and Philip stayed at the royal monastery at El Escorial, which prompted one poet to declare, "The Moon and Sun occupy / the Escorial."[21] Using the sun and moon

to symbolize a husband and his loyal wife had an important precedent in a moralizing emblem that Sebastián de Covarrubias Orozco had published in 1610 (fig. 72). With a motto of *Clarior absens* ("The brighter one is absent")—a variation on Ovid, *Metamorphoses* 11.424, *Carior absens* ("The dearer one is absent")—it employs the increased brightness of the moon when it is farthest from the sun as a metaphor for wifely fidelity to an absent husband.[22] Inasmuch as Philip's death removed him from his wife, who did not remarry and who continued to serve his wishes by acting as regent, the example of the emblem might have contributed to the sense that lunar imagery was appropriate for Mariana at Philip's exequies. In addition, a few hieroglyphs portray the royal children, Charles II and Margarita María, as suns—in effect, solar progeny of the sun and moon. As a result, as many as three suns might be found in one hieroglyph (fig. 17).

A related planetary image that recurs in the hieroglyphs is the terrestrial globe, which signifies the territories of the Monarchy. This image lends itself to the interpretation of Philip's epithet, the Planet King, as a reference to the worldwide extent of his empire, and when it is combined with the sun, the two neatly express the relationship between the monarch and his dominions. To Philip's loyal subjects, the world was a Spanish globe. Méndez Silva expressed this notion in striking fashion upon the birth of Fernando Tomás, which occurred about thirteen months after the birth of Felipe Próspero: "The name Tomás, which in Hebrew signifies *Mellizo* [Twin] or *Gemelo* [Twin], is worthy of note, because

18. *Relacion breve de la muerte del Rey N. S.*, n.p.

19. Hortensio F. Paravicino [Arteaga], *Panegyrico funeral a la gloriosa memoria del Señor Rey D. Filipe Tercero El Piadoso*, 7.

20. Rodrigo Méndez Silva, *Nacimiento, y bautismo del Serenissimo Infante de España, D. Fernando Tomas de Avstria*, fol. 6.

21. *Relaciones breves*, 506.

22. Sebastián de Covarrubias Orozco, *Emblemas morales*, centuria II, emblema 41.

D. Fernando Tomás was born with the same felicity as the Prince D. Felipe Próspero, his brother (although not in one delivery); so that being two most unshakable Poles, Arctic and Antarctic, they may sustain the resplendent Spanish, and Austrian, Globe, and may rule the peoples who inhabit the face of the earth."[23]

Another recurrent symbol for the late king in the hieroglyphs is the royal crown, which signifies his person or his soul, just as the crown that rested atop the *tumba* symbolized his person. In fact, each of the other attributes that would have lain on his *tumba*—a scepter, a sword, and a collar of the Order of the Golden Fleece—turns up at least once in the hieroglyphs. There are also hieroglyphs in which multiple crowns, like multiple suns, signify other members of the royal family.

Conventional symbols of death and mortality abound in the hieroglyphs. Death is personified by a skull or by a skeletal arm emerging from a cloud. (She does not appear as a full-length skeleton, which is in keeping with the avoidance of full-length figures in all but two of the hieroglyphs.) In contrast, a flesh-covered arm emerging from a cloud represents the intervention of Divine Providence. Candles and sandglasses, which crop up several times, are traditional symbols of mortality and earthly transience— candles because they burn brightly until their wax has been consumed, and sandglasses because they measure the finite time allowed to each person on earth.[24] A scythe, the lethal implement with which Death mows down human lives, appears twice.

Some hieroglyphs depict unpopulated landscapes of rolling plains dotted with scrub that recede to distant mountains rising abruptly out of the terrain (for example, fig. 13). These recall the arid, sedimentary plains that separate Madrid from the mountains that lie in every direction. Including the local landscape in the hieroglyphs would have reminded spectators at the exequies that the king whom they were mourning had ruled the Crown of Castile. Moreover, a tree stump is found in the foreground of many of these landscapes. In part, the motif is a compositional device that defines the plane of space closest to the viewer; however, it may have more profound significance because tree stumps can symbolize rebirth and resurrection.[25] At a ceremony in which Masses were celebrated for the salvation of a dead man's soul, resurrection symbolism was indisputably apt.

Although the terrain in such landscapes appears ordinary, the skies overhead are sometimes enlivened by supernatural forces that carry off crowns, scepters, and other objects representing Philip's soul. Clouds part before them as they ascend to Heaven. The viewer never sees the heavenly host, but the glare of brilliant light from above is enough to suggest the profound difference between the Kingdom of God and the mundane world below.

The forty-one hieroglyphs proclaim Philip's greatness, console those who mourn his death with assurances that his soul has been saved, and declare with confidence that Charles's accession and Mariana's regency bode well for the Monarchy. By presenting the ruling family as extraordinary persons for whom special places are reserved in both

23. Méndez Silva, *Nacimiento, y bautismo*, fol. 14[v].
24. Tervarent, *Attributs*, cols. 70 and 330–31.

25. Susan D. Kuretsky, "Rembrandt's Tree Stump: An Iconographic Attribute of St. Jerome," 573.

this world and the next, they constitute an elaborate tribute that no single hieroglyph could have expressed so fully. This paean to the House of Austria comprises a variety of themes, but in general, the hieroglyphs that express them can be divided into three categories: biographical, consolatory, and political.

The *biographical hieroglyphs* concern themselves with the king's behavior on earth. Although a few allude to specific events, for the most part from his last days, the majority report the different virtues that Philip demonstrated throughout his life in order to portray him as a paragon of royal comportment. These include secular virtues that governed his relations with other human beings, but references to the spiritual virtues that characterized his demeanor toward God are more numerous. For all his failings, Philip was a fervent Catholic, and the hieroglyphs lay great weight upon that aspect of his personality.[26] The messages concealed within them range from general declarations that he had lived a pious life to precise references to specific doctrines he had espoused.

In particular, the hieroglyphs repeatedly proclaim Philip's attitudes toward two of the most important causes of the Catholic Counter-Reformation. The first is his devotion to the Sacrament of the Eucharist. Throughout his life the doctrine of Transubstantiation that informed Catholic understanding of the Eucharist was under attack by Protestant reformers whom Philip regarded as heretics. Philip never wavered in his adherence to Church teachings about the mysteries of the Blessed Sacrament. Indeed, the Habs-

burgs attributed their rise to power to an act of devotion that their ancestor, Holy Roman Emperor Rudolf I, had paid the Eucharist. According to family tradition, one day when Rudolf, then Count of Habsburg, was hunting on horseback, he encountered a priest carrying the Viaticum to a dying man. Dismounting from his horse so that the priest could ride in his place, Rudolf conducted the Host to the death-chamber on foot. The Habsburgs credited this deed with winning Rudolf divine favor, which enabled him to become the first of his house to be elected Holy Roman Emperor. Thereafter the Habsburgs venerated the Eucharist with special fervor. When the dying Philip IV commanded that the Viaticum be brought to him in public procession rather than in secret, he was openly declaring his reverence for the sacrament. It was fitting that a painting of the *Act of Devotion of Rudolf I* (fig. 76) hung over his deathbed—a circumstance that was recorded with approval in one of the epitaphs at La Encarnación (Appendix B, Courtyard Epitaph 1) and in Rodríguez de Monforte's account of his death.[27]

The hieroglyphs also acknowledge Philip's profound devotion to the cult of the Virgin Mary, whose unique role within the Church as Queen of Heaven and intercessor for mankind was denied by Protestant reformers. His ardor manifested itself not only in his observance of her feast days and his veneration of her miraculous images, but also in his pressing the Church to institute additional feasts in her honor and to adopt the doc-

26. There is no better testimony to the king's religiosity than his own letters; see *Cartas de Sor María de Jesús de Agreda y de Felipe IV*, ed. Carlos Seco Serrano.

27. Rodríguez de Monforte, *Descripcion*, fol. 23ᵛ. The painting can be identified from inventories of the royal art collection—see Yves Bottineau, "L'Alcázar de Madrid et l'inventaire de 1686," 302–3, no. 618; and Matías Díaz Padrón, *Museo del Prado, catálogo de pinturas. I: Escuela flamenca, siglo XVII*, 1:323–24, no. 1645.

trine of the Immaculate Conception as dogma. Two feasts that he promoted, the Feast of the Name of Mary and the Feast of the Patronage of the Virgin, were adopted in his lifetime, and although debate over the Immaculate Conception persisted well after his death, the Immaculist camp scored important gains during his reign.[28]

The *consolatory hieroglyphs* address themselves to Philip's afterlife in order to comfort those who mourn his passing. Such works provide two kinds of solace. The first is to remind the viewer that earthly existence is ephemeral and that every life must end. Hieroglyphs of this sort are essentially *vanitas* or *memento mori* images. They alone would not alleviate grief without a second, more direct assurance that Philip has attained eternal salvation in Heaven. By far the majority of the consolatory hieroglyphs are those that assert that in dying, the king has gone to a better place.

The *political hieroglyphs* concern themselves as much with Philip's survivors as with Philip himself. Their function is to assure the viewer that although the king has died, he has left a worthy successor who will govern the Monarchy well. In other words, they defend the legitimacy of Charles II's accession. Solar imagery proves especially helpful in conveying this theme by depicting Philip as a setting sun that yields the sky to Charles's rising sun. This equates the succession with the regularity and inevitability of the sun's daily course from east to west.

The continuity of the royal line was the object of acute concern throughout much of Philip's reign because few of his legitimate children enjoyed good health and

because he had more daughters than sons. Five of his offspring lived for less than a year, and at his death only three children survived him (see Table 1). His first four children by Isabella of Bourbon were short-lived daughters, all of whom went to the grave before Baltasar Carlos was born on October 17, 1629. The safe delivery of the long-awaited male heir inspired jubilant celebrations at the court.[29] Before she died on October 6, 1644, Isabella gave birth to two more daughters: María Antonia, who lived less than two years, and María Teresa, who proved more sturdy. Although Philip was left a widower, the royal succession appeared secure. Baltasar Carlos received the *juramento* of Castile in 1632, and in 1646 he swore to uphold the *fueros* (traditional rights) of Aragon, Valencia, and Navarre in separate ceremonies that confirmed him as heir apparent to those kingdoms. When the prince died of smallpox on October 9, 1646, it was a shattering blow to the Monarchy. Suddenly the king found himself with a single legitimate daughter, no male heir, and no wife to give him one.

Philip responded to this dilemma by marrying his niece, Mariana of Austria, who had been betrothed to Baltasar Carlos. On their wedding day, November 7, 1649, she had not yet reached her fifteenth birthday, whereas Philip had passed his forty-fourth. Their first child was a daughter, Margarita María, who was born July 12, 1651. Not until December 7, 1655, did Mariana deliver their second child, María Ambrosia, who died within two weeks. As the 1650s wore on, the royal family found itself caught in a diplomatic vise from which

---

28. For example, Rodríguez de Monforte, *Descripcion*, fols. 118–19, notes his promotion of these causes.

29. *Relacion del feliz parto que tuuo la Reyna nuestra Señora, en 17. de Octubre de 1629 . . .* ; and *Relaciones breves*, 379–90.

only the birth of a son could release it. Spain and France had been engaged in a debilitating war since 1635, and the prospect of a match between Louis XIV and Philip's elder daughter, María Teresa, was a compelling inducement to the French to end hostilities. The French raised the possibility of such a match during peace negotiations in 1656, but the Spanish rejected the suggestion. Philip knew that if the marriage took place and he died without leaving a male heir, the French would press María Teresa's claim to the Spanish throne. He feared that if they succeeded, the Monarchy would eventually pass to her firstborn son, and Spain would be ruled by a Bourbon king of France. For that reason, as long as Philip had no son, he could not permit the marriage.[30]

Excerpts from a series of *avisos* written at the time by Jerónimo de Barrionuevo underscore the royal dilemma. One, dated January 1, 1656, reports that members of the government were advocating that María Teresa receive the *juramento* of Castile, but the king would have none of it: "The Council of State and the Cortes are petitioning His Majesty that the Infanta be sworn to and that she go to Zaragoza this summer [to swear to uphold the *fueros* of Aragon]. He does not receive this well in order not to offend his wife, responding that soon he will have a male offspring, as if he had him in his pocket, and that this being so, it will not be considered as good [an idea] afterward as it is now."[31] Another *aviso* dated two weeks later opens bluntly, "Since Sunday the King [has been] sleeping with the Queen. God give him blessed sons for the tranquility of Spain and the defense of the faith, and above all for peace, which is that which is most meet for us."[32]

Mariana became pregnant again in 1657. In an *aviso* dated November 28, 1657, Barrionuevo states, "They are already putting in order the theatrical machines for a great *comedia* and entertainment that is ordered for the Queen's parturition. If it is a male, it will be in the Theater in the Retiro, and if it is a female, in the Great Hall of the Palace [the Alcázar]. Very soon, God being served, we shall be free of this uncertainty."[33] The distinction in how the birth would be celebrated—with a boy meriting the translation of the royal household from the Alcázar to the Buen Retiro, but not a girl—betrays the king's eagerness for a son. Barrionuevo evidently compiled this *aviso* in several sittings because it ends by reporting that a boy had been born at 11:30 A.M. on November 28.[34]

The infant was Felipe Próspero, whose birth triggered exuberant festivities at the Spanish court.[35] At last, the Monarchy again had a male heir to the throne. Even allowing for the exaggerations inherent in court flattery, the panegyric writings celebrating the prince's birth testify to the immense relief with which Felipe Próspero was greeted. To Méndez Silva, the birth proved that the Monarchy still enjoyed divine favor:

Our Spain, finding herself afflicted for want of a male [heir] who would succeed in her Catholic Crown, vast Monarchy, and sovereign Empire, did not cease to continuously implore Divine favor, until the infinite mercy,

30. Philip himself expressed his concern over the succession in some of his letters to Sor María de Jesús de Agreda in the period 1654–1656; see *Cartas de Sor María*, 1:335 and 2:15, 20, and 42.

31. Barrionuevo, *Avisos*, 2:252.

32. Ibid., 2:266–67.

33. Ibid., 3:395.

34. Ibid., 3:397.

35. Ibid., 3:405, 412, 415, and 433–35; Deleito y Piñuela, *El Rey se divierte*, 234–35; and "Epitome," fols. 605–5ᵛ.

hearing such gracious petitions and humble entreaties, granted her greatest desires. With which you will see quickly, O illustrious head of Europe, the obscure darkness of night end in the smiles of Dawn; for the climacteric year of your painful infirmity has passed. You revive, you become inspired, you gain strength, for the Princes of the Universe have to work changes at the sound of your desires; and in tranquil peace, you will enjoy golden ages, for the Most High has always carried you like his firstborn, hanging from his paternal breast, bound in his loving arms, and protected in the loving gaze of his eyes.[36]

And another author exulted,

Among the great benefits that Princes receive from the Celestial Clemency, a happy succession and peace in the Realm should be esteemed the best, because all the rest are useful and brilliant consequences [of these two things] and because they are so absolutely dependent upon Divine Providence that human prudence never has a part in the one and seldom in the other. This is proved with a singular example in this vast and honored Empire—which, having a King who is Just, Prudent, Pious, and for so many talents and faculties Great, and his Councils being composed of such wise and experienced men—this Great Monarchy finds itself obligated to defense against many enemies, with long-lasting wars in different places, and it was without a Male [heir] who would succeed in her. This was a concern that wearied the soul of the vassals, and when relief was closest (hope assuring it with the third pregnancy of the Queen our Lady), there still remained the uncertainty of the outcome, all the more feared because so much desired.

All was cleared up Wednesday, November 27 [sic], at 11:30 in the morning, the Prince being born with the Heavens in such a felici-

tous disposition (in the judgment of the Astrologers) that the Stars did not seem arranged at random, but rather positioned for what was desired.[37]

Another son, Fernando Tomás, was born on December 21, 1658. In the meantime negotiations to end the war with France had proceeded with renewed vigor. The Peace of the Pyrenees, as the settlement was called, provided for the marriage of Louis XIV and María Teresa, which the sudden abundance of Spanish royal sons had made possible. Louis dispatched an ambassador, the Marshal-Duke of Gramont, to Madrid, where on October 16, 1659, the ambassador formally asked Philip for María Teresa's hand on his sovereign's behalf.[38] Although Fernando Tomás died a week later, Felipe Próspero continued to secure Spain's future. On June 7, 1660, Philip presented his daughter to her bridegroom at the Isle of the Pheasants on the Franco-Spanish border. However, the expectation that Felipe Próspero would succeed his father proved false, for the prince died on November 1, 1661. Five days later Mariana gave birth to her last child, the future Charles II. In the space of a few days, the hopes of the Monarchy had been dashed and restored.

The new hope of Spain did not inspire confidence, for from his earliest years Charles showed signs of physical debility and mental incapacity. At his father's death, he was still being breast-fed by wet-nurses (which ceased upon his accession out of concern for royal decorum), and though nearly four years old, he had not yet learned to walk because his legs

---

36. Rodrigo Méndez Silva, *Gloriosa celebridad de España en el feliz nacimiento, y solemnissimo bavtismo de sv Deseado Principe D. Felipe Prospero . . .*, fols. 1–1*v*.

37. Luis de Ulloa, *Fiestas qve se celebraron en la Corte por el nacimiento de Don Felipe Prospero, Principe de Asturias*, n.p.

38. On this ceremony and its artistic consequences, see Orso, *Alcázar of Madrid*, 37–41 and 105–7.

could not support his weight.[39] On October 28, 1665, while Mariana was retired from public in mourning, Charles granted his first audience to the ambassadors to the court, who had come to the Alcázar to deliver the *pésame*, a traditional expression of condolence, for the death of his father. Georges Dubesen, the French ambassador, could not attend owing to the illness that also prevented him from participating in Philip's royal exequies two days later, but he sent home a report based upon the Venetian ambassador's account of the audience: "The king was propped up by the back of an armchair that was placed on a dais in his apartment; and his governess, who was behind the chair, held him by a ribbon attached to his robe. He said to these gentlemen, *Cubríos* (Cover yourselves), at the start of the discourse that the nuncio made, and at the end, *Agradezco mucho* (Thank you very much). One did not see that royalty had given him new strengths; and somebody always has him fastened by a not very long ribbon when he walks."[40]

Dubesen had an opportunity to confirm this account on November 16, 1665, when he accompanied the Marquis of Bellefond and two gentlemen, whom Louis XIV had sent to pay his respects to the Spanish court, to their audience with the king. Four days later he wrote to Louis,

We had the time to consider the king of Spain well during various compliments that M. de Bellefond made to him in French on the part of Your Majesty, on that of the queen and queen mother, and of M. le Dauphin, which I

explained in Spanish, and I finished by presenting those gentlemen who had come with him. The king of Spain was standing, propped up on the knees of the *señora* Miguel de Texada, a *menina*, who held him up by the ribbons of his gown. He wore a small bonnet in the English fashion on his head that he did not have the strength to pull off, as he would have otherwise done when I approached him with M. le Marquis de Bellefond. We were not able to draw any word from him, except that which he said to me, *cubríos* (cover yourself), and his governess, who was to the right of the *menina*, made some replies to our compliments.

He seemed extremely weak, his visage pale and his mouth open wide, which indicates some indisposition of his stomach (so the doctors stand in agreement on it); and although it is said that he walks on his own feet and that the *menina* only has him by the ribbons in order to prevent him from making a misstep, I would doubt that strongly. And I saw that he took the hand of his governess to support himself upon withdrawing. Be that as it may, the doctors are pessimistic for his long life; and it seems that here one takes that foundation as the basis for all deliberations.[41]

Fate had selected this pathetic child to be the guarantor of the ideals and aspirations of the Monarchy, and Mariana's regency government had no choice but to put the best possible face on such bleak prospects. Claiming that the ribbons that kept Charles from falling on his face were not really necessary was one way of doing so, and seeing to it that Philip's royal exequies included hieroglyphs that characterized Charles as a legitimate and capable successor was another. After any king's death, the people needed to be reassured of the continuity of the royal line, and in 1665 the need was extraordinary.

For her part, Mariana needed to estab-

39. Henry Kamen, *Spain in the Later Seventeenth Century, 1665–1700*, 21.

40. *Négociations relatives*, 1:402. The command "Cover yourselves" permitted the ambassadors to wear their hats in Charles's presence.

41. Ibid., 1:403–4.

lish her authority as queen governor in the public mind. The provisions of Philip's will that named her regent created a situation last seen in Spain 259 years earlier, when the death of Henry III of Castile had brought John II to the throne at the age of twenty-two months.[42] Mariana was ill prepared for the task before her, and she was not disposed to rely upon the advice of the junta that Philip had constituted to assist her, or upon the aristocratic elite who sat on the royal councils. She was also determined to resist the maneuverings of Juan José de Austria, Philip's son by the actress María Calderón and the only one of his bastards whom he had legally recognized as his natural child.[43] Until his death in 1679, Juan José vied with Mariana for influence over Charles and the power that it brought.

42. Caparrós, "Enfermedad," 182–83.

43. Mariana surely would have known that Juan José had attempted to see his father when he lay on his deathbed; however, Philip had refused to receive him (Stradling, *Philip IV*, 329).

Whatever her limitations, Mariana would have realized from the outset that maintaining her authority required that she impress upon her subjects the unique standing that she enjoyed as Philip's widow, Charles's mother, and the regent whom Philip had named as tutor of their son. Some of the hieroglyphs from Philip's exequies make those very points, thereby defending the legitimacy of the regency as forcefully as others defend the legitimacy of Charles's accession.

Thus, the hieroglyphs from Philip's royal exequies are a melange of emblems intended to glorify the deceased, comfort his subjects, and promote the new regime. However, they are not divided rigidly into biographical, consolatory, and political categories. Because each hieroglyph combines a verse, a motto, and visual symbols into a sophisticated message, more than one idea can inform its meaning. As a result, some hieroglyphs straddle two of these categories, and a few address the concerns of all three.

9
CATALOGUE OF THE HIEROGLYPHS

In the catalogue that follows, each hiero-glyph is designated by the number that corresponds to its position in the sequence in which the hieroglyphs appear in Rodríguez de Monforte's book. Hieroglyphs 1 through 16 hung in the courtyard and atrium of La Encarnación, and Hiero-glyphs 17 through 41 hung in the nave. The entry for each hieroglyph consists of four parts: (*a*) the Latin motto, its translation, and a confirmation of its source (when known); (*b*) the Spanish verse with a prose translation; (*c*) a description of the symbolic image; and (*d*) an explanation of the hieroglyph's meaning.

HIEROGLYPH 1 (fig. 10)

Motto: *AGNVS, ET LEO. Apc 5. 6.*
"The lamb and the lion" (source: see below)

Verse: *Mansedumbre, y fortaleça*
De Cordero, y de Leon
Yacen en vn Coraçon.
"The gentleness and fortitude of a Lamb and a Lion exist in one Heart."

Image: A lion rears up in an open land-scape, props its right forepaw on a boulder, and turns its head to regard the viewer. It wears a collar of the Order of the Golden Fleece.

This biographical hieroglyph asserts that Philip demonstrated gentleness and fortitude while he lived, and the parallel-isms of the motto and verse suggest they were present in equal measure. The lion is a conventional symbol of fortitude.[1] What is more, as the "king of beasts" the lion is an apt symbol for the King of Spain; in fact, *el león de España* ("the lion of Spain") is one of Philip's epithets.[2] Leonine imagery is also pertinent because in astrology the constellation Leo the Lion is the House of the Sun, another symbol for the king at his exequies.[3]

The lion's pose is that of the heraldic lion rampant guardant: body facing dexter, head turned toward the viewer, trunk inclined upward, forepaws elevated with the dexter above the sinister, standing on the sinister hindpaw, and tail flourished upward and curved over to the sinister. The present lion differs from the heraldic type in two ways. It does not raise its dexter hindpaw (in order to keep its balance), and it does not stick out its tongue (which would show fierceness, not gentleness). Had it not been necessary for the lion to display its collar, its pose could have been that of the more familiar lion rampant (with its head seen in profile) found on the arms of several realms of the Monarchy (figs. 26–29). The collar, which enhances the lion as a symbol of the king because Philip commanded the Order of the Golden Fleece, introduces the lamb that signifies his gentleness.[4] In

1. Ripa, *Iconologia*, 179–81; and Tervarent, *Attributs*, col. 243.
2. For example, *Relaciones breves*, 461.
3. Tervarent, *Attributs*, cols. 247–48.
4. Ibid., cols. 2–3; and Ripa, *Iconologia*, 42.

this the inventor of the hieroglyph has indulged in artistic license because the "lamb" is a ram—that is, the miniature ram's fleece that depends from the collar.

The putative source that the banderole gives for the motto, Apocalypse 5:6, is only loosely tied to the phrase *agnus et leo*. The word *lion* appears in Apocalypse 5:5; the word *lamb* appears in Apocalypse 5:6. In the Spanish verse the verb *yacen* can also mean "lie in the grave," a variant reading that would have suited the exequies as well.

Hieroglyph 1 recalls a passage from a sermon that Philip IV had Hortensio Félix Paravicino Arteaga deliver in honor of Philip III that was later published by the court. In it the Trinitarian preacher spoke of a lion and a lamb in conjunction with Saint John's vision of the Apocalypse:

St. John proclaimed that the Lion conquered, and at the end it was the Lamb that opened the seals of the book, and to which they sang the glory with particular mystery. For the Lion of Spain does not carry the Lamb of Austria on its chest by accident, but rather in order to show the world that he has the claws of a Lion for his enemy, and the kindness of a Lamb for his vassal.[5]

Perhaps this praise for Philip III inspired the hieroglyph for Philip IV.

HIEROGLYPH 2 (fig. 11)

Motto: *ORIETVR IN TENEBRIS LVX.* Isai. 58
"Light will arise in darkness." (Isaiah 58:10)

Verse: *En los rayos de la Luna*
Viue ardiendo otro farol:
No es noche aunque murio el Sol.
"In the rays of the Moon another light lives burning; it is not night although the Sun died."

Image: In the left background of a rural landscape, a sun shrouded in clouds sets behind a mountain. To the right a smaller sun that is cradled within the points of a crescent moon shines brightly, unhindered by clouds.

The sun setting in the distant gloom is Philip, the dead sun of the verse. The second sun, which has risen in its place, represents his son Charles, and it is smaller because Charles has succeeded his father while he is still a child. The moon that protects the smaller sun is Mariana, who is to serve as queen governor during Charles's minority. Hieroglyph 2 acknowledges the legitimacy of the succession (which proceeds in as regular and as orderly a fashion as a sunrise follows a sunset) and the desirability of the regency. Because the smaller sun and the moon occupy a cloudless expanse of sky, the hieroglyph also suggests that their day (that is, Mariana's regency and Charles's adult reign) will be free from misfortune.

HIEROGLYPH 3 (fig. 12)

Motto: *NVNC IN EORVM CANTICVM VERSVS SVM.* Iob. 30.
"Now I am turned into their song." (Job 30:9)

Verse: *En el morir considero*
Vn goço tan superior,
Que afecto cantar mejor
En albricias de que muero.

5. Paravicino [Arteaga], *Panegyrico fvneral*, 27–28. A similar hieroglyph was displayed at the exequies that the city of Toledo celebrated in Philip IV's honor on December 23, 1665; see Hurtado, *La Philipica oracion*, 66.

"In dying, I consider a joy so superior that I make a show of singing better, in joy of which, I die."

Image: A swan dies beside a harp that stands at the edge of a vast body of water. Another swan swims close to the shore and watches.

Antique legend holds that a swan will sing its most beautiful song immediately before it dies (hence the idiom *swan song*).[6] Here the dying swan represents Philip, the joy that he has considered is the salvation of his soul, and his last song is his good death—that is, his display of steadfast devotion to the Faith on his deathbed. Philip dedicated his last days to acts of contrition, which he carried out with dignity and patience in spite of his illness. He prayed and confessed at length; he took Communion even after receiving Extreme Unction; he had images of Christ on the Cross and the Virgin Mary mounted on the curtains of his bed for his contemplation; and he died while adoring the crucifix that Charles I, Philip II, Philip III, and Baltasar Carlos had revered at their deaths. All these actions constituted a "good death" that prepared his soul for heavenly judgment. The living swan may represent Charles, whom Philip has left as a survivor.

The harp, a symbol of joy, signifies the spiritual joy of salvation to which the verse alludes.[7] Indeed, the Book of Psalms repeatedly identifies the harp as an instrument with which to praise the Lord, as in such verses as "Give praise to the Lord on the harp" (Psalm 32:2), "To you, O God my God, I shall give praise upon the harp" (Psalm 42:4), and "Sing praise to

the Lord on the harp" (Psalm 97:5). Because it was the instrument on which David played (as in I Kings 16:23), the harp may also be intended to compare Philip to the Old Testament king, a mighty ruler who had enjoyed God's favor.

The Spanish verse and studies for the two swans and the harp are found on one of Herrera Barnuevo's preparatory drawings for the exequies decorations (fig. 70).[8] He probably sketched them to guide the artist who painted the hieroglyph, just as the studies of coats of arms that fill the greater part of the sheet were probably intended to guide the artists who painted the coats of arms for the church nave.

HIEROGLYPH 4 (fig. 13)

Motto: *VSQVE AD OCCASVM LAVDABILE. Malach. 2.*
"Unto the end praiseworthy" (Psalm 112:3, with an echo at Malachi 1:11; not from Malachi 2)

Verse: *Viernes santo amanecio*
Sol, que Cruz, y Eucharistia
En su exaltacion junto
Y en Iueves su dia espiro
Con el nombre de Maria.
"The Sun that joined the Cross and the Eucharist in its exaltation rose on Good Friday, and on Thursday its day ended with the name of Mary."

Image: Clouds obscure the sun as it shines over a landscape.

Like the clouds that obscure the setting sun in Hieroglyph 2, the clouds in this

6. Tervarent, *Attributs*, cols. 138–39 and 141.
7. Ibid., col. 209.

8. AHN, Códices 288b, fol. 27^{v}; as first noted by Marías and Bustamante, "Apuntes arquitectónicos," 36–38.

image suggest that Death has claimed the personage whom the sun represents. The verse makes it clear that the deceased is Philip. He was born (sunrise) on a Good Friday (April 8, 1605). While he lived (the solar day), he was a good Christian who venerated the Cross, on which Christ had died to redeem mankind, and the Sacrament of the Eucharist, which offered him salvation. His death (sunset) occurred on Thursday, September 17, 1665, the Feast of the Holy Name of Mary. The feast had significant associations with Spain and the king. It had been instituted in Cuenca in 1513, and in response to Philip's petitioning, Pope Gregory XV had extended its observance to the entire Archbishopric of Toledo in 1622. Upon Philip's death in 1665, several writers cited his role in obtaining the extension as evidence of his devotion to the Virgin.[9]

HIEROGLYPH 5 (fig. 14)

Mottoes: *NONDVM ERAT LVX. Iuan. 1.*
"There was not yet light." (Variation on John 1:4, 8, or 9)
SEMEL MORI. Ad Hebr. 9.
"To die once" (Hebrews 9:27)

Verse: *De que duracion presumes*
Luz, si entre sagradas ruinas
Si no ardes, no illuminas,
Y si ardes te consumes?

9. Rodríguez de Monforte, *Descripcion*, fols. 24 and 117[v]–19; Caparrós, "Enfermedad," 182; Díaz de Ylarraza, *Relacion*, n.p.; Bartolomé García de Escañuela, *Penas en la mverte, y alivios en las virtvdes de el rey catholico de las Españas N. S. Felipe IV . . .* , 5; Frederick G. Holweck, "Name of Mary, Feast of the Holy"; Lezana, *Memorial*, fol. 15[v]; *Relacion de la enfermedad*, n.p.; and untitled *gaceta*, BNM, Ms. 2,392, n.p.

"How long do you presume to last, Light, although among sacred ruins, if you don't burn, you don't illuminate, and if you do burn, you are consumed?"

Image: Two objects float over an empty plain: an unused taper in which a royal scepter is embedded and a lighted taper which has a royal crown for its candlestick.

This *vanitas* image acknowledges the inherent tragedy of human life by equating the opportunity that a king (symbolized by the scepter and the crown) has to rule with the capacity of a candle to shed light. For the king to rule, he must be born as a human being, just as the candle must be lighted if it is to illuminate. However, to be a human being is to face inevitable death, just as a candle will burn out when it has consumed all its wax. Hence, Philip's passing was the inescapable price of his earthly greatness.

The verse reference to "sacred ruins" is puzzling. Perhaps it is a metaphor for the catafalque, which bore hundreds of lighted candles during the king's exequies. The ambiguity may have been necessary to provide *ruinas* as a rhyme for *iluminas*.

HIEROGLYPH 6 (fig. 15)

Motto: *ESTO FIDELIS VSQVE AD MORTEM, ET DABO TIBI CORONAM VITÆ. Apoc. 2.*
"Be faithful unto death, and I shall give you the crown of life." (Apocalypse 2:10)

Verse: *En Philipo si se advierte*
Ay bentaja conocida,

De lo que le dio la vida,
A lo que le dio la muerte.
"In Philip, indeed, it is seen that there is a noticeable advantage in that which death gave him over that which life gave him."

Image: A royal crown sits balanced on top of two terrestrial globes that rest on the bare earth. The skeletal hand of Death emerges from a cloud and holds a second crown above the first. In the background alternating light and dark arcs fill the sky.

The two globes symbolize the Old World and the New World, and the single crown that rests atop them signifies the dominion that Philip exercised over his territories in both. This earthly crown of temporal power is "what life gave him"—an empire to which he was heir from birth. In fact, *el rey de dos mundos* ("the king of two worlds") is one of his epithets.[10] Death, on the other hand, holds out the heavenly crown of eternal life—that is, the Christian salvation of Philip's soul—to which the motto refers. This gift of God's grace surpasses all temporal honors in value. It is the "noticeable advantage" that Death, to whom all must yield as the prelude to salvation, has conferred upon the king. The arcs that fill the background are probably meant to represent the celestial spheres through which Philip's soul passes as it ascends to the empyrean.[11]

This hieroglyph has a notable Spanish precedent in an emblem with the motto *Non magna relinquam* ("I shall not leave great things behind" [Ovid, *Metamorphoses* 7.55]) that was devised by Covarrubias Orozco (fig. 73). It shows a king who discards a crown, a scepter, an orb, and a mantle (four symbols of earthly rule) as he pursues another crown that appears in the sky. In his commentary Covarrubias Orozco explains that kings owe their empires to God. If they govern well, they will have hope of attaining greater glory (salvation), but if they lose sight of the eternal Kingdom of God, their earthly powers will serve only to worsen the sins in which they become embroiled.[12]

HIEROGLYPH 7 (fig. 16)

Motto: *PLANGENTES ADONIDEN SVVM. Eccech. 8.*
"Weeping for your Adonis" (Variation on Ezekiel 8:14)

Verse: *Sola vna Muerte se llora*
Pero las Viudas tres son
Piedad, Reyna, y Religion.
"Only one Death is mourned, but the Widows are three: Piety, Queen, and Religion."

Image: A crowned skull hovers in the sky. Below it, left to right, are a church built to a circular plan, a crowned eagle in flight, and a butte on which an adult pelican pierces its breast so that its two young can feed on its blood.

The use of the crowned skull illustrates how symbols with dual meanings can en-

10. For example, Lezana, *Memorial*, fol. 4.
11. For representations of the cosmos in terms of concentric celestial spheres, see S. K. Heninger, Jr., *The Cosmographical Glass: Renaissance Diagrams of the Universe*, esp. 14–80.

12. Covarrubias Orozco, *Emblemas morales*, centuria III, emblema 7. This may also have informed two similar two-crown hieroglyphs at the royal exequies for Isabella of Bourbon; see *Pompa Fvneral Honras*, fols. 19ᵛ and 24ᵛ–25.

rich a hieroglyph. The motif can be interpreted as a representation of *mors imperator*—that is, of Death as the empress who exerts absolute power over all who inhabit the temporal world. Another interpretation is to regard the crown as Philip's soul, which Death (the skull) carries off to Heaven. Both readings accord with the funereal concerns of the hieroglyph.

Philip is the Adonis of the motto who is mourned, and it is his death that has left the three widows who are listed in the verse. Religion is symbolized by the church.[13] Calling Religion a widow implies that when Philip died, the institutional Church lost one of its most ardent defenders. The queen (Mariana) is a widow because she has lost her husband, and she is represented here by the eagle, whose crown indicates her royal status. The bird is an appropriate symbol of royalty because the eagle is traditionally regarded as the king of birds. (Presumably king eagles had queen eagles as mates.) Moreover, the eagle is an attribute of Royal Majesty.[14] Like the lion (see Hieroglyph 1), the eagle is also a heraldic creature found on the arms of several realms of the Monarchy (figs. 26 and 29). Naming Piety as the third widow declares that Philip believed in the Christian promise of salvation. Here his piety is signified by the pelican that feeds its young with its blood, which is a traditional symbol of Christ's death for the redemption of mankind.[15]

It may be intentional that the pelican feeds two chicks because two royal children, Charles and Margarita María, survived Philip at the Spanish court. There is

no reference to his other surviving legitimate child, María Teresa, in this or in any other hieroglyph. When she married Louis XIV in 1660 and became Queen of France, she renounced her rights of inheritance to the Spanish throne. In 1665 it suited the political interests of Spain to avoid suggesting that any such rights still existed. Nor is there any reference to Philip's natural son, Juan José, because ignoring him served Mariana's need to minimize his political influence.

HIEROGLYPH 8 (fig. 17)

Motto: *IMPEDITVS EST SOL, ET VNA DIES FACTA EST, QVASI DUO. Ecles. 46*
"The sun was halted, and one day made like two." (Ecclesiasticus 46:5)

Verse: *No llore esta Monarchia*
Si impedido, no apagado
Mira al Sol, pues le an quedado
Otros dos en solo vn dia.
"This Monarchy should not mourn. Although [it is] hindered, [it is] not extinguished. It looks to the Sun, for two others have remained to it in only one day."

Image: Three suns arranged in an equilateral triangle shine on a terrestrial globe that rests in an open landscape. Clouds obscure the uppermost sun from view.

The sun that clouds hide from the globe is Philip, whom the Monarchy has lost. The two suns that remain in view on the day of his death are his children, Charles and Margarita María. As in Hieroglyph 7, María Teresa and Juan José are ignored for political reasons.

13. Ripa, *Iconologia*, 455.
14. Ibid., 326.
15. Tervarent, *Attributs*, col. 302.

HIEROGLYPH 9 (fig. 18)

Motto: *ET HABITAVIT ARCA DOM-INI IN DOMO OBEDEDON.*
2 Reg. 6.
"And the Ark of the Lord abode in the house of Obededom." (II Kings 6:11)

Verse: *Catholico Obededon*
No solo al Arca dio asiento,
Pero al mismo Sacramento
Dio en su casa habitacion.
"The Catholic Obededom gave a place not only to the Ark, but to the Sacrament itself he gave a dwelling place in his house."

Image: An altar covered with fringed and embroidered frontals stands in an arched niche or chapel. Two seraphim flutter over a covered box that sits on top of the altar, and above them floats a glowing Host.

This hieroglyph uses an Old Testament prefiguration to praise Philip's devotion to the Sacrament of the Eucharist. The motto refers to the time when David refrained from implementing his plan to bring the Ark of the Covenant into Jerusalem out of fear of the Lord. Instead he placed it in the house of Obededom the Gittite, whereupon "the Lord blessed Obededom and all his household" (II Kings 6:9–11). Philip became the "Catholic Obededom" of the verse when he secured permission from Pope Urban VIII to have the Holy Sacrament installed in the Royal Chapel of the Alcázar of Madrid on a permanent basis. That raised the Royal Chapel to the status of a parish church. The installation took place on March 10, 1639, when the Host was car-ried in a solemn procession from the church of San Juan (which until then had been the Alcázar's parish church) to the Royal Chapel.[16] The prefiguration is straightforward: Whereas the Ark (the box on the altar) held the tablets of the Old Law that signified the Old Covenant between God and the Jews, the Sacra-ment of the Eucharist (the glowing Host) confirmed the New Covenant of Christ's redemption of mankind by His death on the Cross. When Philip died, the installa-tion of the Holy Sacrament in the Royal Chapel was among the deeds that were cited as evidence of his devotion to the Eucharist.[17]

HIEROGLYPH 10 (fig. 19)

Motto: *OPTIMAM PARTEM ELEGIT.*
Luce. 10.
"He has chosen the best part." (Luke 10:42)

Verse: *Bien hiciste gran Monarcha*
(Aunque lagrimas nos cueste)
En dejar este, por este.
"You did well, great Monarch (although it may cost us tears), by relinquishing this, for this."

16. *Cartas de algunos PP.* 3:190 and 194–97; "Epitome," fols. 188–88ᵛ; Antonio de León Pi-nelo, *Anales de Madrid (desde el año 447 al de 1658),* ed. Pedro Fernández Martín, 316; "Papeles varios" [*noticias* from 1637–1642], fols. 85–90ᵛ; and *Relaciones breves,* 461–64.

17. Lezana, *Memorial,* fol. 15; Manuel de Ná-jera, *Sermon funebre ... En las svmptvosas lvgvbres exeqvias que hizieron a su Magestad en el Colegio Imperial de la Compañia de Iesus ...,* 15; Rodríguez de Monforte, *Descripcion,* fols. 118ᵛ–19; and "Tratado de las ceremonias," fols. 8ᵛ–9. Rodríguez de Monforte, *Descripcion,* states that Pope Gregory XV authorized the installation, but that appears to be part of a confusion that also mis-takenly ascribes Gregory's bull authorizing the ex-tension of the Feast of the Holy Name of Mary (see Hieroglyph 4) to Pope Urban VIII.

Image: A terrestrial globe sits in an open landscape. Above it clouds part before the approach of a rising scepter. A hand emerges from the clouds at the left and points upward while another hand emerges from the right and points down at the globe.

In dying, Philip has relinquished his dominion over the Monarchy (the terrestrial globe). By doing so, he has attained the greater glory of eternal salvation in the Kingdom of Heaven, into which the scepter that represents him ascends. Although his subjects may grieve at his death, Philip has gone to an undeniably better place. The hands of Providence that point at Heaven and the globe signify that the king's salvation is God's will.

HIEROGLYPH 11 (fig. 20)

Motto: *ET SVSCITABO EI GERMEN IVSTVM ET REGNAVIT REX. Hiere. 23*
"I shall raise up to him a righteous branch, and he will reign as king." (Variation on Jeremiah 23:5)

Verse: *Las obras parten los dos*
Por enriquecer vn marmol,
Si la parca corta el arbol,
El pinpollo guarda Dios.
"The powers divide the two in order to enrich a marble; although death cuts the tree, God protects the shoot."

Image: The skeletal arm of Death emerges from an empty sepulcher and pulls the trunk of a great tree into the tomb. A bough that branches off the trunk continues to grow upward.

This hieroglyph employs the metaphor of the "family tree" to assert the legitimacy and the continuity of the royal succession. The tree is Philip, whose royal corpse will soon enrich the marble sepulcher. The branch that grows from the tree trunk is his son Charles, whose reign lies ahead. Under God's benevolent protection, which the hieroglyph prophesies for him, Charles will grow to greatness like his father. This hieroglyph may have been inspired by the same emblematic tradition that informs Hieroglyph 35 (see below).

HIEROGLYPH 12 (fig. 21)

Motto: *ELEVATUS EST SOL, ET LVNA STETIT IN ORDINE SVO. Abac. 3.*
"The sun rose, and the moon stood in its place." (Variation on Habbakuk 3:11)

Verse: *Esta Luna con luz nueua*
Viue a pesar de esse monte,
Que el Sol en otro oriçonte
No falta, quando se eleua.
"In spite of this mountain, this Moon lives with new light because the Sun on another horizon is not wanting when it rises."

Image: A butte surmounted by a skull dominates the center of the image. In the sky at the upper left a cloudbank begins to conceal the sun from view. On the other side of the butte the moon rises wearing a crown. It is in a crescent phase, but the remainder of its circumference is indicated faintly.

Once again a skull symbolizes Death, and its preeminence in relation to the surrounding landscape signifies the inevitability of death in the mundane world. The sun is Philip, the moon is Mariana, and their placement on opposite sides of the butte represents their having been separated by the king's death. The clouds that have begun to conceal the sun likewise allude to Philip's death, and the moon's crown signifies that Mariana has assumed the duties and authority of the regency.

If Philip's sun were still the moon's source of light, its crescent would appear on the left side of its sphere, but it is the right side that is illuminated. This means the moon has a new source of light, a sun that lies beyond the right edge of the composition. That would be the sun "on another horizon" from the verse, which must be Charles's sun rising in the east. Thus, the hieroglyph underscores the political relationship between Mariana and her child. As regent, she presides over the Monarchy (the landscape), but her authority results from her relationship to Charles, the new source of the moon's light. The hieroglyph predicts he will be a good king, for as the verse says, the new sun "is not wanting."

HIEROGLYPH 13 (fig. 22)

Motto: *TRANSIVIMVS PER IGNEN, ET AQVAM. Psal. 65.*
"We have passed through fire and water." (Psalm 65:12)

Verse: *Si al mar de la muerte entrega*
Su Imperial corriente clara
Philippo, llega, y no para
Aunque para, donde llega.
"Although Philip delivers his clear, Imperial current to the sea of death, it arrives and does not stop, although it stops where it arrives."

Image: A river flows into a turbulent, flaming sea on which a skull floats. Instead of mixing with the sea, however, the river twists across its surface and ascends into the sky as a column of water.

The river symbolizes Philip's earthly life, which ends when the river reaches the sea where Death (the skull) presides—"it [his life] stops where it [the river] arrives." However, the sea does not consume his current, which abruptly changes course and rises into the sky. This signifies that Death has conquered only Philip's mortal part. His immortal soul has been saved, and it ascends into Heaven—"it arrives [at Death] and does not stop."

Depicting the sea of Death as a vast, flaming ocean was probably inspired by the "pool of fire and brimstone" into which the Bible says the damned will be cast at the Last Judgment (see Apocalypse 19:20; 20:9–10 and 14–15; and 21:8). Philip, however, has not been damned, but saved. In contrast to the flaming brimstone, the clarity of his current (to which the verse alludes) may represent the piety and goodness that have earned him salvation.

HIEROGLYPH 14 (fig. 23)

Motto: *RENOVABITVR VT AQUILA. Ps. 102.*
"He will be renewed like the eagle." (Psalm 102:5)

Verse: *En esse, Renuebo mio,*
(Que esta presente a mi vuelo)
Le queda al mundo el consuelo.
"In that one, my Renewal (who is present at my flight), consolation is left to the world."

Image: As it flies over an open plain, an eagle sheds its feathers and looks back at a second eagle that regards its flight from a nest atop a butte.

As in Hieroglyph 7, the eagles in this image signify members of the royal family, Philip (in flight) and Charles (in the nest). This hieroglyph refers to two kinds of "renewals." First, it alludes to the ancient belief that aged eagles could rejuvenate themselves by a process that entailed flying toward the sun to burn off their old feathers.[18] The ongoing renewal of the flying eagle represents Philip's rejuvenation into a new life—the eternal life of the Christian soul in Heaven. The flight also lends itself to this interpretation because Spanish royal exequies were regarded as modern adaptations of the funeral rites of the ancient Roman emperors. When the funeral pyre of a Roman emperor was set ablaze, an eagle was released in order to symbolize the apotheosis of his soul.[19] Second, the "Renewal" of the verse is Charles, the nestling that stays behind while its father flies away. By carrying on in his father's place, Charles renews the Habsburg dedication to defending the Monarchy and the Catholic Faith.

Such imagery had been used at the court well before 1665. In 1603 the decorations for the exequies that the Jesuit College in Madrid staged in honor of the Empress María featured a hieroglyph in which an eagle shed its feathers in order to rejuvenate itself (fig. 77). The motto,

a slight variation on Psalm 102:5 (the source for the motto of Hieroglyph 14), declared, *RENOVABITVR VT AQVILÆ IVVENTVS MEA* ("My youth will be renewed like the eagle's"). The verse stated,

Bate el Aguila Imperial
Las alas al Sol, do dexa
La pluma y la vida vieja,
Para viuir la inmortal.

(The Imperial Eagle flaps its wings in the Sun, where it relinquishes its feathers and its old life, in order to live the immortal [life].)

According to the book recording the event, this hieroglyph stood for the increasing piety and religious fervor that the empress had displayed in her later years—that is, for her spiritual renewal.[20]

Five years later, when the future Philip IV received the *juramento* of Castile as a two-year-old, he fell asleep in the middle of the ceremony. That prompted one observer to write, "The Renewal of the royal Eagle of Spain slept in the rays of the Sun, his father [Philip III]."[21] In a similar vein, an anonymous account of Baltasar Carlos's first meeting with his father after Isabella of Bourbon died refers to the prince as the "Renewal of his [Philip's] Greatness."[22]

HIEROGLYPH 15 (fig. 24)

Motto: *ABIIT, NON OBIIT.*
     "He has departed, not died."

Verse: *Para que vuelba a Reynar*
    (Equibocando la suerte)
    Me dio sus alas la Muerte.

18. *Libro de las Honras qve hizo el Colegio de la Côpañía de Iesvs de Madrid, à la M. C. de la Emperatriz doña Maria de Austria . . .* , fol. 59ᵛ; Tervarent, *Attributs*, col. 8; and Rudolf Wittkower, "Eagle and Serpent: A Study in the Migration of Symbols," 313.

19. See Berendsen, "Catafalques," 156–57; and Giesey, *Royal Funeral Ceremony*, 148–49.

20. *Libro de las Honras*, fols. 59ᵛ–60.
21. *Relaciones breves*, 60.
22. *Escrivense los svbcessos de Espana, Flandes, Italia, y otras partes de la Europa, desde Março de 44. hasta el mismo de 45*, n.p.

"So that I could reign again (overcoming fate), Death gave me her wings."

Image: Clouds part before a crowned, winged skull that flies over the countryside.

The winged skull is Death, who carries Philip's soul (the crown) into the Kingdom of Heaven, where Philip will "reign again"—that is, where he will live forever amid the heavenly host. The "fate" he has overcome is the mortality of his flesh, the common frailty of all mankind. Only the death of his body could release his soul to Heaven. For that reason, the verse has Philip credit Death for helping his soul to ascend to God. Thus, in the words of the motto, the king's soul "has departed, not died."

HIEROGLYPH 16 (fig. 25)

Motto: *VISVS SVM OCVLIS INSIPI-ENTIVM MORI. Sap. 3.*
"In the eyes of the unwise I seemed to die." (Variation on Wisdom 3:2)

Verse: *Ignorante juzgo el mundo*
Que dejaua de viuir,
Y fui dichoso en morir.
"The world judged foolishly that I stopped living, and I was fortunate in dying."

Image: A *tumba* standing in a darkened chamber atop a three-stepped dais supports a cushion on which a royal crown and scepter lie. Six large candlesticks with lighted tapers line the lateral sides of the bottom step at regular intervals.

The motto and verse offer Philip's mourners the consolation that he has gone to a heavenly reward that surpasses all his earthly glories. This assurance is all the more forceful because both texts have Philip address the viewer in the first person. He dismisses as foolish those who think his death is his misfortune. The image combines elements from a royal lying-in-state and from royal exequies to create a funeral monument that signifies that the king has died. According to the *etiquetas* of 1647–1651, at a lying-in-state, "The body is put in the Great Hall [of the Alcázar of Madrid], and for this a platform three steps in height is built at the head of the hall . . . and it is carpeted. A canopy is hung, and below it an opulent bed is set up."[23] In lieu of a royal corpse lying in an open coffin on a bed of sorrow, this hieroglyph substitutes a *tumba* similar to one that would be found inside a royal catafalque. As a result, the crown and scepter on the cushion draw attention to the royal authority that Philip has had to surrender to attain his heavenly reward.

HIEROGLYPH 17 (fig. 30)

Motto: *SOL, ET LVNA STETERVNT IN HABITACVLO SVO. Abac. 3.*
"The sun and moon stood still in their habitation." (Habakkuk 3:11)

Verse: *El Sol en el Sacramento,*
Y la Luna de Maria,
Haran esta Noche Dia.
"The Sun in the Sacrament and the Moon of Mary will make this Night Day."

23. "Etiquetas generales de la Casa R! del Rey nˉ̃ro. S: para el Uso y exerzicio de los ofizios de sus Criados," fol. 579; see also Rodríguez Villa, *Etiquetas*, 151–52.

Image: A royal crown sits on the lid of a stone tomb that bears a cartouche inscribed *SEPVL-CHRVM EIVS GLORIOSVM. Isa. 15.* ("His sepulcher [is] glorious" [Isaiah 11:10]). The sun and moon shine overhead.

The crown on the sepulcher signifies that Philip is dead. Although this circumstance might occasion sorrow (the "Night" of the verse), the king's death has been transformed into something worthy of joyous celebration ("Day"): the eternal salvation of his soul through the intervention of the sun and the moon. In this case the two heavenly bodies do not represent members of the royal family. The sun is Christ, who offers redemption through His corporeal presence in the Eucharistic Host ("the Sun in the Sacrament") in accordance with the Catholic doctrine of Transubstantiation.[24] The moon is the Virgin Mary, who intercedes on behalf of Philip's soul as a reward for his devotion to her cult. In particular, the moon calls to mind Philip's persistent defense of the doctrine of the Immaculate Conception, which teaches that the Virgin was conceived free from Original Sin. Although the doctrine is now Catholic dogma, in the seventeenth century it was still being debated within the Church, and Philip ardently championed its cause.[25] When he died, his perseverance and achievements in the campaign for its adoption as dogma were cited by many as proof of his devotion to the Virgin.[26] Artists of his

time customarily represented the doctrine with an allegorical composition in which Mary stood on a crescent moon (see figs. 79 and 80). The "Moon of Mary" in the hieroglyph is both a general allusion to the Virgin and a specific reference to Philip's Immaculist beliefs.

Hieroglyph 17 may also admit a political reading similar to those of other hieroglyphs that use the sun and moon to symbolize Charles and Mariana (for example, Hieroglyph 2). If such associations are intended here, then the hieroglyph also declares that the glorious promise of Mariana's regency and Charles's reign ("Day") will dispel the gloom that Philip's death has brought ("Night"). Because "Mariana" is a compression of "María Ana," the phrase *Luna de María* can be read in this fashion with ease. However, the difficulty of relating the phrase *Sol en el Sacramento* to the name *Carlos* restricts this interpretation to a secondary one at best.

HIEROGLYPH 18 (fig. 31)

Motto: *LATET VLTIMVS DIES, VT OBSERVENTVR OMNES. August de Doct christ.*
"The last day lies hidden, so that all [days] will be watched for." (Augustine, *Sermon* 39.1; not from *On Christian Doctrine*)

Verse: *Cada dia a morir vamos,*
Qual a de ser no sauemos,
Y es, si lo consideramos,
Piedad que el vno ignoremos,
Porque todos los temamos.
"Every day we are going to die. We do not know which one it is

24. On the sun as a symbol of Christ, see Kantorowicz, "*Oriens Augusti*," 135–49.

25. Suzanne L. Stratton, "The Immaculate Conception in Spanish Renaissance and Baroque Art," 216–22 and 236–47. See also Stradling, *Philip IV*, 344–46.

26. Díaz de Ylarraza, *Relacion diaria*, n.p.; Lezana, *Memorial*, fols. 14–15; *Relacion de la enfermedad*, n.p.; Rodríguez de Monforte, *Descripcion*,

fols. 24^v and 118^v–19; and untitled *gaceta*, BNM, Ms. 2,392, n.p.

to be; and it is, if we consider it, a mercy that we are ignorant of the one, because we fear them all."

Image: The skeletal hand of Death emerges from a cloud holding a lighted taper. Its flame attracts a ring of seven moths, each of which has the astronomical symbol of a heavenly body on its left wing and a Roman capital letter on its right.

Each moth represents a day of the week. Its astronomical symbol corresponds to the heavenly body that is traditionally associated with its day, and its Roman letter is the initial letter of the day in Spanish. Clockwise from Death's hand, they are as follows:

Sun—*Domingo* (Sunday)
Luna (Moon)—*Lunes* (Monday)
Mars—*Martes* (Tuesday)
Mercury—*Miercoles* (Wednesday)
Jupiter—*Jueves* (Thursday)
Venus—*Viernes* (Friday)
Saturn—*Sabado* (Saturday)

The burning candle, a common symbol for the transience of earthly life, holds a fatal attraction for the moths that surround it.[27] The hieroglyph reminds the viewer that the achievements of mundane existence are ephemeral vanities and that all men eventually die. This is the inevitable tragedy of human life, and its only mystery is that a person cannot foretell the specific day of his death. For that reason he must live every day piously in preparation for the judgment of his soul.

27. Tervarent, *Attributs*, col. 70, for the candle; for an emblematic tradition of moths drawn to flames, see also Rafael García Mahiques, "Las 'Empresas Sacras' de Núñez de Cepeda: un lenguaje que configura al prelado contrarreformista," 30–31.

The presence of this *memento mori* at Philip's exequies implied that he had conducted his life in such a manner.

HIEROGLYPH 19 (fig. 32)

Motto: *NON MORIAR, SED VIVAM. Psal. 117.*
"I shall not die, but live." (Psalm 117:17)

Verse: *Que importa al que Phenix hace*
De sus ceniças la hoguera
Que desde que nace muera
Si muere desde que nace?
"What does it matter to the Phoenix that he makes the bonfire from his remains (since he is dying from [the moment] when he is born, and he is born from [the moment] when he dies)?"

Image: A phoenix standing in a fire looks upward and spreads its wings. It is unharmed by the flames.

According to its legend, when a phoenix reached the end of its life (sometimes put at 500 years), it burned itself on a fragrant funeral pyre that it fanned with its wings (hence, the outstretched wings in the image). A new, youthful phoenix was born from the ashes of the pyre, and the life cycle of the fabulous bird commenced anew. On the basis of this legend the phoenix became a conventional symbol of renewal and resurrection.[28] Here it meets the needs of Philip's exequies in the same manner as the eagle that rejuvenates itself in Hieroglyph 14. The rebirth of the phoenix symbolizes Philip's spiritual rebirth into the eternal life of Christian salvation. Moreover, the youthful phoenix born of the flames can also signify

28. Tervarent, *Attributs*, cols. 304–5.

Charles, the renewal of the deceased who emulates his father's glorious example.

Phoenix imagery had been employed to honor the royal family before 1665. In his previously cited sermon in honor of Philip III, Paravicino Arteaga had written of his accession after the death of Philip II, "Saint Ambrose could say of it, what he already said of Theodosius, that from the ashes of the dead phoenix, with a natal end and a fecund death, the same Bird would arise copied in the flaming virtues of his son."[29] When Philip III died, the exequies that the city of Murcia celebrated for him included a hieroglyph in which a phoenix renewed itself on a flaming pyre. An accompanying verse declared,

El Fenix fue sin igual,
Que con su muerte en el suelo
Se renovò para el Cielo.[30]

(The Phoenix was without equal [in that it] renewed itself for Heaven with its death on earth.)

The phrase el fénix de Austria ("the phoenix of [the House of] Austria") is another epithet that was applied to Philip, one that lent itself to the Habsburgs' predilection for associating themselves with the qualities and achievements of their predecessors.[31] In the same vein, Rodríguez de Monforte refers to Charles II as "the Phoenix of the Fragrant Remains of the [House of] Austria."[32]

29. Paravicino [Arteaga], Panegyrico fvneral, 13.

30. Alonso Enríquez, Honras y obsequias que hizo al Catholico, y Christianissimo Rey Don Filipo Tercero nuestro Señor su muy Noble y muy Leal Ciudad de Mvrcia, 302.

31. For example, see Lezana, Memorial, fol. 12v.

32. Rodríguez de Monforte, Descripcion, fol. 119v.

HIEROGLYPH 20 (fig. 33)

Motto: *IVSTITIA VERO LIBERABIT A MORTE. Prou. 10.*
"But justice will deliver from death." (Proverbs 10:2)

Verse: *Con Iusticia procedi,*
Y con Piedad goberne,
A otra Corona aspire.
"I proceeded with justice and governed with piety; I aspired to another crown."

Image: Clouds part as a royal crown ascends into the sky. To the lower right a sword floats in the air with its blade pointed straight up. To the lower left a fruit-bearing tree stands apart on an open plain.

This work was inspired by the arms of the Inquisition (see fig. 60), in which an olive branch (dexter) is juxtaposed with a naked sword (sinister). The olive branch, symbol of peace, represents the mercy with which the Inquisition would treat those who were reconciled with the Faith; whereas the sword represented the stern justice that awaited those who defied the Faith.[33] The hieroglyph, which enlarges the olive branch to an olive tree, adapts this device to praise the late king: He, too, ruled with both Christian mercy (the olive tree) and justice (the sword). Of course, the painted sword in the hieroglyph had a counterpart at the king's exequies in the real sword on the *tumba* that symbolized the same virtue. The ascent of the crown confirms that Philip's justice and piety have earned him salvation. In Heaven he will set aside his

33. Rafael Sabatini, Torquemada and the Spanish Inquisition: A History, 249.

earthly crown for the crown of eternal life, the "other crown" to which the verse refers (compare Hieroglyph 6).

HIEROGLYPH 21 (fig. 34)

Motto: *ERVNT SIGNA IN SOLE, LVNA, ET STELIS. Luce. 21.*
"There will be signs in the sun, the moon, and the stars." (Luke 21:25)

Verse: *Eclipsado el Real Planeta*
Llorã la infausta Fortuna,
Mal presagio de vn Cometa
Funestos Astros, y Luna.
"The Royal Planet [is] eclipsed; Funeral Stars and the Moon mourn the unhappy Fate [that was] the ill omen of a Comet."

Image: A blazing comet that trails a royal crown in its tail shares the sky with dark stars and a solar eclipse.

Early in December 1664, a comet was sighted in Spain that remained visible until February 1665. Comets were then believed to foretell—if not cause—the deaths of great princes and other calamities, and after Philip's death, the comet was held to have warned of his demise.[34] The year 1665 was marked as well by solar and lunar eclipses, which were also regarded as signs of great import.[35] One reason such phenomena were taken seriously in Spain was that they had heralded the deaths of Philip's predecessors on the throne. Comets appeared from one to twenty-eight months before the deaths of

Philip I, Charles I, and Philip III (two comets were sighted in his case), and Philip II's death was preceded by a solar eclipse and two lunar eclipses.[36]

The belief that the astronomical events of late 1664 and 1665 foretold Philip IV's death informs this hieroglyph. Its comet carries off a crown, a recurrent symbol for the king, while another familiar symbol, the sun (the "Royal Planet" of the verse), is eclipsed. The significance of the "Funeral Stars" of the verse is not immediately evident, but presumably they are to be identified with the ominous, dark stars in the image. Perhaps they represent an unfavorable configuration of stars and planets that astrologers at the court surely would have found in order to account for Philip's death. The moon that mourns the eclipse in the verse could refer to Mariana, the royal widow who mourns her husband's death.

HIEROGLYPH 22 (fig. 35)

Mottoes: *COR REGIS IN MANV DOMINI. Prob. 21.*
"The heart of the king is in the hand of the Lord." (Proverbs 21:1)
CONCVPIVI SALVTARE TVVM DOMINE, ET LEX TVA MEDITATIO MEA EST. Ps. 118.
"I have longed for your salvation, Lord, and your law is my meditation." (Psalm 118:174)

Verse: *A quanto en mi vida obre*
Nunca le llego a faltar
El deseo de acertar.
"The desire to be right never

34. Rodríguez de Monforte, *Descripcion*, fols. 19ᵛ–22; Díaz de Ylarraza, *Relacion diaria*, n.p.; and Lezana, *Memorial*, fols. 3ᵛ and 10ᵛ.
35. Lezana, *Memorial*, fol. 3ᵛ; and Díaz de Ylarraza, *Relacion diaria*, n.p.

36. Lagomarsino, "Habsburg Way of Death."

came to be lacking in all that I wrought in my life."

Image: Beneath the first motto a hand of Providence emerges from a cloud holding a crowned, winged heart in its palm. Beneath the second motto another hand of Providence emerges from a cloud grasping a winged scepter.

Speaking the verse in the first person, Philip declares that he never lost sight of "the desire to be right"—that is, while he lived, he was a good, Christian prince who sought to save his soul. The rest of the hieroglyph attests that he succeeded. The heart is a soul (a play on *corazón*, which means both "heart" and "soul"), its crown identifies it as Philip's, and its wings enable it to return to Heaven for judgment now that the body in which it has been confined has died. Illustrating the first motto literally demonstrates that the king's soul is the Lord's to judge. The care with which He supports it suggests that He is admitting the soul into Heaven.

The winged scepter poses a greater ambiguity in interpretation. If it is another symbol of Philip, then its wings, like those of the heart-shaped soul, can be understood as helping him to ascend into Heaven. On the other hand, if it is regarded as a divine scepter wielded by the Providential hand, then it may signify the Law of God (by which Philip is understood to have lived) that is cited in the accompanying motto.

HIEROGLYPH 23 (fig. 36)

Motto: *MELIOR EST DIES MORTIS, DIE NATIVITATIS. Ecles. 7.*

"The day of death is better than the day of birth." (Variation on Ecclesiastes 7:2)

Verse: *Prospera, y feliz Fortuna,*
Halle en morir, no en nacer,
Y assi mas llego a deuer,
A la muerte, que a la cuna.
"I found a prosperous and happy Fate in dying, not in being born, and thus, I come to owe more to death than to the cradle."

Image: An unadorned *tumba* stands beside an empty cradle.

The verse to this *memento mori* has Philip himself console those who mourn his death. Its point, and that of the motto, is that in dying, Philip has gone to a better place, the Kingdom of Heaven. The juxtaposition of the cradle, signifying his entry into this world at birth, and the *tumba*, signifying his departure from this world at death, reiterates the contrasts drawn by the motto and the verse.

HIEROGLYPH 24 (fig. 37)

Motto: *SOL OCCIDIT, ET ORITVR Ecles. 1.*
"The sun goes down, and it rises." (Variation on Ecclesiastes 1:5)

Verse: *Aunque vn Sol muere entre sombras*
No ay tiniebla que enbarace
Porque luego otro Sol nace.
"Although a Sun dies among shadows, there is no darkness that may perplex because immediately another Sun is born."

Image: While a sun sets amidst clouds at the left horizon of a rural landscape, another sun rises from the right horizon into a clear sky.

As in Hieroglyph 2, the natural progression of a sunrise following a sunset symbolizes Charles's orderly, legitimate accession after his father's death. To imply the successor will rule well, the motto corrupts its biblical source. The correct text from Ecclesiastes 1:5 is *Oritur sol et occidet* ("The sun rises, and it will set"). Because the inventor of this hieroglyph switched the verbs, the motto culminates optimistically with the brilliant prospects of the rising sun (Charles), rather than with the gloomy end of the setting sun (Philip).

This hieroglyph may have been inspired by one that the College of Cuenca displayed at the exequies that the University of Salamanca celebrated for Philip III in 1621. It showed one sun setting with the motto *Sol cognovit occasum suum* ("The sun knows its setting" [Psalm 103:19]), and another sun rising with the motto *Dulce lumen: & delectabile est oculis videre solem* ("The light is sweet, and it is delightful for the eyes to see the sun" [variation on Ecclesiastes 11:7]). An accompanying verse declared,

Si el Sol se puso, tambien
Comiença otro nueuo Sol
A desplegar su arrebol.[37]

(If the Sun sets, another new Sun also begins to display its red sky [to dawn].)

If this inspired Hieroglyph 24, then it may not be coincidental that the first of the two mottoes from 1621 also ap-

37. Angel Manrique, *Exeqvias. Tvmulo y pompa fvneral, qve la Vniversidad de Salamanca hizo en las honras. Del Rey nuestro Señor don Felipe III . . .* , 32.

peared at Philip IV's royal exequies on the ceiling painting in the catafalque (Appendix C, 13).

HIEROGLYPH 25 (fig. 38)

Motto: *FRVMENTVM ELECTORVM. Zach. 9.*
"The corn of the elect" (Zachariah 9:17)

Verse: *El acimo pan que Elias,*
Ayuno quarenta auroras,
Redujo a quarenta horas.
"He compressed into forty hours the unleavened bread that Elijah fasted upon for forty dawns."

Image: Three loaves of unleavened bread are piled on an altar. The altar frontal bears the inscription *PROPTER ELECTOS BREVIABVNTVR DIES. Math. 24* ("For the sake of the elect the days will be shortened" [Matthew 24:22]).

This hieroglyph employs an Old Testament prefiguration to acclaim Philip's devotion to the Sacrament of the Eucharist. The verse associates the loaves of unleavened bread in the image with the hearthcake that an angel brought Elijah to sustain him in the desert for forty days (III Kings 19:5–8). The life-giving property of the hearth-cake makes it an obvious prefiguration for the Eucharistic Host. The "forty hours" of the verse are the Forty Hours' Devotion. In this rite, which originated in Milan in the early sixteenth century, the Holy Sacrament is exposed to view in a church for forty hours, during which time prayers are said before it continuously. What is more, the devotion can be held in a succession of churches within a diocese so that when the forty hours end at one church, they begin at another. In Philip's time the devotion was often performed for supplicatory purposes.[38]

Philip's respect for the Forty Hours was considerable. He had the devotion performed in the Royal Chapel of the Alcázar of Madrid every month, ordinarily on its first Thursday, Friday, and Saturday.[39] Moreover, in July 1643, he ordered the churches in Madrid to begin celebrating it in succession. His apparent purpose was to persuade Heaven to grant him military victory, for the order coincided with his departure for Aragon that month to direct the ongoing war against France from a position closer to the front.[40] After Philip died, his predilection for the Forty Hours' Devotion was cited as evidence of his faith in the mysteries of the Eucharist.[41]

HIEROGLYPH 26 (fig. 39)

Motto: *RETRO REDIIT SOL, ET AD-DIDIT REGI VIAM. Eccles. 48.* "The sun went backward, and it lengthened the king's life [*vitam*]." (Ecclesiasticus 48:26)

Verse: *Quando va el Sol a espirar*
Buelue a nueba luz su Rueda,
Para enseñar al que queda
El camino de Reynar.
"When the Sun is going to ex-

pire, its Wheel returns to a new light in order to teach the one that remains the way to govern."

Image: A terrestrial globe rests on an open plain, and the four points of the compass are marked about its circumference: *Septentrion* (North), *Oriente* (East), *Mediodia* (South), and *Poniente* (West). Two horses that have drawn an uncrowned sun to the western side of the globe in a carriage turn back toward a crowned sun in the east. Two dotted lines indicate the path that the horses take between the eastern and western extremities of the globe.

Like Hieroglyphs 2 and 24, this employs a sun that rises while another sun sets as a metaphor for Charles's accession after his father's death. Philip, the western sun, has died (sunset) and no longer wears the crown, which has passed to Charles, the sun awaiting its carriage in the east (sunrise). In accordance with the motto, Charles will lengthen the late king's life by carrying on the Habsburg mission in his father's place. The image departs from the motto in that it is not the sun but its horse-drawn carriage that reverses course. (The verse uses *rueda* [wheel] to fit an *a b b a* rhyme scheme.) The carriage represents Mariana, whom Philip named as governor of the Monarchy and tutor of their son during his minority. She will teach the new king "the way to govern," which is represented by the solar path across the globe.

This conceit calls to mind the myth of another child of the sun: Phaëthon, the mortal son of Apollo, who obtained his father's permission to drive the solar

38. Herbert Thurston, "Forty Hours' Devotion," 151–52; and J. M. Champlin, "Forty Hours Devotion."
39. "Tratado de las ceremonias," 1:fols. 22ʳ–23, 29, and 100ʳ–108.
40. *Cartas de algunos PP.*, 5:145–46; and León Pinelo, *Anales*, 328.
41. Lezana, *Memorial*, fol. 12ʳ; and Rodríguez de Monforte, *Descripcion*, fols. 23 and 117ʳ.

chariot for a day. Because he lacked sufficient training for the task, Phaëthon lost control of the chariot and was killed (Ovid, *Metamorphoses* 2.153–328). Hieroglyph 26 implies that under Mariana's prudent guidance, Charles will fare better.

HIEROGLYPH 27 (fig. 40)

Motto: *VITAM ETERNAM POSIDEBO. Luc. 10.*
"I shall possess eternal life." (Luke 10:25)

Verse: *Quien con su muerte pago*
La comun fatalidad,
Al tienpo no se rindio,
Pues su vida al tienpo hurto,
Para hacerla eternidad.
"He who paid the common destiny with his death did not yield to time, for He stole his life from time in order to make it an eternity."

Image: The hand of Providence emerges from a cloud and hoists a royal crown with a scythe. Other clouds part before the crown's approach.

Philip's mortal body has succumbed to the passage of time, "the common destiny" of mankind. Nevertheless, he has triumphed over death because the Lord has admitted his soul into Heaven. For that reason it is the hand of Providence, not the skeletal arm of Death, that lifts the crown (Philip's soul) into glory. In this case the scythe is better understood as an attribute of Time, rather than of Death.[42]

42. Tervarent, *Attributs*, cols. 164–65.

HIEROGLYPH 28 (fig. 41)

Motto: *MORS IN LVCE*
"Death [is] in the light."

Verse: *La engañosa Vanidad*
Es esta Luz presumida,
Huyendo se halla la vida.
"This presumptuous Light is false Vanity; shunning it, one finds life."

Image: A candle mounted in a candlestick burns atop a simple table in a dark room. One moth is drawn to its flame, but another shuns it.

As in Hieroglyph 18, the fatal attraction that flames hold for moths informs a *vanitas* image. The candle, which shines brightly but consumes itself, is a common symbol of the transience of earthly glories. Just as the moth that shuns the flame will live, so persons who are not beguiled by earthly vanities will gain eternal salvation. However, those who are ensnared by earthly vanities will be punished, just as the flame will burn the moth that succumbs to its allure.

HIEROGLYPH 29 (fig. 42)

Motto: *ANIMA MEA ILLI VIUET, ET SEMEN MEVM SERVIET IPSI. Psal. 21*
"For Him my soul will live, and my seed will serve Him." (Psalm 21:31)

Verse: *La aclamacion adelanta*
De dos coronas el celo,
Vna se lebanta al cielo,
Otra el cielo la lebanta.
"The acclamation advances the devotion of two crowns; one is

raised to Heaven, the other Heaven raises up."

Image: A pennon bearing a quartered coat-of-arms surmounted by a crown stands on a wooden platform set on an empty plain. Above it clouds roll back to reveal a vision of two crowns above and below the main facade of the Alcázar of Madrid.

The key to this complex hieroglyph is the idiom *levantar el pendón*, "to raise the pennon." Spain had no formal coronation ceremony with which to mark the accession of a king. Instead, a new ruler was publicly proclaimed in Madrid by "raising the pennon." The performance of this ceremony upon Charles's accession was typical.[43] On October 8, 1665, the *regidores* (magistrates) of Madrid rode in procession on horseback from the Town Hall to the Plaza Mayor, where a wooden platform had been erected. The *corregidor* (chief magistrate) and the senior *regidor* mounted this platform along with the secretaries of the town council and four kings-at-arms. The senior *regidor*, the Duke of San Lúcar and of Medina de las Torres, carried a pennon bearing the arms of Castile and León. The senior king-at-arms quieted the spectators by calling out, "Silence! Silence! Silence! Hear ye! Hear ye! Hear ye!" Then the duke proclaimed, "Castile, Castile, Castile, for the Catholic King Don Carlos the Second of that name, our lord, whom God protect!" while lifting the pennon three times. The crowd roared back,

"*Vive! Vive! Vive!*" The proclamation and the crowd's response were repeated two more times. Then the magistrates made their way to the square in front of the Alcázar, where they mounted another platform and performed the same ceremony while Charles watched from the royal balcony over the main entrance to the palace. They repeated the ceremony two more times, at the convent of the Descalzas Reales and at the Town Hall.

The platform, pennon, and view of the Alcázar in the hieroglyph recall the acclamation of Charles in front of the palace, and the two crowns illustrate the same distinction between earthly and heavenly crowns that informs Hieroglyph 6. The verse unites these motifs into a coherent whole by playing upon the verb *levantar* (to raise) from the idiom *levantar el pendón*. The lower crown is the earthly crown of Charles's dominion over the Monarchy, and the verse relates it to the heraldic crown on the pennon that "is raised to Heaven" (hoisted skyward) at the proclamation of a king. The upper crown is a crown of eternal life that "Heaven raises up"—it symbolizes Philip's soul, which the Lord has admitted to heavenly glory.

HIEROGLYPH 30 (fig. 43)

Motto: *SPIRITVS DOMINI RAPVIT PHILIPPVM. Actor. 1.*
"The Spirit of the Lord took away Philip." (Acts 8:39; not from Acts 1)

43. This account follows *Aclamacion Real, y Publica de la Coronada Villa, y Corte de Madrid . . . por su Augusto, y Catolico Rey Carlos II. que Dios guarde*. See also José Amador de los Rios and Juan de Dios de la Rada y Delgado, *Historia de la villa y corte de Madrid*, 3:429–32 n. 1; APM, SH, Proclamaciones de Reyes, caja 117, "Levantamiento del Pendon pᵃ el Rey nro sᵣ dⁿ Carlos 2ᵒ;" and untitled *gaceta*, BNM, Ms. 2,392, fols. 237ᵛ–38.

Verse: *Quando del mundo faltó*
Quiso la muerte tener
A Philippo en su poder
Mas Dios se le arrebato.

"When he was missing from the world, Death tried to hold Philip in her power, but God took him from her."

Image: The skeletal arm of Death reaches out from an open sepulcher to pull a royal crown into its cavity. The tomb bears the inscription *NEC EST REX QVI RESISTAT EI. Prob. 30* ("Nor is there a king who can resist her" [Proverbs 30:31]). A second crown above the first ascends into the sky between clouds that part before its approach.

Hieroglyph 30 depends upon the same distinction between heavenly and earthly crowns found in Hieroglyphs 6 and 29. Philip's mortal body has died, which this hieroglyph depicts as Death pulling the earthly crown of Philip's temporal authority into the tomb. However, Death is irresistible only insofar as Philip's mortal part is concerned. God has judged Philip's soul worthy of redemption, and its salvation is represented by the ascent of the second crown, a crown of eternal life.

HIEROGLYPH 31 (fig. 44)

Motto: *O MOMENTVM, O ÆTER-NITAS.*
"O moment, O eternity!"

Verse: *Vn instante de Maria,*
Que celebro mi piedad
Me a dado vna Æternidad.
"An instant of Mary that my

piety celebrated has given me an Eternity."

Image: Parting clouds make way for three ascending objects: a garland, a sandglass, and a crescent moon. A roaring dragon on the ground below cringes at the sight of them.

Like Hieroglyph 17 this work declares that Philip's devotion to the Virgin Mary and the doctrine of her Immaculate Conception has earned him salvation. The doctrine holds that Mary was created free from Original Sin, and the "moment" of the motto, the sandglass in the image, and the "instant of Mary" of the verse all allude to the instant of time in which she was immaculately conceived. The crescent moon and the dragon are conventional motifs from allegorical representations of the doctrine, in which the Virgin stands on a crescent moon in triumph over a dragon or serpent that symbolizes sin (see fig. 79).[44] The garland admits several interpretations. It appears to be composed of laurel leaves, and laurel crowns are attributes of virtue.[45] That could apply both to the Virgin, for her freedom from Original Sin, and to Philip, for his pious promotion of her cult. Laurel crowns also symbolize victory, and both the Virgin's victory over sin and Philip's victory over death (the redemption of his soul) may be intended here.[46] Finally, the garland is circular, and circles can symbolize eternity because they lack beginnings and ends.[47] That may refer to the

44. Stratton, "Immaculate Conception," 108–38 passim.
45. Ripa, *Iconologia*, 541–42; and Tervarent, *Attributs*, col. 129.
46. Ripa, *Iconologia*, 546–47.
47. Ibid., 150.

"eternity" of the verse and motto: the eternal salvation that Philip has attained as a result of his devotion to the Virgin and her intercession on his behalf.

HIEROGLYPH 32 (fig. 45)

Motto: *DEDVCET TE MIRABILITER DEXTERA MEA. Psal. 44.*
"My right hand will conduct you wonderfully." (Variation on Psalm 44:5)

Verse: *Como la Fe a de caer*
(Aunque mas ser ciega muestra)
Si es Philippo quien la adiestra?
"How is Faith to fall (however much she proves to be blind) if it is Philip who guides her?"

Image: An arm emerges from a cloud to guide a blindfolded woman who walks barefoot through the countryside carrying a chalice and Host.

The verse identifies the woman as the personification of Faith, and her attributes—the blindfold, chalice, and Host—confirm that reading.[48] More surprising is the identity of the person whose arm guides her steps. By analogy with other hieroglyphs (10, 22, and 27), it might be the hand of Providence, but the verse identifies it as Philip's. This implies the dead king has been admitted to the elect of Heaven, whence he continues to intercede on behalf of the Faith in the mundane world he has left behind. This is striking testimony to Philip's piety, which has earned him salvation and which moves him to persevere in protecting the Faith, even after death. Implicit in this hi-

eroglyph, too, is a reiteration of his devotion to the Sacrament of the Eucharist, to which the chalice and Host carried by Faith refer.

HIEROGLYPH 33 (fig. 46)

Motto: *MELIVS EST MICHI MORI, QVAM VIVERE. Ione. 4.*
"It is better for me to die than to live." (Jonah 4:8)

Verse: *Quando lo entendi perder,*
Hallo en la muerte el viuir;
Luego se debe decir
Que el dexar de ser, es ser.
"When I understood that I had lost him, he found life in death; therefore, it is to be said, that giving up being, is to be."

Image: A royal crown sits on a cushion atop a *tumba*.

This is a simplified version of Hieroglyph 16. The anonymous mourner who speaks the verse assures the viewer that Philip has left this world for a better place. Dying ("giving up being") was the prelude to the release of Philip's soul and its judgment by God. Because Philip was good, his soul has been saved and admitted to Heaven for all eternity ("to be"). That is the "life in death" the verse declares him to have found.

HIEROGLYPH 34 (fig. 47)

Motto: *CVM OMNI GLORIA SVA ACCEPIT IN PORTVM. 1. Macheb. 14.*
"With all his glory he took a harbor." (I Maccabees 14:5)

Verse: *Feliz puerto ira a goçar*
Naue cuya ligereça

48. Ibid., 161–62; and see above, chap. 7, n. 10.

El austro pudo, ynspirar
Y es su norte la pureça
De la Estrella de la mar.
"The ship whose lightness the south wind was able to blow is going to enjoy a happy port, and its polestar is the purity of the Star of the Sea."

Image: An armed vessel glides across the open sea with its sails billowing in a strong wind.

"Star of the Sea," a traditional epithet of the Virgin, signals that this hieroglyph has Marian significance. The epithet implies that a good Christian puts his faith in the Virgin and accepts her guidance just as sailors navigate by the North Star. Owing to this association, ships often appear in paintings of the Immaculate Conception (see fig. 80).[49] By this association, the Virgin's conception free from Original Sin is the "purity" to which the verse refers. The ship guided by the star is Philip, who has venerated Mary and has defended the doctrine of her Immaculate Conception. As a reward for his devotion, he will "enjoy a happy port"—that is, his soul will enter Heaven. "Star of the Sea" imagery in praise of the dead king was not limited to his royal exequies. A posthumous tribute to him published in 1665 refers generally to princes who steer themselves by the North Star of religion, and twice refers specifically to the Virgin Mary as the North Star by which Philip steered.[50]

The inventor of this hieroglyph drew upon a fertile emblematic tradition. Among the precedents he might have known is one that was devised by the most influential of emblematists, Andrea Alciati (fig. 81). With the motto *Spes proxima* ("Hope is near"), it portrays a ship that has passed through a tempest stirred up by strong winds. The sky has cleared, and the twin stars Castor and Pollux, whose sighting is a good omen to sailors, have appeared. By substituting the Star of the Sea for Castor and Pollux, whoever conceived Hieroglyph 34 transformed the general hope of Alciati's sailors into Philip's specific hope for salvation through the intercession of the Virgin.[51]

Another work that may lie behind this hieroglyph is an emblem with the motto *Fortuna in porto* ("Fortune in the port" [Petrarch, *Sonnets* 231.12]) that was devised by Covarrubias Orozco (fig. 74). It depicts a ship that violent winds cause to founder at the mouth of a harbor. For Covarrubias Orozco this signifies that although a man may pass most of his life virtuously, he may still fall into unworthy action [*fealdad*] and danger—that is, into sin and peril for his soul—at the end of his life, just as a ship may sail from distant isles across dangerous seas only to

49. Stratton, "Immaculate Conception," 222.
50. Lezana, *Memorial*, fols. 11–11ᵛ, 13ᵛ, and 15ᵛ.

51. For Alciati's influence in Spain, see Andrea Alciati, *Emblemas*, ed. Santiago Sebastián with prologue by Aurora Egido, 7–26 and passim; Ledda, *Contributo*, esp. 151–204 passim; and Sánchez Pérez, *La literatura emblemática española*, 61–71 and 82–88. Figure 81 is taken from an influential Spanish commentary on the emblems' meanings: Diego López, *Declaracion magistral sobre las emblemas de Andres Alciato con todas las Historias, Antiguedades, Moralidad, y Doctrina tocante a las buenas costumbres*, fol. 144.
The inventor of Hieroglyph 34 may also have known the commentary on Alciati's emblem in López, *Declaracion magistral*, fols. 144–46ᵛ, that interprets the ship as the Christian Republic, and the two stars as the Pope and Charles I, who guide its course. López further identifies Castor and Pollux's sister Helena, who figures in the verse of the emblem, as the Roman Church.

sink at the entrance to its port. For this reason, no man should be called fortunate until he is counted among the dead.[52] This emblem may have prompted the author of Hieroglyph 34 to use the safe arrival of a ship at its harbor as a metaphor for the salvation of Philip's soul.

The records of funerary honors for other members of the royal family may also have inspired this hieroglyph. The royal exequies for Isabella of Bourbon in 1644 had featured a hieroglyph comparing her death to a ship that sinks.[53] Even earlier, in 1621, the city of Murcia had staged exequies for Philip III at which a hieroglyph had depicted a ship that approached its "North Star," a fleece hanging from the sky. The motto stated, *Bonum certamen certabi. Paul ad Thimot. 4* ("I have fought the good fight" [II Timothy 4 : 7]), and the verse read

Dexando el Tuson del suelo
Sin impedimento humano,
Conquista el Iasson Christiano
El Vellocino del Cielo.[54]

(Leaving behind the Fleece of the earth without any human impediment, the Christian Jason acquires the Fleece of Heaven.)

This work made a familiar symbol of the king's commitment to defending the Faith into the polestar by which his ship sailed. It declared that Philip III, the "Christian Jason" who had commanded of the Order of the Golden Fleece (the "Fleece of the earth"), had died and gone to Heaven because Christ had redeemed his soul. Christ's mercy was the "Fleece of Heav-

en," a play upon His epithet, "the Lamb of God."

Hieroglyph 34 has a second meaning conveyed by a pun in its verse. The word *austro*, which signifies the south wind, plays upon the Habsburg family name, the House of *Austria*. Accordingly, the ship can be understood as the Ship of State, which the House of Austria propels to a safe harbor. This praises not only Philip IV, but also his Habsburg predecessors and survivors (especially Mariana and Charles). Viewed in this light, the banks of cannon with which the ship is armed signify the might of the Spanish armies, which the Habsburg kings of Spain stand ready to direct against the enemies of the Virgin and the Faith.

HIEROGLYPH 35 (fig. 48)

Motto: *LIGNVM HABET SPEM SI PRECISVM FVERIT, RAMI EIVS PVLLVLANT. Iob. 14.*
"A tree has hope: If it be cut, the boughs thereof sprout." (Job 14 : 7)

Verse: *Que importará tu rrigor*
Si aunque la rama cortaste
Los renuebos nos dejaste?
"What will your severity matter if, although you cut the branch, you left us the shoots?"

Image: The skeletal arm of Death emerges from a cloud and lops off the crowned top of a tree trunk with a single stroke of her scythe. Two boughs with smaller crowns are left unharmed. One bough is taller than the other, and its crown is slightly larger.

This work elaborates the "family tree" conceit that underlies Hieroglyph 11.

---

52. Covarrubias Orozco, *Emblemas morales*, centuria III, emblema 32.
53. *Pompa Fvneral Honras*, fol. 19ᵛ.
54. Enríquez, *Honras y obseqvias*, 280.

Once again the main trunk of the tree is Philip, whom Death has felled. The two branches are his two legitimate children who survived him at the court, Charles and Margarita María. Although Charles was younger than his sister, the taller branch with the larger crown probably represents him because he is the first in the line of succession. As in Hieroglyphs 7, 8, and 11, this one makes no allusion to Philip's other children, María Teresa and Juan José, for political reasons.

The hieroglyph has an important precedent in one that the Jesuit College in Madrid displayed at its funerary honors for Empress María of Austria in 1603 (fig. 78). In it Death has chopped down a tree with an ax, and small shoots sprout from the stump. The motto *SVCCIDE AR-BOREM, ET GERMEN. RELINQVE* ("Cut down the tree, and leave the seed"), is a variation on Daniel 4:20 and 23, and the verse reads

Hermosos pimpollos dexa,
Donde se conserue, y viua,
El que oy la muerte derriba.

(What Death fells today leaves beautiful shoots, wherein it may be preserved and live.)

The commemorative book recording the event explains this hieroglyph as follows: "The aged are compared to old and robust trees, already decayed with their many years—thus Lucan pictured the Captain Pompey. This same tree, already felled and brought down, thus comes to be fitting for what death did in felling this lady with her blow. But shoots from this tree remain, from which it proceeds to renew itself again; these are her glorious sons and daughters, whose memory is and will be eternal throughout the world,

whose glory [is and will be] without equal, and whose greatness [is and will be] admirable."[55]

A variation on this idea appeared at the royal exequies for Isabella of Bourbon in a hieroglyph that was displayed in the cloister of San Jerónimo.[56] It showed Death using her scythe to cut down a palm tree on which Baltasar Carlos and María Teresa bloomed as flowers. The severed trunk of the palm was inscribed *Vita* ("Life"), and the scythe, *Succidi* ("I cut"). Above the image were the words *Ex morte vita* ("Life from death"). Below the image was a motto, *Vt Palma sine radice florebit* ("Like the Palm it will flower without roots" [variation on Psalm 91:13]), and a verse that read,

Como es Palma el Alma justa,
Aunque la raiz le falta,
En sus renuevos se exalta.

(The just Soul is like the Palm: Although it is lacking its root, it is exalted in its shoots.)

Although the palm tree (Isabella) has died, its glory lives on in its flowers (her two surviving children).

Another inspiration may have been an emblem devised by Covarrubias Orozco (fig. 75) in which a disembodied arm wields an ax to chop the branches off a tree, from which new foliage sprouts. Its motto declares, *Ab ipso ducit opes animumq.* ("It [the tree] draws wealth and spirit from it [the ax]" [Horace, *Carmina* 4.4.59–60]). As Covarrubias Orozco explains, this teaches that the Lord afflicts those whom He loves with hardships in order to strengthen their faith through adversity, much as a laborer prunes a tree so that it will bring forth new shoots

55. *Libro de la Honras*, fols. 52ᵛ–53.
56. *Pompa Fvneral Honras*, fol. 91.

and sweet, abundant fruit.[57] Adapting this emblem to the concerns of Hieroglyph 35 would have posed little difficulty.

HIEROGLYPH 36 (fig. 49)

Motto: *INTER CÆTEROS DIES FESTOS HANC HABETOTE ET CELEBRATE EAM. Esth. C. 16.* "You shall count and celebrate this one among other festival days." (Esther 16:22)

Verse: *Nuebe Triumphos que tenia*
De mis ojas el dominio
Hico diez el Patrocinio
Que dio Philipo a Maria.
"Of the nine Triumphs over which my leaves had dominion, the Patronage that Philip gave Mary made ten."

Image: A solitary tree stands on an open plain. Mounted on its branches and trunk are ten wreaths, within which appear the names of ten feasts dedicated to the Virgin Mary. Clockwise from the top, they are *Assumtio* (Assumption), *Ad Niues* (Our Lady of the Snows), *Spectatio* (Expectation), *Purificatio* (Presentation of Christ), *Presentatio* (Presentation of the Virgin), *Patrocinio* (Patronage), *Conceptio* (Immaculate Conception), *Nativitas* (Nativity of the Virgin), *Visitatio* (Visitation), and *Anuntiatio* (Annunciation).

There does not appear to be any pattern to the arrangement of the festival wreaths other than the apt placement of the Assumption at the highest point. Although it is implicit in this hieroglyph that Philip kept all the feasts of the Virgin, its principal concern, which the verse makes manifest, is to celebrate his having promoted the *Patrocinio*—the Feast of the Patronage of Our Lady. In response to Philip's petitioning, Pope Alexander VII issued a bull that authorized this rite for Spain and its dominions on July 28, 1656. Each diocese was to select a Sunday in November on which to observe the feast. Most chose the third Sunday, but Philip had it celebrated in the Royal Chapel of the Alcázar of Madrid on the second. The observance spread from Spain to other nations, but early in this century it fell victim to reforms of the liturgical calendar. Since 1915 it has been observed only at titulary churches and other institutions consecrated to it.[58] Philip's sponsorship of the *Patrocinio* was among the demonstrations of his devotion to the Virgin that his panegyrists recalled at his death.[59]

HIEROGLYPH 37 (fig. 50)

Mottoes: *QVI CERTAVERIT CORONABITVR. 2. ad Thim. 2* "The one who shall have struggled will be crowned." (Variation on II Timothy 2:5)
VIDI STELAM DE CŒLO CECIDISSE IN TERRAM. Apoc. 9. "I saw a star had fallen from

---

57. Covarrubias Orozco, *Emblemas morales*, centuria I, emblema 32.

58. Barrionuevo, *Avisos*, 2:152, 158, and 186; "Patrocinio"; and "Tratado de las ceremonias," 1, fol. 29[v].

59. García de Escañuela, *Penas en la muerte*, 6; *Relacion de la enfermedad*, n.p.; and Rodríguez de Monforte, *Descripcion*, fols. 24–24[v] and 118–19.

Heaven on the earth." (Apocalypse 9:1)

Verse: *Subiose al Cielo vn Laurel,*
Y vino al suelo vna Estrella,
Porque alla luzga el por ella,
Y ella aca supla por el.
"A Laurel ascended to Heaven, and a Star came to earth in order that it [the laurel] may shine there for it [the star], and it [the star] may substitute here for it [the laurel]."

Image: Beneath the first motto a laurel garland rises into the sky. Beneath the second motto an eight-pointed star lies in a clump of different flowers.

The ascent of the laurel garland, a symbol of victory, signifies Philip's triumph over death through the eternal salvation of his soul; it may also signify his virtuous character (see Hieroglyph 31). The star that has plummeted from the firmament refers to the common belief in his time that "falling stars" (comets and meteors) foretold imminent deaths.[60] Because flowers, which bloom for a short time and then wilt, are conventional symbols of the brevity of earthly life, the fact that the king's star has landed among blossoms underscores the point that his mortal life has ended.[61]

HIEROGLYPH 38 (fig. 51)

Motto: *DEDIT DE CŒLO PLVVIAM.*
Deuter. 11.
"He gave rain from the sky."

60. As in Nájera, *Sermon funebre*, 2; see also Hieroglyph 21.
61. Tervarent, *Attributs*, col. 191.

(Variation on Deuteronomy 11:11)

Verse: *Como es del Cielo el Rocio,*
Transformado en blanca nube
Otra vez al Cielo sube.
"While the Dew comes from Heaven, transformed into a white cloud, it rises to Heaven again."

Image: Rain falls from dark clouds onto a landscape, and a new, white cloud rises from the earth into the sky.

The continuous cycle in which clouds produce rain ("Dew") that falls and evaporates to form new clouds symbolizes regeneration in this hieroglyph. Like the rejuvenation of the eagle in Hieroglyph 14 and of the phoenix in Hieroglyph 19, this has a twofold significance. First, the fall of rain and the formation of the new cloud respectively signify the descent of Philip's soul from Heaven to occupy his body while he lived, and its return to glory following its release when he died. Second, the formation of one cloud from the rain that fell from another represents Charles's natural succession to the throne following his father's death.

HIEROGLYPH 39 (fig. 52)

Motto: *VENIT HORA. Ioa. 13.*
"The hour has come." (John 13:1)

Verse: *Si cõsideras la vida*
Doce lustros, que el Sol dora
No tienen mas, que vna ora.
"If you consider life to be twelve lustra that the Sun shines, they possess no more than an hour."

Image: A winged sandglass and a crowned skull fly through the air.

The winged sandglass signifies the transience of earthly existence and the swiftness with which time passes.[62] As in Hieroglyphs 7 and 15, the crowned skull represents Death carrying off Philip. The verse unifies these two motifs. The "twelve lustra that the Sun shines" are the sixty years that Philip lived (one lustrum equals five years). From the perspective of his mourners, the sixty years passed all too swiftly, as if they were "no more than [the sixty minutes of] an hour." In that sense, the motto alludes not only to the hour of Philip's death but also to the seeming brevity of his life when it is considered in retrospect.

HIEROGLYPH 40 (fig. 53)

Motto: *CONSIDERANTI VULT.' NA-TIVITATIS IN SPECVLO.* Ia-cob. 1

"[Like] a man beholding the face he was born with in a mirror" (James 1:23)

Verse: *Ese christal en que atenta*
Mirandote vida estas,
Por fragil te enseña mas.

"That looking-glass in which you are gazing at yourself attentively, Life, teaches you more because it is perishable."

Image: A candle burns brightly in a darkened chamber. It is mounted in a candlestick that stands on top of a claw-footed table covered with a tablecloth. A mirror hanging on a nearby wall in an ornate frame reflects the candle's image.

Once again a burning candle symbolizes the brevity of earthly life (see also Hieroglyphs 5, 18, and 28). Its reflection underscores the fugacity of life because mirror reflections are transient and insubstantial. Thus, the anonymous speaker of the verse instructs the living (the candle) that their lives are no more permanent than their reflections in a mirror.

The claw feet of the table may be more than an incidental decorative touch. If they belong to lions, then perhaps the tablecloth should be understood as a kind of shroud concealing the Lion of Spain (that is, the late king) from view, much as clouds conceal the sun from view in other hieroglyphs. (For leonine imagery, see Hieroglyph 1.) In fact, Philip was associated with tables that were supported by lions and stood near mirrors. In the early 1650s he had ordered the construction of six porphyry tables carried by gilded bronze lions for the decoration of one of the most important state chambers in the Alcázar of Madrid, the Hall of Mirrors.[63] To be sure, their designs, which are known from state portraits of Charles and Mariana by Juan Carreño de Miranda, do not match those of the furnishings in Hieroglyph 40. Nevertheless, the possibility remains that the author of the hieroglyph intended his claw-footed table beside a mirror to make a sly allusion to the king.

HIEROGLYPH 41 (fig. 54)

Motto: *VT REQVIESCAT A LABO-RIBVS SVIS, OPERA ENIM ILLIVS SEQVNTVR ILLVM.* Apoc. 14

"He should rest from his labors, for his works follow him." (Variation on Apocalypse 14:13)

62. Ibid., cols. 329–32.

63. Orso, *Alcázar of Madrid,* 66–67.

Verse: *Desde que enpeço a Reynar*
Siguio a estas virtudes fiel,
Y ellas le siguen a el,
Quando se ua a descansar.
"Ever since he began to Rule, he pursued these virtues faithfully, and they follow him when he goes to rest."

Image: A crowned, winged heart flies into the sky between parted clouds. Seven kneeling figures who carry different objects (see below) bid it farewell as they float above the earth.

This was the colossal hieroglyph (twice the height and width of the others) that hung on the tribune at the rear of the nave of La Encarnación. In keeping with its preeminent size and its placement where the spectators would have seen it as they filed out of the church after the exequies had ended, it sums up many of the themes from the decorative ensemble. As a biographical hieroglyph, it declares that Philip had lived a life of virtue; as a consolatory hieroglyph, it celebrates the salvation of his soul; and as a political hieroglyph, it suggests that he has left behind a worthy queen who will govern well as regent.

As in Hieroglyph 22, the crowned, winged heart is Philip's soul, which ascends to heavenly glory following its release from his mortal body. The seven figures who regard its ascent are the personifications of virtues that he practiced in life ("he pursued these virtues faithfully"). They have testified to the goodness of his soul, and God has judged it worthy of admission into Heaven ("they follow him when he goes to rest"). Each personification carries an appropri-ate attribute. The three Theological Virtues kneel at the front: Faith with her chalice and Host, Hope with her anchor, and Charity with the infants for whom she cares.[64] Next come three of the four Cardinal Virtues: Justice with her sword, Prudence with her mirror, and Fortitude with her oak branch.[65] Religion, who wears a nun's habit and carries a Cross, takes the place of the fourth Cardinal Virtue, Temperance.[66]

The substitution of Religion for Temperance facilitates a visual pun that introduces a political theme into the composition. It was customary in the seventeenth century for a highborn Spanish widow to abandon her usual dress for a nun's habit. Although Mariana remained in retirement until the royal honors for her husband had been completed, the courtiers in Madrid must have anticipated her change of garb. In fact, she did conform to custom, as her state portraits from after 1665 show.[67] Thus, including a figure wearing a nun's habit among the virtues who bid Philip farewell becomes more than a declaration of his religiosity. It is also a discreet representation of Mariana as the virtuous widow who has survived him. Furthermore, placing her where the viewer expects to find Temperance comments favorably upon the temperance with which she will carry out responsibilities as regent.

64. Ripa, *Iconologia*, 71–73, 161–62, and 497; and Tervarent, *Attributs*, cols. 28 and 175. See also Hieroglyph 32.

65. Ripa, *Iconologia*, 179–81, 202–4, and 441–43; and Tervarent, *Attributs*, cols. 156 and 271–72.

66. Ripa, *Iconologia*, 456–57; see also *Relaciones breves*, 73, for the description of a personification of Religion on the catafalque at the royal exequies for Margarita of Austria in 1611.

67. See Orso, *Alcázar of Madrid*, 41 and 179–81.

10
A RECORD FOR POSTERITY

Once the royal exequies for Philip IV had ended, it remained for the court to publish its commemorative account of the event, the *Descripcion de las honras*. Its title page (fig. 8) identifies the author, Pedro Rodríguez de Monforte, as a private chaplain to the king, a censor of the Council of the Inquisition, a synodal examiner in the Archbishopric of Madrid, and a curate of the church of San Juan in Madrid. It was the first of these positions—*capellan de honor* to the king—that was most significant, for in that capacity he witnessed firsthand many of the events his book recounts. It was he, acting as chaplain of the week (*capellan de semana*), who celebrated the Communion Mass at the dying king's bedside the morning of September 16, and he was one of twelve private chaplains who participated in the funeral procession to El Escorial.[1] At the royal exequies he was one of six *capellanes de honor* who assisted Cardinal Colonna at the vigil service, and he was the chief (*asistente mayor*) of seven *capellanes de honor* who assisted at the three Masses of the exequies proper.[2] Thus, much of what he reports is based upon direct observation. Furthermore, as a member of the royal household, he was well placed to obtain any information he needed to round out his chronicle from the appropriate officials.[3]

In many ways, the *Descripcion* is an expanded version of the *Pompa Fvneral Honras*, the commemorative book that chronicles the royal exequies for Isabella of Bourbon. Rodríguez de Monforte repeatedly interrupts his narrative with disquisitions on antique precedents for the decorations and ceremonies that he describes. He opens with an account of the king's last days and his death (fols. 1–29^v), followed by accounts of the lying-in-state (fols. 29^v–35) and the procession that conveyed the royal corpse to El Escorial for interment (fols. 35–50). Then he explains how the court came to celebrate the exequies at La Encarnación rather than at San Jerónimo (fols. 50^v–54), which leads him to describe the decorations for the courtyard and atrium of the convent church (fols. 54–60^v) and for the church interior (fols. 61–71). The arrival of the celebrants for the vespers service provides him with the usual opportunity to name the dignitaries in attendance and to describe the seating arrangements (fols. 71–87^v), followed by a brief summary of the service itself (fols. 87^v–88^v). The exequies proper are described more fully (fols. 88^v–113), with the greater part of that section devoted to the complete text of the funeral sermon

---

1. Rodríguez de Monforte, *Descripcion*, fols. 14^v–15 and 39^v.
2. Ibid., fols. 87–87^v and 88^v.
3. For example, see APM, SH, Hf, caja 76, Fe-

lipe IV (1665), for a letter from Rodríguez de Monforte to the Marquis of Malpica, who had overall charge of the king's exequies. In it Rodríguez de Monforte refers to a memorandum on the royal councils and to the texts of five epitaphs that were displayed at the exequies that Malpica has said will be provided to him.

(fols. 92–110^v). The author concludes with his own lengthy tribute to Philip IV, at once a capsule biography of the king and an epitaph to his memory (fols. 113–20^v). The one section of the *Pompa Fvneral Honras* that does not have a counterpart in the *Descripcion* is the lengthy account of the decorations that were displayed in the cloister at San Jerónimo. There were no such adornments at La Encarnación.[4]

The illustrations to Rodríguez de Monforte's text (figs. 8–66) likewise expand upon the precedent of the *Pompa Fvneral Honras*. As in the earlier volume, there are a title page, an allegorical portrait of the deceased, a view of the catafalque from the nave, a plan of the church, and a view of the ceiling painting that hung over the *tumba*. The forty-one hieroglyphs are illustrated more lavishly with individual plates rather than four to a page. Four more plates reproduce the coats of arms of the Spanish realms that lined the nave, and nine small vignettes depict the coats of arms of the royal councils that sat in the nave. There is no view of the decorations outside the church, as there is in the *Pompa Fvneral Honras*, most likely because their disposition did not lend itself to a single perspective view. Nor is the epitaph that stood against the *tumba* illustrated with a separate plate; instead, Rodríguez de Monforte transcribes it in his text.

Forty-six of the illustrations are documented as having been engraved by Pedro de Villafranca y Malagón, who, since his participation in the ill-fated exequies book for Baltasar Carlos, had become the king's chief engraver (*grabador de cá-*

mara). At 200 *reales* per plate, he received 9,200 *reales* for his work.[5] By virtue of their superior quality, these plates can be distinguished easily from the remaining, mediocre illustrations: the four plates of arms of the Spanish realms (figs. 26–29) and the nine vignettes of the arms of the royal councils (figs. 58–66). When it is recalled that Villafranca, Juan de Noort, and Herman Panneels had engraved five plates of coats of arms of Spanish realms and the royal councils for the abandoned exequies book for Baltasar Carlos, the explanation is at hand: The five plates were salvaged for use in the *Descripcion*. Four plates illustrating the arms of the realms were printed unchanged, and the fifth plate, the arms of the royal councils, was cut into the nine vignettes.[6]

Sorting out the three hands that engraved the original five plates poses no great difficulty. The four sheets of territorial arms are indisputably the work of two different hands. One sheet (fig. 26) is markedly inferior to the other three, as a comparison of its insipid heraldic lions with those on the others makes clear. What is more, its lettering, with serifs on the letters *C* and *S*, differs from that on the others. None of the four is good

4. I assume that although it was permissible to open the cloister of a monastery to the public for a few days, to open the cloister of a convent was unthinkable.

5. AGS, CM3, leg. 1,362, Obras del Alcázar, fols. 23bis-23bis^v; and AGS, CM3, leg. 1,810(2), Gastos del Alcázar, fols. 172–73bis.

6. The median dimensions of the slightly irregular plate marks of Figures 26–29 are about 17.8 x 12.6 centimeters, and those of Figures 58–66 are about 3.9 x 3.7 centimeters. The close similarity between these plates and Herrera Barnuevo's study sheet for the coats of arms in the church nave (fig. 70) invites an obvious conclusion: the architect worked from impressions of the plates when he made his drawing. Thus, as in the prints, the devices of the individual realms are displayed on simple shields with appropriate crowns, except for the seigniories of Vizcaya and Molina, in which the shields are uncrowned and mounted on more elaborate cartouches.

enough to be the work of Villafranca, which means that they must be assigned to Noort and Panneels. Signed plates by Noort for the *Pompa Fvneral Honras*—and, for that matter, plates by Villafranca—are lettered with C's and S's that have no serifs.[7] Therefore, Panneels engraved Figure 26 and Noort carried out Figures 27 to 29. As for the vignettes, all nine display Panneels's mediocre draftsmanship, but the letters *C* and *S* in their brief inscriptions lack serifs. Apparently either Noort or Villafranca attended to the lettering.[8]

Most of the illustrations to Rodríguez de Monforte's book are familiar by now, but two that were created expressly for the book have yet to be considered: its title page and an allegorical portrait of Philip IV that appears just before the start of the text. By virtue of their placement at the beginning of the work, they prepare the reader for the panegyric text and illustrations that follow.

The title page (fig. 8) is charged with drama. In a miraculous vision that suddenly appears before the reader, four cherubim in the upper corners push back heavy curtains to reveal a retable from which two more cherubim hang a cloth inscribed with the book's title. The rest of the retable is an armature for a profusion of symbols, inscriptions, and allegorical personifications whose presence comments upon the sober contents of the

book. The credit for inventing this page belongs not to Villafranca, however, but to Sebastián de Herrera Barnuevo, the architect who designed the exequies decorations. His preparatory drawing for the page has survived (fig. 82), and Villafranca's engraving follows it faithfully.[9]

The fundamental conceit of the design equates Philip's life and death with the passage of the seasons and its effect upon different flowers. Two figures stand on projecting socles flanking the book's title: Spring, a young woman who wears a floral garland and holds a cornucopia full of blooms, and Autumn, an old man who wears a garland of acorns and oak leaves, and who grasps a withered tree. Their Spanish names, *Primavera* and *Otoño*, are inscribed on the piers behind them with the dates of Philip's birth (April 8) and death (September 17). The other imagery on Spring's side of the page likewise relates to the king's birth, whereas that on Autumn's side relates to his death. Thus, an inscription on Spring's socle quotes Psalm 102:15, *TANQUAM FLOS AGRI SIC EFFLOREVIT* ("As the flower of the field, so will he flourish"), whereas one on Autumn's socle cites Isaiah 40:7, *EXICCATṼ EST FŒNṼ ET CECIDIT FLOS QUIA SPIRIT' DÑI SUFFLAVIT IN EO* ("The grass is withered, and the flower is fallen because the spirit of the Lord has blown upon it"). Two emblems below these inscriptions maintain this opposition of birth and death. That of Spring, a crown with the letters *PHS* (for *Philippus* [Philip]), quotes Canticles 4:8, *VENI CORONAVERIS* ("Come, you will be crowned"). It reminds the reader that

7. For example, see Noort's signed plan of San Jerónimo as it was furnished for the royal exequies for Isabella of Bourbon in *Pompa Fvneral Honras*, between fols. 20[v] and 21.

8. Although Noort, Panneels, and Villafranca are all named in records of payments for the five plates of coats of arms, it is not necessarily the case that Villafranca worked on any of them. Because they also engraved the twenty-two lost plates for a Baltasar Carlos royal exequies book, it is possible they divided the labor among themselves in a manner not reflected in the royal bookkeeping.

9. See Jonathan Brown, "Spanish Baroque Drawings in the Sperling Bequest," 376–77, on which most of the following iconographic analysis depends.

Philip had been destined from birth to rule the Monarchy. Autumn's emblem is a heart that illustrates a grim motto from Jeremiah 4:9, *PERIBIT COR REGIS* ("The heart of the king will perish").

The floral conceit is elaborated at the base and the summit of the retable. Between the projecting socles two grieving cherubim lean against a cartouche that depicts a lily growing amid other plants. An accompanying motto from Canticles 2:2, *SICVT LILIVM INTER SPINAS* ("As a lily among thorns"), praises the virtue of the king. Another flower grows at the top of the retable, and an accompanying banderole quotes Job 14:2, *QVASI FLOS EGREDITVR ET CONTERITVR* ("He comes forth like a flower and is destroyed").[10] Two winds that breathe upon the flower determine its fate. At the left (Spring's side) is Austro, the young and gentle South Wind, who puffs life into the flower, as the word *VIVE* ("It lives") inscribed on his gust makes clear. At the right (Autumn's side) is Boreas, the old and harsh North Wind, whose chill blast will kill the flower, as the inverted word *MVERE* ("It dies") confirms. A crown floating above the flower indicates that the bloom represents the king. An inscription above the crown, *AVSTER DIVERSA MINISTRAT* ("The South Wind brings many things"), makes a Latin pun based upon the family name, the House of Austria, that recalls the Spanish pun seen at the king's exequies in Hieroglyph 34. The *Auster* of Spring brought Philip into the world, and Philip was an *Austria* who wrought many deeds while he lived.

The *Allegorical Portrait of Philip IV* (fig. 9) displays a sophistication of alle-

gorical thinking comparable to what is seen in the title page. It, too, can be attributed to Herrera Barnuevo, for a sheet of drawings from his hand includes studies of two motifs found in the composition, a lion and an eagle (fig. 83). Moreover, in his signature at the bottom left of the portrait, Villafranca claims only to have engraved it, not to have invented it.[11] The portrait pays flattering tribute to Philip's greatness as a monarch and acknowledges his subjects' profound grief at his passing. In doing so, it makes inventive use of imagery that is compatible with the hieroglyphs from the exequies without lapsing into stale repetition.

The composition is dominated by a bust portrait of the king adapted from one Velázquez painted in the mid-1650s (frontispiece).[12] Whereas Velázquez depicts the king in a simple black outfit, the engraving dresses him in armor with a commander's sash and a collar of the Order of the Golden Fleece. This change of costume characterizes Philip as the glorious commander of the Spanish armies. A funeral wreath surrounds the bust, and through it twists a banderole inscribed, *PHILIPPVS. IV. HISPANIARVM REX* ("Philip IV, King of the Spains"). Two putti hovering at the left carry his crown and scepter, while two at the right bear the royal coat of arms. All three insignia of his rule had figured prominently at his exequies.

The pedestal on which the bust rests is nothing less than the terrestrial globe, which is borne aloft by the personifica-

10. Herrera Barnuevo incorrectly cites Job 4 as the source on his preparatory drawing.

11. As noted by Marías and Bustamante, "Apuntes arquitectónicos," 36–38; Herrera Barnuevo's drawing is in AHN, Códices 288b, fol. 28.

12. As noted in Matilde López Serrano, "Reflejo velazqueño en el arte del libro español de su tiempo," in *Varia velazqueña: homenaje á Velázquez en el III centenario de su muerte 1660–1960*, 1:512.

tions of four continents.[13] At the front left is Europe, represented by Europa riding the Jovian bull. Behind her is Africa, a black woman who wears a turban-crown and whose other attribute, a crocodile, pokes its head out from behind the bull. Most of the background is dark, but the sun glows behind Africa. From its position in the west relative to the globe, it must be a setting sun, a recurrent symbol of the king's death in the hieroglyphs. At the front right is Asia, who wears another turban-crown and carries a flaming brazier embellished with a crescent moon. Behind her is America, an Indian woman whose attributes include a feathered headdress, a bow, a quiver of arrows, and two ears of corn. A parrot perches between the two continents on what seems to be America's knee. A banderole that runs beneath the globe quotes Ecclesiasticus 2:16, *VÆ HIS QVIA PERDIDERVNT SVSTINENTIAM* ("Woe to them, for they have lost [their] support"). Interpreting *sustinentiam* as "support" rather than as the more conventional "patience" provides the basis for understanding the role of the continents. One of Philip's epithets was "the Spanish Atlas." Just as Atlas bore the weight of the celestial globe on his shoulders, so Philip was understood to bear the weight of the terrestrial globe on his. The *Allegorical Portrait* reverses this metaphor. Because Philip has died, the continents have lost the Spanish Atlas who supported them. To honor his passing, they now support him as the pedestal that carries his bust. Whoever devised this motif may have been inspired by a passage in an epitaph at La Encarnación that addressed the

13. Although the personifications do not match the prescriptions of Ripa, *Iconologia*, 355–61, perfectly, there are sufficient correspondences to confirm the identifications that follow.

four continents by name (see Appendix B, Courtyard Epitaph 1). What is more, the striking image of Philip surmounting the globe inevitably recalls another of his epithets, "the Planet King."

Beneath the global pedestal the personification of Madrid sits with her coat of arms mourning her sovereign's death. A banderole lying on a cartouche below her expresses her sentiments with words from Jeremiah 4:31, *VÆ MIHI QVIA DEFECIT ANIMA MEA* ("Woe is me, for my soul has fainted"). Her presence is triply appropriate because Madrid was the capital of the Monarchy that Philip had ruled, the place of his death, and the setting for his royal exequies. At her sides are a lion and eagle, whose status as the king of beasts and the king of birds alludes to the royal standing of the deceased. As heraldic creatures from the arms of different realms of the Monarchy, they hint at the extent of the dominions where Philip is mourned. The lion, which may also symbolize the king's fortitude (as in Hieroglyph 1), holds the sword of the king's justice and a globe that signifies his dominion over the Monarchy. The eagle, which is the Jovian eagle, clutches thunderbolts (indicating Philip's might) and a garland (symbolizing his victories) in its talons. This accords with the portrayal of Philip as a commander as well as a king.

When all was ready, Rodríguez de Monforte supervised the publication of the *Descripcion* in an edition of 1,750 copies. The printer Francisco Nieto received 10,150 *reales* for the costs of the paper and the actual printing of the text; the stamper Felipe de Felipe collected 9,196 *reales* for printing 87,500 large plates and 15,750 small ones (that is, the fifty large plates and the nine vignettes for the complete edition); and bookbinders were paid 5,250 *reales* for binding all 1,750 copies.[14] It is not documented how the book was distributed, but the court surely used it to expand the audience for the king's funerary honors to include his distant contemporaries and his posterity. As a royal commission, it was inextricably bound up in the regime's efforts to present itself in the best possible light. The most telling measure of the book's success is the most obvious: Without it, our capacity to appreciate the royal exequies for Philip IV would be negligible.

14. AGS, CM3, leg. 1,810(2), Gastos del Alcázar, fols. 173bis-73bis^r; and APM, SH, Hf, caja 76, Felipe IV (1665).

AFTERWORD

With their capacity to engage the mind and delight the eye, the decorations at the royal exequies for Philip IV provided his survivors with a seductive means to set the agenda of public affairs. Even after more than three centuries, the decorations retain their capacity to impress us, but we should not let the glare of the candles blind us to the limitations of the ensemble. Exequies decorations were hortatory. They could celebrate the virtues of the royal family until verging on hagiography, and they could proclaim the ideals of the regime in the loftiest terms—but their practical effects were limited. In 1665 the exequies decorations for Philip IV declared that he had left a worthy successor in Charles II and a wise regent in Mariana of Austria, but what secured their positions were the laws of inheritance and their power to enforce them. Their confident assurances notwithstanding, the hieroglyphs could not guarantee the new regime would rule well—and history's judgment of Mariana's regency and Charles's reign is far from glowing.

The power of royal exequies was psychological: Funerary honors extended the healing powers of ritual to a grieving court that mourned a beloved leader. To Philip's loyal subjects, his death was a personal loss that unsettled the political order. His demise must have been felt especially keenly in Madrid. Unlike most citizens of the Monarchy, the Madrilenians saw the Habsburgs firsthand, and many of them served in the bureaucracies that administered the empire at the king's behest. Royal exequies eased their grief by providing them with a framework within which they could take their leave of Philip and come to terms with his death. The subsequent exequies staged by other institutions throughout the Monarchy served the same end for the citizens of other locales.

This need to console the people at a time of national grief has remained a concern of modern statecraft. Americans old enough to remember the assassination of John F. Kennedy can recall how a nation sat transfixed by live television coverage of his state funeral. The public solemnities in Washington, D.C., enabled the people to pay homage to their fallen president and to accept the reality of his untimely death. The rituals and images from those first days of mourning—the presidential coffin lying in state in the Capitol rotunda, the riderless horse in the funeral cortege with the boots of its fallen commander mounted backward in its stirrups, the widow lighting an eternal flame at the grave in Arlington National Cemetery—remain vivid memories for those who shared in the national trauma. To the courtiers of Madrid in 1665, the royal exequies for Philip IV were no less compelling to the eye, and no less soothing to the heart.

The king's funerary honors addressed not only the immediate past, but also the imminent future. As a vehicle for royal propaganda, the exequies enabled his survivors to proclaim their goals and be-

117

liefs in a forum that was sure to capture the attention of the public—especially of the elite who served in the upper levels of the government. So well had the royal family and its servants mastered the language of catafalques and hieroglyphs that even to this day, the decorations for the royal exequies for Philip IV can tell us how the Habsburgs perceived themselves, how they sought to make their world a better place, and how they aspired to salvation in the afterlife that awaited them.

Appendix A
THE ETIQUETTE FOR ROYAL EXEQUIES FOR PERSONAGES OTHER THAN KINGS, QUEENS, AND *PRÍNCIPES JURADOS* OF SPAIN

In addition to prescribing how royal exequies were to be celebrated for kings, queens, and *príncipes jurados* of Spain, the *etiquetas* of 1647–1651 also specified how royal exequies were to be arranged for two other groups of dignitaries with ties to the royal house:[1]

HONORS FOR FOREIGN EMPERORS AND EMPRESSES, KINGS AND QUEENS, OR PRINCES AND PRINCESSES

The honors of emperors and empresses, kings and queens, or princes and princesses who are fathers or mothers of the queens of Spain are celebrated in the same manner as and with the said ceremonies of the honors for the kings and queens of Spain, as are those of brothers and sisters [of a king of Spain] who are crowned kings and queens. The catafalque[2] is of more or less grandeur according to the church or chapel where it is executed by the superintendent of the [royal] works in conformance with the order that His Majesty gives. Most ordinarily it is in the royal convent of the Descalzas. Usually the councils are not present, although sometimes Their Majesties have ordered it. It was done thus at the honors for the Most Serene Doña Juana, Princess of Portugal [and] sister of the lord King Philip II, that were celebrated in the Descalzas Reales in Madrid at the end of September in 1573.

And it was in those for the Most Serene Maria, Archduchess of Austria, the mother of the queen our lady Doña Margarita (who is in glory), in the royal monastery of San Benito in Valladolid on August 11, 1608, that the *chancillería* was present because the court was in Madrid and there were no councils [in Valladolid]. And it has been seen [thus] on other occasions, the three Pontifical Masses and only one Responsory being said.

The coats of arms of the kings-at-arms and the escutcheons of the catafalque, the hangings, and the candles are customarily the arms of the deceased and of his four grandparents. His own are put in the most preeminent place.

HONORS FOR INFANTES OF SPAIN AND ARCHDUKES AND ARCHDUCHESSES OF AUSTRIA

In the honors for *infantes* of Spain and for Archdukes and Archduchesses of Austria the church is hung in black. A catafalque[3] with steps is set up, and the *tumba* is put on top [of the steps]. It is adorned with candlesticks and with *agujas* at the corners. On it, on the altar hanging, and on the candles [are] coats of arms and some trophies. The kings-at-arms [are] atop the platform, the macebearers are on the ground to one side and the other of the catafalque, and the chapel is in the ordinary form. Three Pontifical Masses and only one Responsory are said. This same was done

---

1. For the sources on which the following texts are based, see chap. 1, n. 19.

2. Some versions give *capella ardente* for "catafalque" (*túmulo*).

3. Some versions give "platform" (*tablado*) for "catafalque" (*túmulo*).

[at the honors for] the king and queen of Denmark.

When they are celebrated in the Descalzas [Reales], His Majesty comes out from the quarters that he has in that convent and descends by the staircase that gives onto the cloister. He enters by the door of the chapel of Saint Sebastian with the ordinary accompaniment.

Appendix B
The Epitaphs

The epitaph displayed on the catafalque and the seven epitaphs displayed in the courtyard of La Encarnación at the royal exequies for Philip IV are transcribed below.[1] Courtyard Epitaphs 1 and 2 appeared on two freestanding dossals that were erected in the corners formed by the church facade and the courtyard walls. Courtyard Epitaphs 3 to 7 were placed in two frames on the piers flanking the central entrance portal. To judge from their lengths, numbers 3 to 5 would have occupied one pier, and numbers 6 and 7 the other.

The Catafalque Epitaph

D. O. M. / *PERGE GRADV, QVI REGIAM* / *HANC MOLEM CONSVLIS.* / CADVNT *DE MONTIBVS* / *VMBRÆ,* / PHILIPPVS QVARTVS CATHO- / LICVS HISPAN-IARVM / MONARCHA. / *SOLIS INSTAR IN VMBRAS* / *VERGIT.* / HEV MORTIS AEQVVS PES! / MONTIVM PLANITIES! / AST SI VMBRA CECIDIT, VIR- / TVTES PERSTANT. / *RELIGIO, PIETAS, CLE-* / *MEN-* / *TIA, CONSTANTIA.* / QVIBVS NVLLI SECVNDVS, / RELIGIONE SVPE-ROS IMPEN- / SE COLVIT. / PIETATE SVBIECTOS BENIGNE / EXCEPIT. / *CLE-* / *MENTIA OFFENSOS PER* / *HVMANITER* / *ABSOLVIT.* / CONSTANTIA LABORES HER- / CVLEOS AEQVANIMITER / EXA-LAVIT, / ET SI SIT REGALE FASTIGIVM / ÆRVMNARVM IMPATIENS / PATIENTIA LEVIORA FIVNT, / QVAE NEFAS EST, CO- / RRIGAS, / FVGACEM MAGNITVDINIS / VMBRAM EXVIT, / PERENNITATEM IND-VIT. / *XV.KALEND AS OCTOBRIS* / *ANNO CIↃ.IC.ↃLXV.* / *ÆTATIS* LX. / DIE

BEATISSIMAE VIRGINIS / MARIAE MEL-LITO NOMINE / SACRO, / CVIVS SPE-CIEM PRIMAEVAM / ARDENTER ADA-MAVIT, / *NASCITVR PINCIÆ, MATRITI* / *DENASCITVR.* / CVM IMPERII CVLMEN IN / VTRAQVE FORTVNA / SVBIVGAS-SET. / *ANNIS XLV. SED SEMPER* / *IDEM.* / ET CHARISSIMAM CONIVGEM / EX AVGVSTA SORORE / FILIAM. / PRO-SVPERSTITE *CAROLO* / *QVADRIMO FI-LIO* / *ORBI MAXIMOPERE* / *CHARO.* / NOMINE *SECVNDO,* O ASPI- / RENT NVMINA! NIMIVM / *SECVNDO.* / IN SCEPTRI CVRAS VIRITIM / ASCIVISSET. / NVLLIVS SIBI MAGIS CONS- / CIVS, QVAM INTERITVS. / VACVAS, SED PRECIOSSAS / ILLAS AVRAS INCOLIT. / *QVAS VI-VENS DESTINARAT* / *RECNICOLARVM VOTVM* / IN LACHRYMAS SOLVITVM, / IN FAVILLA EXCEDENS / MOERORIS MONVMENTVM / POSVIT.

(To God, the Best, the Greatest:

Walk on, you who come to gaze upon this royal structure. The shadows fall from the mountains. Philip IV, Catholic King of the Spains, the likeness of the Sun, fades into the shadows. Alas, Death the leveler! Flattener of mountains! But if the shadow has fallen, the virtues stand fast: Religion, Piety, Clemency, [and] Constancy, in which he was second to none. In Religion, he worshiped God earnestly. In Piety, he treated his subjects kindly. In Clemency, he forgave most humanely those who had offended him. In Constancy, he [performed][2] Herculean labors calmly.

And if his royal dignity was indignant at hardships, by his patience, they became lighter. What is wicked, may you correct. He

---

1. As given in Rodríguez de Monforte, *Descripcion*, fols. 54ᵛ–60ᵛ and 69ᵛ–71.

2. *Exalavit* is undoubtedly a corruption.

121

has put off the fleeting shadow of greatness, and has put on eternity.

17 September 1665.

Age 60.

[He died] on the day sacred to the Most Blessed Virgin Mary, whose name is honeyed, whose youthful image he adored ardently. He was born at Valladolid [and] died at Madrid. Though he had subdued the height of empire in both [good and bad] fortune for forty-five years, he was always the same.

And his dearest wife [is] the daughter of his august sister. His fourth son, the surviving Charles, the second of that name—O ye gods, too much the second—[is] to the world especially dear. O, may the divine powers favor [him]! Would that he [Philip] had introduced him [Charles] to the cares of the scepter one at a time.

Thinking[3] of nothing save death, he dwells in the breezes, empty but precious, which he had chosen when he was alive. The prayer of his subjects [*regnicolarum*] turned to tears [*solutum*], departing in the ash, established this monument of grief.)

Courtyard Epitaph 1

D. O. M. / PHILIPPO IV. HISPANIARVM / REGI CATHOLICO, / ORBIS GENVIS [*sic*] MÆRENS / PARENTABAT. / Siste viator, lachrymas comprime, vt / attentius / Legas, & perpendas. / OBIT PHILIPPVS; PROH DO-LOR! INGRESVS EST VIAM / VNIVERSÆ CARNIS. / QVID MIRVM? / Pelle; ossibus, & nerbis compactus, cur / non dissolueretur? / Virtutibus Christiano, Regibus / circumceptus, / Cur non ad melius Regnandum / assumeretur? / Si doles EVROPA, AFRICA, AS-SIA, / AMERICA, quod talem, / Actantum dominatorem perdideris, / Sortem tuam doleas. / Regiæ fœlicitati non inuideas. / Regnare non desijt, sed incæpit, qui / sceptrum mutauit / In melius. / Pro terreno cœleste: pro

3. From *Nullius sibi magis conscius* . . . onward, the Latin of the epitaph is difficult, obscure, and possibly corrupt.

temporali / æternum apprehendens. / Quid dubitas? / PIETATEM INSPICITO, RELI- / GIONEM ATTENDITO. / Propicium Filium habeat necesse est, qui / fauentem habuit Matrem. / Quid vltrà dubitas? /SACRORVM MISTERIORVM / CVLTOR ASSIDVVS, mistarum / defensor acerrimus. / IMMACULA-TAE CONCEPTIO- / NIS INCONCVSSVS, AC AMAN- / TISSIMVS ASSERTOR / AN-TESIGNANVS / PRAECIPVVS. / Quid ni Matrem, quid ni Filium propi- / tium; & defensorem habeat? / Audite Insulæ, & attendite Populi / de longe. / PHILIPPVS VESTER REGNAT, / non obijt, si obijt, vt Regnet fœlicius, / Fortuito si humanè, si Christianè inspi- / cias, non fortuito inestibali Auleo / Vitam finiuit Princeps, & casu, sed non / casu Regium Thalamum / Sub ea pictura estrauere Ministri, quæ / Attauorum Principis, / Et subsequentium nepotum / Gloriæ, & amplitudinis referret initium, / & promissum finem / Non habituræ in terris, donec iugue Sa- / crificium durat in Cœlis; / Donec nuptiæ Agni Immaculati / perdurabunt. / Sic decuit Austriadum perenne designare / Imperium. / Sub referente pictura Rodulfum Parro- / cho famulantem obijt PHILIPPVS. / PHILIPPVS, qui cum Rodulfo pari, si / non simili obsequio. / Venerabatur dum viueret admi- / randum Catholicæ Fidei / SACRAMENTVM / Mortem, ad se gradu celeri venientem, / prospexit. / Qui mortem non expauit. / Illam exomologesi facta exarmauit. / Se ad singulare certamen commu- / niuit. / SACRA SINAXI repetita, / Si quid residum fuit, VNTIO / abstersit vltima, / Quam postulauit. / Domesticis, publicisque, vt Principem / decet Maximum, / Compositis, firmatisque negotijs, ea / animi æqualitate, / Qua semper prospera, aduersaque / substinuit. / ANNVM AETATIS AGENS. LX. / REGNORVM. XLIV. / SA-ECVLI LXV. / Die Iobis mensis Septembris. XVII. / hora sex. / Qui quinta Matutina. / Inter suos mærentes, & plangentes, / vltimum / Exhalauit spiritum. / ET APPOSITVS EST AD PA- / TRES SVOS. / Prosequere Viator planctum, resume / lachrymas, / Refunde, de tua sorte dolens, de / PHILIPPI nostri. / Gloria nihil dubitans. / Quia si tu in mæstitia, & squalore / insepultus viuis. / ILLE AETER-NAM REQVIES- / CIT IN PACEM.

(To God, the Best, the Greatest:

In honor of Philip IV, the Catholic King of the Spains, the genius of the world sadly offers sacrifice.

Come to a stop, traveler, and repress tears in order to read and consider more attentively. Philip is dead. Alas! He has gone the way of all flesh. What is the great surprise? Being made of skin, bones, and sinews, why would he not dissolve away? A Christian for his virtues, why should he, surrounded by kings, not be taken up to a better reigning?

Europe, Africa, Asia, and America: If you grieve that you have lost such and so great a master, it is *your* lot for which you are lamenting. You should not be envious of the royal felicity. He has not ceased to reign; rather, he begins—he who has changed his scepter for a better one, a heavenly one for an earthly one, grasping an eternal one for a temporal one. Why do you hesitate?

Consider his piety, take heed of his religion. The Son must be propitious toward him, he for whom the Mother is watchful. Why hesitate further?

[He was] a regular attender of sacred mysteries and a fierce defender of priests. [He was] an unshaken and most loving proponent and an outstanding standard-bearer of the Immaculate Conception. Why should the Mother and why should the Son not be propitious toward him and defend him? Hear ye, Islands, and give heed ye peoples from afar: Your Philip reigns. He does not die, if he dies to reign more happily. If, perchance, you examine humanely, if [you examine] like a Christian, [you will see that] not by chance has the prince finished his life in the summer apartments. By chance, but not by chance, have the ministers laid out the royal bedchamber beneath this picture, which reports the origin of the glory and the grandeur of the grandfathers of the prince—[glory and grandeur] that will have their promised end not on earth, as long as the constant sacrifice in Heaven endures, as long as the nuptials of the Immaculate Lamb endure. So [by hanging this picture here] it befitted the everlasting empire of the Austrias to be marked out. Philip, who, with Rudolf, by an equal (if not identical) reverence, venerated the admirable Sacrament of the Catholic Faith while he lived.

He saw Death approaching him with a swift stride. He did not fear Death; his confession having been made, he disarmed it. He fortified himself for [this] single combat. He sought out the Sacred Liturgy, and the Extreme Unction he asked for cleansed him of any remaining [sin]. [He died] as befits the greatest prince, among his servants and his courtiers, with his affairs having been arranged and settled with that evenness of soul with which he always endured in prosperity and adversity.

He breathed his last breath amid the weeping and lamenting of his subjects at the sixth hour, which is the fifth hour of the morning, on Thursday, September 17, in the sixty-fifth year of the century, the sixtieth year of his life, and the forty-fourth of his reign. And he was set in the company of his fathers. Traveler, continue your lament and weep tears again. Pour them out and grieve for your lot. But do not hesitate at all with regard to the glory of our Philip, because while you live unburied, grieving and unkempt, he reposes in eternal peace.)

COURTYARD EPITAPH 2

D. O. M. / MAVSOLEVM Posthumæ ac / perennis Gloriæ. / Pulchritudine egregium, Arte / ingeniosum. / SOLEMNE OPVS. / Nobili virtutum animatum cælatura. / Illustri pietatis titulo inscriptum. / Vnico nominis elogio satis elegans, satis / laudabile. PHILIPPO QVARTO. / Catholico Hispaniarum Regi. / Ingenti, ac mæstissimo planctu commu- / ni malo præpopero fato erepto, sancto / demum fine quiescenti erectum. / Qui inter Christianissimos Magnus, & / inter pijssimos Maìor. / Et inter purè, illibatèque Catholicos / affatim Maximus. / Cultu in Deiparam summus. / Pro cuius immuni à labe Conceptu / asserendo. / Adeò nullis pepercit studijs, nullis / sumptibus ac vigilijs. / Vt natura lenissimus non solum inde- / uitos, sed et sontes. / De Genitricis Dei puritate cogitans. / Nunquam non Fortis, Acer Inconcussus, / Vindex, ac Propugnator exarserit. / RELIGIONE, IVSTITIA, PIETA- / TE, CONSTANTIA / Tam abundè præditus, & ornatus. / Vt cum ipso pariter tumulari / videantur. / Qua propter si Regem discooperires, / PHILIPPVM, deligeres: Quem / deligeres, deligeres. / Qui variè flantem, ac reflantem / fortunam, immobili, Semper / animo tulit. / Ex Elisabetha Galliarum Regibus orta. / Gallicis Regnis, Mariam Theresiam / dedit Reginam. / Ex Maria-Anna Imperatoris filia, Filiam / imperaturam, spopondit Imperio. / CAROLO II nomine, quem, & numine / apprecamur secundum, Nullique / secundum Virtute ominamur. / Quadriennio Principe spe, & delicio / nostri sæculi Rege successore / Inaugurato. / Maria-Anna Augustissima. / Ex Sorore Nepte dilectissima, ex mori- / bus Vxore. / Hispaniarum Regnis Moderatrice relicta, / Tandem miserias huius sæculi beato / exitu absoluit. / Die XVII. Septembris diei Iobis, hora / quarta matutina. Anno M.DC.LXV. / SISTE HOSPES. / Cerne Regis Monumentum (inquam) / virtutum operosam Molem. / Hoc Tumulo clauditur, quod micat in / Orbe terrarum decus / Funere raptus est AEteris invidia. / Vt in æternum viuat.

(To God, the Best, the Greatest:

A mausoleum: for [keeping] after death and for everlasting glory; remarkable for its beauty, clever in its artistry; a solemn work enlivened by a noble ceiling [*caelatura*] of virtues lettered with a distinguished inscription attesting to his piety; quite elegant enough, quite praiseworthy for the unique praising of his name. To Philip IV, Catholic King of the Spains.

With great and saddest lament, this is erected for him reposing at last in a holy rest, whom over-hasty fate snatched away to the common detriment, who among the most Christian people was great, [who] among the most pious [was] greater, and [who] among the most purely and unimpairedly Catholic [was] quite the greatest.

Unsurpassed in reverence for the Mother of God, he spared no effort, no cost, and no lack of sleep in asserting his veneration of her conception free from sin. [He was] by nature most gentle not only toward the innocent, but also toward the guilty, thinking of the purity of the Genetrix of God. Always brave, fierce, unshaken, an ardent vindicator and champion.

So abundantly endowed with religion, justice, piety, and constancy that they seem equally buried with him.

So if you had uncovered the king, you would love Philip; you would love the one whom you would love. [Philip,] who always endured with unchanging spirit Fortune, variously blowing one way and the other. From Isabella, herself born of the Kings of the Gauls, he gave María Teresa as queen to the Gaulish kingdoms. From Mariana, daughter of the Emperor, he betrothed to the Empire a daughter who would rule. With Charles II, second of that name, whom we pray be second in *numen* and whom we foretell to be second to none in virtue, having been left behind as a four-year-old prince (the hope and delight of our age) and having been inaugurated as successor-king; and with the most august Mariana, beloved niece on his sister's side and by custom wife, having been left as Moderator of the Kingdoms of Spain—finally, he was freed from the miseries of this age with a blessed departure on Thursday, September 17, 1665, at the fourth hour of the morning.

Pause, guest! See, I say, the monument of the king, a structure wrought of virtues. What has shone for adornment to the whole world is shut in this tomb. He has been taken away by his funeral because of the envy of Heaven, that he might live forever.)

COURTYARD EPITAPH 3

D. O. M. / PHILIPPVS IV. / Verè Catholicus. / Christiana pietate / Magnus. / CVIVS / IN /

DEO / Constans Charitas. / IN / Beatissima Maria Virgine, / Deuotio admirabilis, / Interminabilis Amor, / SVAE / Immaculatæ Conceptionis. / Defensor, & Celator Acerrimus. / IN / Sanctos / Veneratio, & Deuotio Eximia. / IN / Suprema Dignitate, / SINE / Acerbitate, erga suos, Grauitas. / IN / Omnes / Benevolentia, & Iustitia, / IN / Primis, Chara Deo, Grata Hominibus. / IN / Vtraque Fortuna / Ipsiusmet Fortunæ Victor / Migravit / AD / Cœleste Beatorum consortium regnan- /tium Anno M.DC.LXV. mense / Septembris: Die XVII. / AEneus est / QVI / Siccis oculis legit.

(To God, the Best, the Greatest:

Philip IV the Great: Truly Catholic; great in Christian piety; whose Charity in God was constant; boundless in his love and admirable in his devotion to the Virgin Mary; Defender and Zealous Protector of her Immaculate Conception; remarkable in his veneration and devotion to the saints; in highest office without bitterness, grave toward his own, benevolent and just toward all; pleasing to men, especially dear to God; victor over Fortune itself in both [good and bad] fortune.

He migrated to the heavenly company of the blessed who reign on September 17, 1665.

He who reads [this] with dry eyes is made of brass.)

COURTYARD EPITAPH 4

D. O. M. / PHILIPPVS IV. / Insignis pietate Vir / Obseruantissimus. / Christianæ Religionis, & Iustitiæ / HAC / In Exigua Vrna / Clauditur! / Heù dolor! / Timete, / O / Principes Deum: / Attendite: Videte: Audite. / Tam paruus Cinis Herculeus Est! / SIT ILLI / Requies, & Dies sine Nocte.

(To God, the Best, the Greatest:

Philip IV, a man most remarkable for piety and most observant of Christian religion and justice, is shut in this little urn. Alas! Fear God, O princes! Heed, see, hear: So little ash is Hercules! To him be repose and day without night.)

COURTYARD EPITAPH 5

D. O. M. / PHILIPPO IV. / VNVS, / Non suficiebat Orbis! / IAM! / Superest Sepulchrum! / MORS / Præripuit, / Anno M.DC.LXV. ætatis suæ LX. / Regni Sui XLIV. Mense Septembris / Die XVII. / QVIS / Temperet A Lacrymis.

(To God, the Best, the Greatest:

To Philip IV one world was not enough! Now the tomb remains! Death snatched him away September 17, 1665, at age 60, in the forty-fourth year of his reign. Who could refrain from tears?)

COURTYARD EPITAPH 6

D. O. M. / PHILIPPVS IV. / IN / Vno, & Altero Hemispherio, / Rex Potentissimus / FVI: / Non Fuit / In Mea Potestate / Prohibere Spiritum: / NEC / Habere Potestatem in Die Mortis: / VIVENS, / Paravi Hoc Sepulchrum: / MORTVVS, / Requiesco In Illo.

(To God, the Best, the Greatest:

I, Philip IV, was the most powerful king in one hemisphere and the other. It was not in my power to keep my soul [in my body], nor to have power over my day of death. Living, I prepared this tomb. Dead, I repose in it.)

COURTYARD EPITAPH 7

D. O. M. / REX PHILIPPVS IV. / Hispanicus: Gothicus: Austriacus: / Lusitanicus: Celtibericus: Cantabricus: / Italicus: Indicus: Flandricus, &c. / Mortuus Est, In Osculo Domini: / Anno Ab Orbe Redempto / M.DC.LXV. / Septembris, / Die XVII. / IMPERATORES! / Mortalia Curato! / VOBIS / Quoque Erit Moriendum! / MIRVM! / Hunc Tumulum Tantum Virum / Posse Condere! / QVI / Legis: Elige: / Inscriptio, & Epitaphia / Vota sunt mea: / Ingeniabat affectus; / AD / Perpetuam recordationem / Augustissimi / REGIS PHILIP. IV. / Vivet post cineres. / Populi Deprecate Omnes, / VT / In præsenti Statu, / Eueniat Hispanis / Illud. / *Regum, lib. 2. cap. 7. vers. 16.* / *Cum, completi fuerint dies tui,* /

Et dormieris cum Patribus tuis / Suscitabo se-men tuum; / QVOD / Egredietur de vtero tuo, / ET / Firmabo / Regnum Eius. / Fiat: Fiat: / Fiat.

(To God, the Best, the Greatest:

Philip IV, King of Spain, of the Goths, of Austria, of Lusitania, of Celtiberia, of Canta-bria, of Italy, of the Indies, of Flanders, etc. has died with the kiss of the Lord, September 17, in the year of the Redeemed World 1665.

Emperors! Think on mortal things. You will also have to die! Marvelous! That this tomb can contain so great a man! [You] who read, choose: the inscription and epitaphs are at my wish. Affection is doubled [*ingemina-bat?*]. To the perpetual memory of the most august King Philip IV. May he live beyond the ashes!

Pray all ye peoples that this may occur for Spain in its present state: "When your days shall be completed and you sleep with your fathers, I shall raise of your seed which shall come forth from your belly, and I shall make its kingdom firm" (II Kings 7:16).[4]

So be it. So be it. So be it.)

4. The correct citation is II Kings 7:12.

Appendix C
THE CEILING PAINTING OVER THE *TUMBA*

To Rodríguez de Monforte the ceiling painting set within the first story of the catafalque at the royal exequies for Philip IV "made a Majestic dossal to the *Tumba*" (fig. 56).[1] The twenty-four inscriptions radiating from its central medallion were:

[1]   Potens in terra Semen eius *Ps. 111*.
      (His seed is mighty on earth. [Psalm 111:2])

[2]   Honor Regis iuditium diligit *Ps. 98*.
      (The king's honor loves judgment. [Psalm 98:4])

[3]   Iudicauit populos in Iustitia *Ps. 9*.
      (He will judge the people with justice. [Psalm 9:9])

[4]   Lex Dei eius in corde ipsius *Ps. 36*.
      (The law of his God is in his heart. [Psalm 36:31])

[5]   Induit eum Dominus loricam fidei *ad Thes. Cap. 5*.
      (The Lord has dressed him in the breast-plate of faith. [Variation on I Thessalonians 5:8])

[6]   Prosperum iter faciet *Ps. 67*.
      (He will make the way prosperous. [Psalm 67:20])

[7]   Virtutem possuit Deus in opera sua *Ecl. Ca. 16*.
      (God has endowed his works with virtue. [Variation on Ecclesiasticus 16:25])

[8]   Similem reliquit post. se *Ecl. Ca. 30*.
      (He has left one behind him who is like himself. [Ecclesiasticus 30:4])

[9]   Iustitia, et pax osculatæ sunt *Ps. 84*.
      (Justice and peace have kissed. [Psalm 84:11])

[10] Virtus ex illo exibat *Luca. Ca. 6*.
      (For virtue went out from him. [Variation on Luke 6:19])

[11] Humiliauit se vsque ad mortem. *ad philip. Ca. 2*.
      (He humbled himself unto death. [Variation on Philippians 2:8])

[12] In corde prudentis requiescit sapientia. *Prob. Ca. 14*.
      (Wisdom rests in the heart of a prudent man. [Proverbs 14:33])

[13] Sol cognouit occasum suum. *Ps. 103*
      (The sun knows his own setting. [Psalm 103:19])

[14] Primus homo de terra terrenus. *1 Corin. Ca. 15*.
      (The first man was of the earth, earthly. [I Corinthians 15:47])

[15] Amauit eum Dominus, et ornauit eum *ex Ecl*.
      (The Lord loved him and adorned him. [The source of this quotation remains to be determined.])

[16] Nomine æterno hereditauit illum *Ecl. Ca. 15*.
      (He shall cause him to inherit an everlasting name. [Ecclesiasticus 15:6])

[17] Inuenit gratiam in conspectu illius *Esth. Ca. 2*.
      (He found favor in his sight. [Esther 2:9])

[18] Anima illius cum ipso delectabitur *Ecl. Ca. 31*.
      (His soul shall be delighted with him. [Ecclesiasticus 31:24])

[19] Renacens girat per meridiem *Ecl. Ca. 1*.
      (Rising again, [the sun] travels round to midday. [Ecclesiastes 1:5–6])

[20] Vir prudens dirigit gresus suos. *Parali. Ca. 2*.

1. Rodríguez de Monforte, *Descripcion*, fol. 68*ᵛ*.

(The wise man makes his steps straight. [Proverbs 15:21, not Paralipomenon])

[21] Mortuus est quasi non mortuus. *Ecl. Ca. 30.*

(He is dead [but it is] as if he were not dead. [Variation on Ecclesiasticus 30:4])

[22] Rex vero letabitur in Deo *Ps. 62.*

(The king will rejoice in God. [Psalm 62:12])

[23] Ex Augusto deposuit imperio *Parali. Ca. 5.*

(He deposed from the imperial authority. [II Paralipomenon 15:16])

[24] Xp̄us perducat eum in vitam æternam. *Exprecib. eclesiæ.*

(May Christ conduct him into eternal life. [The liturgical source for this quotation remains to be identified.])

Like the hieroglyphs (see Chapter 8), the inscriptions can be classified as biographical, consolatory, or political. The biographical ones present Philip as a virtuous monarch by asserting his worthiness in general (7 and 10) and by referring to specific qualities that he displayed: justice (3 and 9), wisdom (12 and 20), righteousness (4), peacefulness (9), and prudence (12). Four consolatory phrases acknowledge that like Adam, he was born mortal (14), that death eventually claimed him (23—that is, Death "deposed" Philip "from the imperial authority"), and that he accepted the inevitability of death with equanimity (11 and 13). Nine other consolatory phrases hint or declare outright that Philip's soul has been judged and saved, and that he has gone to a better reward (2, 5, 6, 15–18, 22, and 24). A biographical phrase alluding to his justice may also refer to the justice with which the Lord judged his soul (3). Four political inscriptions affirm that in dying, Philip left behind him a worthy successor to the crown (1, 8, 19, and 21).

1. Church of San Jerónimo, Madrid (photograph courtesy of Arxiu Mas).

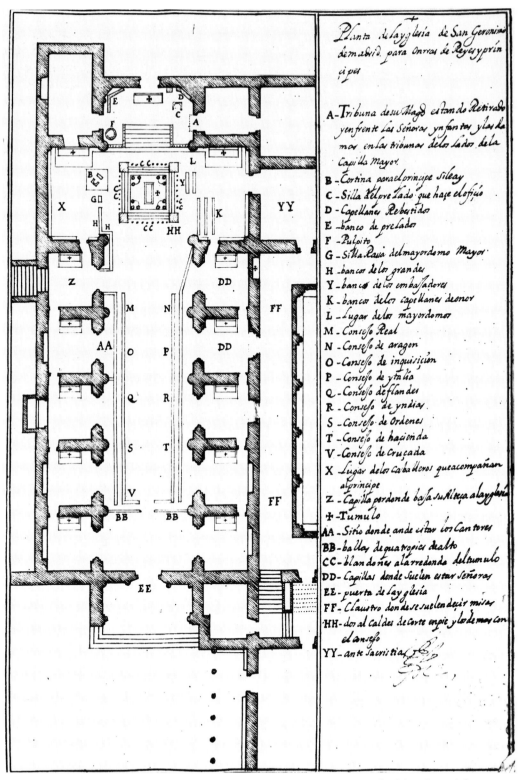

The handwritten legend (right side of the plan) reads:

Planta de la yglesia de San Geronimo
de madrid para Onrras de Reyes y prin
cipes

A – Tribuna de su Magd estando Retirado
   y enfrente Las Señoras ynfantes y las da
   mas en las tribunas delos Lados dela
   Capilla Mayor.
B – Cortina para el principe Si le ay
C – Silla del que Lado que haçe el ofiçio
D – Capellanes Rebestidos
E – banco de prelados
F – Pulpito
G – Silla Rasa del mayordomo Mayor
H – bancos de los grandes
Y – bancos de los embassadores
K – banco delos capellanes de onor
L – Lugar delos mayordomos
M – Consejo Real
N – Consejo de aragon
O – Consejo de inquisiçion
P – Consejo de ytalia
Q – Consejo de flandes
R – Consejo de yndias
S – Consejo de Ordenes
T – Consejo de haçienda
V – Consejo de Cruçada
X – Lugar delos Caballeros que acompañan
   al principe
Z – Capilla por donde basa su Alteza a la yglesia
✝ – Tumulo
AA – Sitio donde ande estar los Cantores
BB – ballas de quatro pies de alto
CC – blandones alarrededor del tumulo
DD – Capillas donde Suelen estar Señoras
EE – puerta de la yglesia
FF – Claustro donde se suelen deçir misas
HH – dos alcaldes de Corte en pie y los demas con
   el consejo
YY – ante sacristia

2. Juan Gómez de Mora, *Plan of the Church of San Jerónimo as Furnished for the Celebration of Royal Exequies* (Madrid, Archivo General de Palacio).

130

3. Chausuble from the "Vestments of the Skulls" (El Escorial, Real Monasterio de San Lorenzo; reproduced courtesy of the Patrimonio Nacional).

131

4. Attributed to Juan de Noort, *View of the Entrance to the Church of San Jerónimo at the Royal Exequies for Isabella of Bourbon* (by permission of the British Library, London).

5. Juan de Noort, *View of the Catafalque at the Royal Exequies for Isabella of Bourbon* (Madrid, Biblioteca Nacional).

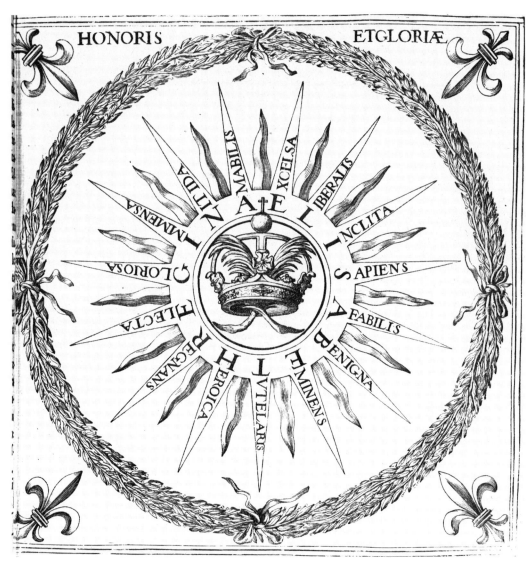

6. Attributed to Juan de Noort, *Ceiling Painting in the Catafalque at the Royal Exequies for Isabella of Bourbon* (Madrid, Biblioteca Nacional).

7. Domenichino, *Exequies for a Roman Emperor* (Madrid, Museo del Prado, all rights reserved).

8. Pedro de Villafranca y Malagón after Sebastián de Herrera Barnuevo, *Title Page for Pedro Rodríguez de Monforte, "Descripcion de las honras . . ."* (by permission of the British Library, London).

9. Pedro de Villafranca y Malagón after Sebastián de Herrera Barnuevo, *Allegorical Portrait of Philip IV* (Madrid, Biblioteca Nacional).

10. Pedro de Villafranca y Malagón, *Hieroglyph 1*, *Royal Exequies for Philip IV* (Madrid, Biblioteca Nacional).

11. Pedro de Villafranca y Malagón, *Hieroglyph 2, Royal Exequies for Philip IV* (Madrid, Biblioteca Nacional).

12. Pedro de Villafranca y Malagón, *Hieroglyph 3*, *Royal Exequies for Philip IV* (Madrid, Biblioteca Nacional).

Pedro de Villafranca y Malagón, *Hieroglyph 4, Royal Exequies for Philip IV* (Madrid, Biblioteca Nacional).

14. Pedro de Villafranca y Malagón, *Hieroglyph 5*, *Royal Exequies for Philip IV* (Madrid, Biblioteca Nacional).

15. Pedro de Villafranca y Malagón, *Hieroglyph 6, Royal Exequies for Philip IV* (Madrid, Biblioteca Nacional).

16. Pedro de Villafranca y Malagón, *Hieroglyph 7, Royal Exequies for Philip IV* (Madrid, Biblioteca Nacional).

17. Pedro de Villafranca y Malagón, *Hieroglyph 8, Royal Exequies for Philip IV* (Madrid, Biblioteca Nacional).

145

ET HABITAVIT ARCA DOMINI
IN DOMO OBEDEDON. 2 *Reg.6.*

Catholico Obededon
Nosolo al Arca dio asiento,
Pero almismo Sacramento
Dio en sucasa habitacion.

18. Pedro de Villafranca y Malagón, *Hieroglyph 9, Royal Exequies for Philip IV* (Madrid, Biblioteca Nacional).

19. Pedro de Villafranca y Malagón, *Hieroglyph 10, Royal Exequies for Philip IV* (Madrid, Biblioteca Nacional).

20. Pedro de Villafranca y Malagón, *Hieroglyph 11, Royal Exequies for Philip IV* (Madrid, Biblioteca Nacional).

ELEVATVS EST SOL, ET LVNA STETIT IN ORDINE SVO. *Abac. 3*

EstaLuna con luz nueua
Víue apesar de eſse monte,
Que el Sol en otro óriçonte
Nofalta, quando se eleua.

21. Pedro de Villafranca y Malagón, *Hieroglyph 12, Royal Exequies for Philip IV* (Madrid, Biblioteca Nacional).

149

22. Pedro de Villafranca y Malagón, *Hieroglyph 13, Royal Exequies for Philip IV* (Madrid, Biblioteca Nacional).

RENOVABITVR VT AQVILA. *Ps. 102*

En esse Renuebo mío,
(Que esta presente a mi vuelo)
Le queda al mundo el consuelo.

23. Pedro de Villafranca y Malagón, *Hieroglyph 14, Royal Exequies for Philip IV* (Madrid, Biblioteca Nacional).

24. Pedro de Villafranca y Malagón, *Hieroglyph 15, Royal Exequies for Philip IV* (Madrid, Biblioteca Nacional).

VISVS SVM OCVLIS INSIPIENTIVM MORI. *Sap. 3.*

Ignorante juzgo el mundo
Que dejaua de viuir,
Yfui dichoso enmorir.

25. Pedro de Villafranca y Malagón, *Hieroglyph 16, Royal Exequies for Philip IV* (Madrid, Biblioteca Nacional).

26. Attributed to Herman Panneels, *Arms of the Spanish Realms, Royal Exequies for Philip IV* (Madrid, Biblioteca Nacional).

154

27. Attributed to Juan de Noort, *Arms of the Spanish Realms, Royal Exequies for Philip IV* (Madrid, Biblioteca Nacional).

155

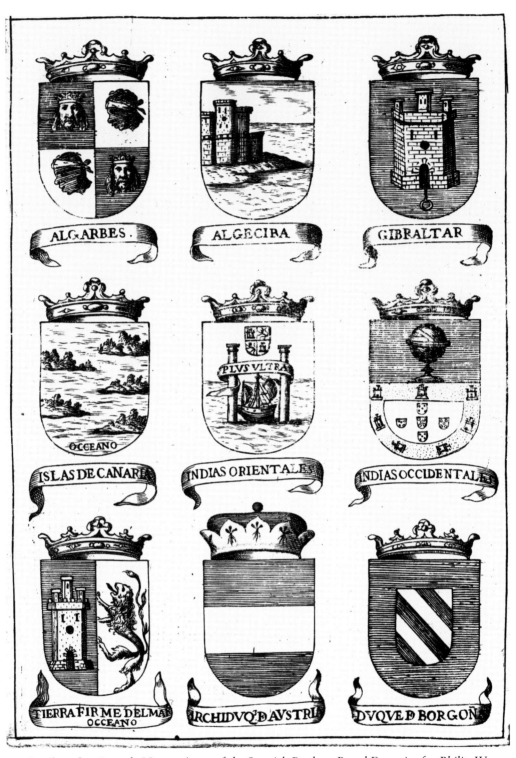

ALGARBES.

ALGECIRA

GIBRALTAR

OCCEANO

PLVS VLTRA

ISLAS DE CANARIA

INDIAS ORIENTALES

INDIAS OCCIDENTALES

TIERRA FIRME DEL MAR
OCCEANO

ARCHIDVQ D AVSTRI

DVQVE D BORGON

28. Attributed to Juan de Noort, *Arms of the Spanish Realms, Royal Exequies for Philip IV* (Madrid, Biblioteca Nacional).

29. Attributed to Juan de Noort, *Arms of the Spanish Realms, Royal Exequies for Philip IV* (Madrid, Biblioteca Nacional).

30. Pedro de Villafranca y Malagón, *Hieroglyph 17, Royal Exequies for Philip IV* (Madrid, Biblioteca Nacional).

31. Pedro de Villafranca y Malagón, *Hieroglyph 18, Royal Exequies for Philip IV* (Madrid, Biblioteca Nacional).

NONMORIAR, SED VIVAM. *Pfal. 117*

Que importa al que Phenix hace
Defus ceniças la hoguera
Que des de que nace muera
Sinuere des de que nace?

32. Pedro de Villafranca y Malagón, *Hieroglyph 19, Royal Exequies for Philip IV* (Madrid, Biblioteca Nacional).

IVSTITIA VERO LIBERABIT AMORTE. *Prou. 10.*

Con Iuſticia procedí,
Y con Piedad goberne,
A otra Corona aſpire.

33. Pedro de Villafranca y Malagón, *Hieroglyph 20, Royal Exequies for Philip IV* (Madrid, Biblioteca Nacional).

ERVNT SIGNA IN SOLE, LVNA, ET STELIS. *Luce. 21.*

Eclipsado el Real Planeta
Llorála infausta Fortuna,
Mal presagio de vn Cometa
Funestos Astros, y Luna.

34. Pedro de Villafranca y Malagón, *Hieroglyph 21, Royal Exequies for Philip IV* (Madrid, Biblioteca Nacional).

35. Pedro de Villafranca y Malagón, *Hieroglyph 22, Royal Exequies for Philip IV* (Madrid, Biblioteca Nacional).

BELIOR EST DIES MORTIS, DIE NATIVITATIS..Eclef.

Prospera, y feliz Fortuna,
Halle en morir, no en nacer,
Yassi mas llego adeuer,
Ala muerte, que ala cuna.

36. Pedro de Villafranca y Malagón, *Hieroglyph 23, Royal Exequies for Philip IV* (Madrid, Biblioteca Nacional).

SOL OCCIDIT, ET ORITVR *Eclef. 1.*

Aunque vnSol muereentresombras
Noay tiniebla queenbarace
Porque luego otro Sol nace.

37. Pedro de Villafranca y Malagón, *Hieroglyph 24, Royal Exequies for Philip IV* (Madrid, Biblioteca Nacional).

38. Pedro de Villafranca y Malagón, *Hieroglyph 25*, *Royal Exequies for Philip IV* (Madrid, Biblioteca Nacional).

39. Pedro de Villafranca y Malagón, *Hieroglyph 26, Royal Exequies for Philip IV* (Madrid, Biblioteca Nacional).

VITAM ETERNAM POSIDEBO. *Luc. 10.*

Quien con su muerte pago
Lacomun fatalidad,
Altienpo no se rindio,
Pues su vida al tienpo hurto,
Para hacerla eternidad.

40. Pedro de Villafranca y Malagón, *Hieroglyph 27, Royal Exequies for Philip IV* (Madrid, Biblioteca Nacional).

MORS IN LVCE

Laengañosa Vanidad
Es esta Luz presumida,
Huyendo sehalla lavida.

41. Pedro de Villafranca y Malagón, *Hieroglyph 28, Royal Exequies for Philip IV* (Madrid, Biblioteca Nacional).

ANIMA MEA ILLI VIUET, ET SEMEN MEUM SERVIET IPSI. Psal.

La aclamacion adelanta
De dos coronas el celo,
Vna se lebanta al cielo,
Otra el cielo la lebanta.

42. Pedro de Villafranca y Malagón, *Hieroglyph 29, Royal Exequies for Philip IV* (Madrid, Biblioteca Nacional).

170

SPIRITVS DOMINI RAPVIT PHILIPPVM. *Actor.1.*

NEC EST REX QVI RESISTAT EI *Prob.30.*

Quando del mundo faltó
Quiso la muerte tener
A Philippo en su poder
Mas Dios sele arrebato.

43. Pedro de Villafranca y Malagón, *Hieroglyph 30, Royal Exequies for Philip IV* (Madrid, Biblioteca Nacional).

171

44. Pedro de Villafranca y Malagón, *Hieroglyph 31, Royal Exequies for Philip IV* (Madrid, Biblioteca Nacional).

DEDVCET TE MIRABILITER DEXTERA MEA. *Pſal. 4ɡ.*

Como la Fe a de caer
(Aunquemas ser ciega mueſtra)
Si es Philippo quien la adieſtra

45. Pedro de Villafranca y Malagón, *Hieroglyph 32, Royal Exequies for Philip IV* (Madrid, Biblioteca Nacional).

MELIVS EST MICHI MORI, QVAM VIVERE. Ione. 4.

Quando lo entendi perder,
Hallo en lamuerte el viuir;
Luego sedebe decir
Que el dexar deser, es fer.

46. Pedro de Villafranca y Malagón, *Hieroglyph 33, Royal Exequies for Philip IV* (Madrid, Biblioteca Nacional).

174

47. Pedro de Villafranca y Malagón, *Hieroglyph 34, Royal Exequies for Philip IV* (Madrid, Biblioteca Nacional).

48. Pedro de Villafranca y Malagón, *Hieroglyph 35, Royal Exequies for Philip IV* (Madrid, Biblioteca Nacional).

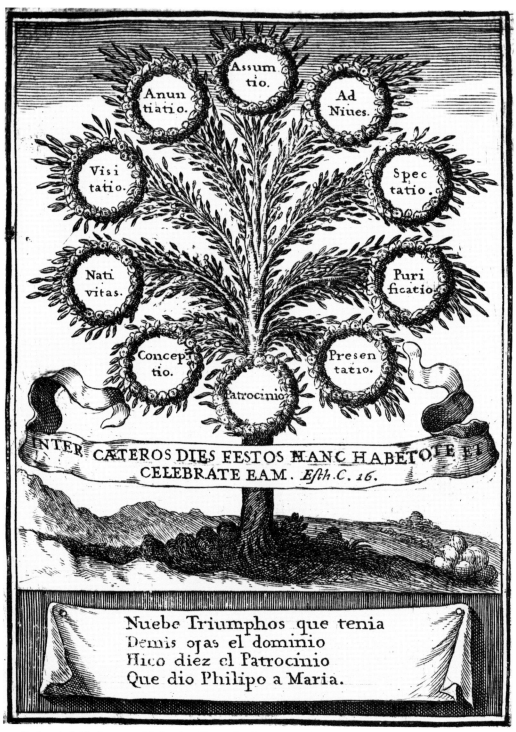

49. Pedro de Villafranca y Malagón, *Hieroglyph 36, Royal Exequies for Philip IV* (Madrid, Biblioteca Nacional).

50. Pedro de Villafranca y Malagón, *Hieroglyph 37, Royal Exequies for Philip IV* (Madrid, Biblioteca Nacional).

DEDIT DE CŒLO PLVVIAM. *Deuter. 11.*

Como es del Cielo el Rocío,
Transformado en blanca nube
Otra vez al Cielo sube.

51. Pedro de Villafranca y Malagón, *Hieroglyph 38, Royal Exequies for Philip IV* (Madrid, Biblioteca Nacional).

52. Pedro de Villafranca y Malagón, *Hieroglyph 39, Royal Exequies for Philip IV* (Madrid, Biblioteca Nacional).

CONSIDERANTI VULT.NATIVITATIS IN SPECULO. Iacob.

Ese christal enque atenta.
Mirandote vida estas,
Por fragil te enseña mas.

53. Pedro de Villafranca y Malagón, *Hieroglyph 40, Royal Exequies for Philip IV* (Madrid, Biblioteca Nacional).

NT REQVIESCAT ALABORIBVS SVIS, OPERA ENIM ILLIVS SEQVNTVR ILLVM. *Apoc. I.*

Desde que enpeço a Reynar
Siguio a estas virtudes fiel,
Yellas lesiguen a el,
Quando seua adescansar.

54. Pedro de Villafranca y Malagón, *Hieroglyph 41, Royal Exequies for Philip IV* (Madrid, Biblioteca Nacional).

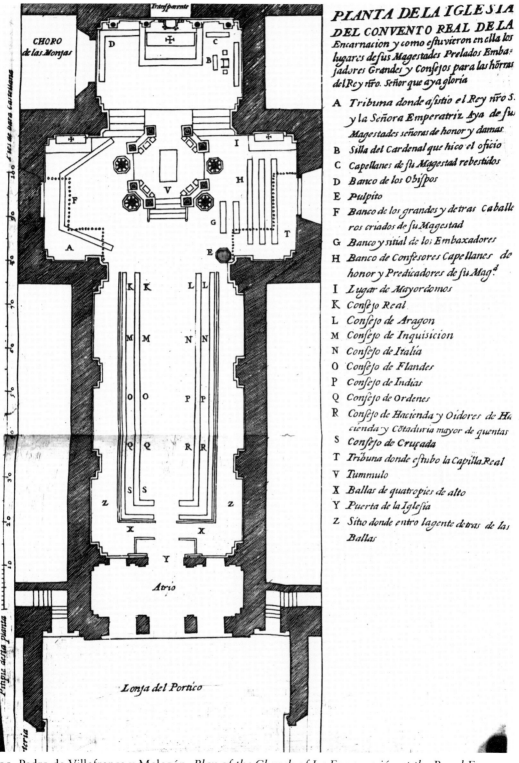

55. Pedro de Villafranca y Malagón, *Plan of the Church of La Encarnación at the Royal Exequies for Philip IV* (Madrid, Biblioteca Nacional).

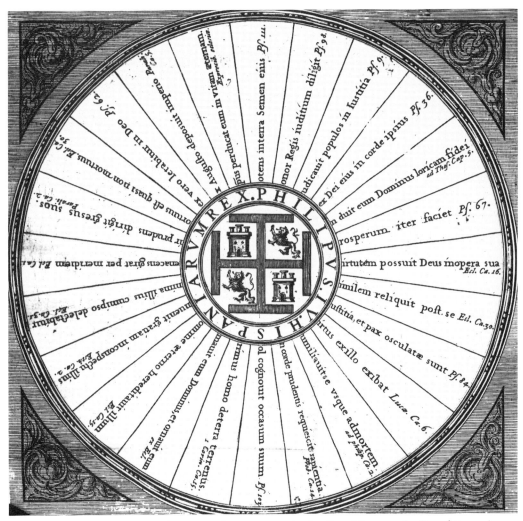

56. Pedro de Villafranca y Malagón, *Ceiling Painting in the Catafalque at the Royal Exequies for Philip IV* (Madrid, Biblioteca Nacional).

57. Pedro de Villafranca y Malagón, *View of the Catafalque at the Royal Exequies for Philip IV* (Madrid, Biblioteca Nacional).

58–66. Attributed to Herman Panneels, *Arms of the Royal Councils, Royal Exequies for Philip IV*: (58) Council of Castile, (59) Council of Aragon, (60) Council of the Inquisition, (61) Council of Italy, (62) Council of Flanders, (63) Council of the Indies, (64) Council of the Orders, (65) Council of Finance, and (66) Council of the Cruzada (by permission of the British Library, London).

186

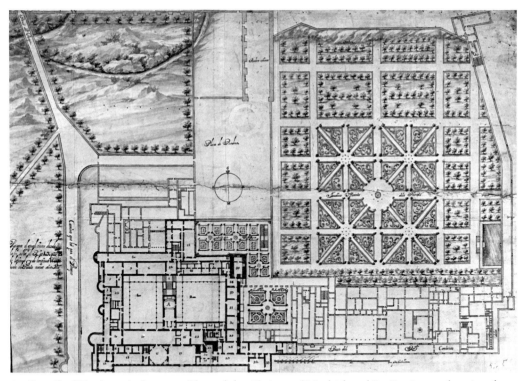

67. Detail of Teodoro Ardemans, *Plan of the Alcázar of Madrid and Its Environs*, showing the Alcázar at the lower left and the royal convent of La Encarnación at the upper right (Paris, Bibliothèque Nationale).

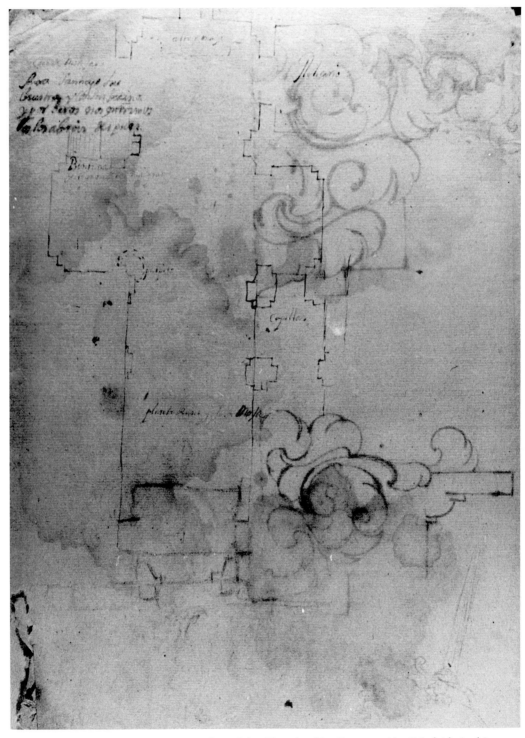

68. Sebastián de Herrera Barnuevo, *Plan of the Church of La Encarnación* (Madrid, Archivo Histórico Nacional).

69. Church of La Encarnación, Madrid (photograph courtesy of Arxiu Mas).

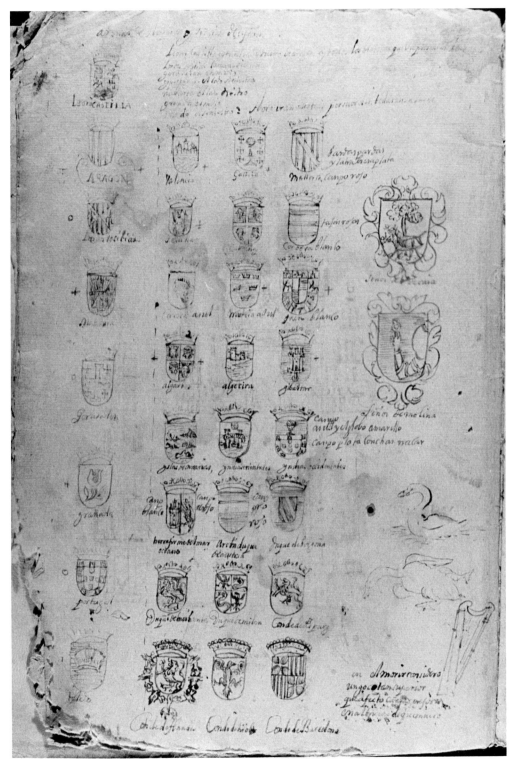

70. Sebastián de Herrera Barnuevo, *Studies for Coats of Arms and a Hieroglyph* (Madrid, Archivo Histórico Nacional).

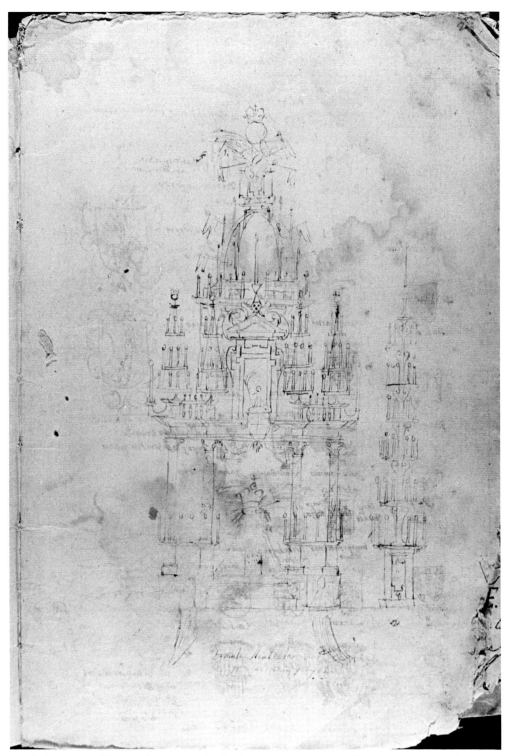

71. Sebastián de Herrera Barnuevo, *Study for the Catafalque at the Royal Exequies for Philip IV* (Madrid, Archivo Histórico Nacional).

72. *Clarior absens*, emblem from Covarrubias Orozco, *Emblemas morales* (reproduced courtesy of the University of Illinois Library at Urbana–Champaign).

73. *Non magna relinquam*, emblem from Covarrubias Orozco, *Emblemas morales* (reproduced courtesy of the University of Illinois Library at Urbana–Champaign).

74. *Fortuna in porto*, emblem from Covarrubias Orozco,
Emblemas morales (reproduced courtesy of the University of
Illinois Library at Urbana–Champaign).

75. *Ab ipso ducit opes animum*, emblem from Covarrubias
Orozco, *Emblemas morales* (reproduced courtesy of the
University of Illinois Library at Urbana–Champaign).

76. Peter Paul Rubens and Jan Wildens, *The Act of Devotion of Rudolf I* (Madrid, Museo del Prado, all rights reserved).

77. *Renovabitur ut aquilae iuventus mea*, hieroglyph at the exequies for the Empress María of Austria at the Jesuit College in Madrid in 1603 (Madrid, Biblioteca Nacional).

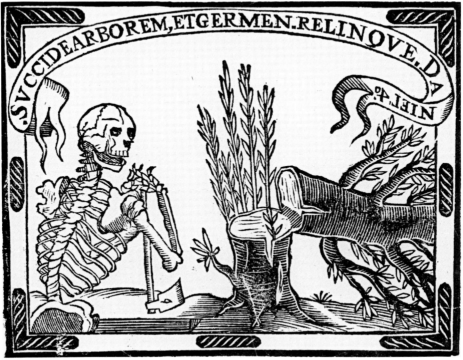

78. *Succide arborem, et germen relinque*, hieroglyph at the exequies for the Empress María of Austria at the Jesuit College in Madrid in 1603 (Madrid, Biblioteca Nacional).

79. Jusepe de Ribera, *Immaculate Conception* (Madrid, Museo del Prado, all rights reserved).

80. Francisco de Zurbarán, *Immaculate Conception* (Madrid, Museo del Prado, all rights reserved).

81. *Spes proxima*, emblem devised by Andrea Alciati, from Diego López,
Declaracion magistral . . . (courtesy of the John M. Wing Foundation,
The Newberry Library, Chicago).

82. Sebastián de Herrera Barnuevo, *Design for the Title Page for Pedro Rodríguez de Monforte, "Descripcion de las honras . . ."* (New York, Metropolitan Museum of Art, Bequest of Harry G. Sperling, 1975 [1975.131.221]; all rights reserved).

83. Sebastián de Herrera Barnuevo, *Studies for Architectural Details and for an Allegorical Portrait of Philip IV* (Madrid, Archivo Histórico Nacional).

Bibliography

Aclamacion Real, y Publica de la Coronada Villa, y Corte de Madrid; en cuyo nombre leuantó el Pendon de Castilla el Excelentissimo señor Duque de San Lucar, y de Medina de las Torres, Conde de Oñate, y Villa-Mediana, Correo mayor general de España, por su Augusto, y Catolico Rey Carlos II. que Dios guarde. Madrid, 1665.

Alciati, Andrea. *Emblemas.* Edited by Santiago Sebastián, with a prologue by Aurora Egido. Arte y Estética, no. 2. Madrid: Ediciones Akal, n.d.

Alenda y Mira, Jenaro. *Relaciones de solemnidades y fiestas públicas de España.* Madrid: Sucesores de Rivadeneyra, 1903.

Almansa y Mendoza, Andrés de. *Cartas.* Colección de Libros Españoles Raros ó Curiosos, vol. 17. Madrid, 1886.

Alpers, Svetlana. *The Decoration of the Torre de la Parada.* Corpus Rubenianum Ludwig Burchard, pt. 9. London and New York: Phaidon, 1971.

Amador de los Rios, José, and Juan de Dios de la Rada y Delgado. *Historia de la villa y corte de Madrid.* 4 vols. Madrid, 1860–1864.

Anderson, Jaynie. "'Le roi ne meurt jamais': Charles V's Obsequies in Italy." *Studia Albornotiana* 36 (1979): 379–97.

Angulo [Iñiguez], Diego, and Alfonso E. Pérez Sánchez. *A Corpus of Spanish Drawings, II. Madrid 1600–1650.* London: Harvey Miller Publishers, 1977.

Aparato fvnebre y real pyra de honor, que erigio la piedad, y consagro el dolor de la mvy insigne, y siempre leal civdad de Manila A Las memorias del serenissimo Principe de España Don Balthassar Carlos, que esté en Gloria. Manila, 1649. Reprinted in *Archivo del Bibliófilo Filipino* 2:105–58. Madrid, 1896.

Azcárate, José María de. "Datos sobre túmulos de la época de Felipe IV." *Boletín del Seminario de Estudios de Arte y Arqueología* 28 (1962): 289–96.

Barrionuevo, Jerónimo de. *Avisos.* Edited by A. Paz y Mélia. 4 vols. Colección de Escritores Castellanos: Historiadores, vols. 94, 96, 99, and 103. Madrid, 1892–1893.

Benavides, Francisco de. *Aparato, y Pompa Fvnebre a las devidas Honras en la Muerte de la Cesarea Magestad la Señora Emperatriz Doña Margarita de Austria Infanta de España. Solemnizadas en la Sacra, y Real Capilla de la Magestad Catolica de Don Carlos Segundo, que viua, y Reyne.* Madrid, 1673.

Berendsen, Olga. "The Italian Sixteenth and Seventeenth Century Catafalques." Ph.D. dissertation, New York University, 1961.

Bonet Correa, Antonio. "La fiesta barroca como práctica del poder." In *El arte efímero en el mundo hispánico,* 43–78. Estudios de Arte y Estética, no. 17. Mexico City: Universidad Nacional Autónoma de México, 1983.

———. *Iglesias madrileñas del siglo XVII.* 2d ed. Madrid: Consejo Superior de Investigaciones Científicas, 1984.

———. "El túmulo de Felipe IV, de Herrera Barnuevo y los retablos-baldaquinos del barroco español." *Archivo Español de Arte* 34 (1961): 285–96.

Borsook, Eve. "Art and Politics at the Medici Court I: The Funeral of Cosimo I de Medici." *Mitteilungen des Kunsthistorischen Institutes in Florenz* 12 (1966): 30–54.

Bottineau, Yves. "L'Alcázar de Madrid et l'inventaire de 1686." *Bulletin Hispanique* 58 (1956): 421–52, and 60 (1958): 30–61, 145–79, 289–326, and 450–83.

———. "Architecture éphémère et Baroque espagnole." *Gazette des Beaux-Arts,* 6th ser., 71 (1968): 213–30.

———. "Aspects de la cour d'Espagne au XVII*e* siècle: l'étiquette de la chambre du roi." *Bulletin Hispanique* 74 (1972): 138–57.

"Breue Relacion De la muerte del Rey Catholico Phelipe Quarto Y su Testamento, y otros papeles que dan noticia de lo que ha sucedido en el tiempo de la menor edad Del Rey Carlos segundo su Hijo." London, British Library, Ms. Add. 18,703, fols. 4–6.

Brown, Jonathan. *Images and Ideas in Seventeenth-Century Spanish Painting.* Princeton Essays on the Arts, no. 6. Princeton: Princeton University Press, 1978.

———. "Spanish Baroque Drawings in the Sperling Bequest." *Master Drawings* 11 (1973): 374–79.

———. *Velázquez: Painter and Courtier.* New Haven and London: Yale University Press, 1986.

Brown, Jonathan, and J. H. Elliott. *A Palace for a King: The Buen Retiro and the Court of Philip IV.* New Haven and London: Yale University Press, 1980.

Bustamante García, Agustín. "Los artífices del Real Convento de la Encarnación, de Madrid." *Boletín del Seminario de Estudios de Arte y Arqueología* 40–41 (1975): 369–88.

Cabrera de Córdoba, Luis. *Relaciones de las cosas sucedidas en la córte de España, desde 1599 hasta 1614.* Madrid, 1857.

Caparrós, José María. "Enfermedad, muerte y entierro del Rey D. Felipe IV de España." *Revista del Centro de Estudios Históricos de Granada y su Reino* 4, no. 2 (1914): 171–89.

Carducho, Vicente. *Diálogos de la pintura: su defensa, origen, esencia, definición, modos y diferencias.* Edited by Francisco Calvo Serraller. Madrid: Ediciones Turner, 1979.

Cartas de algunos PP. de la Compañía de Jesus sobre los sucesos de la monarquía entre los años de 1634 y 1648. 7 vols. Memorial Histórico Español, vols. 13–19. Madrid, 1861–1865.

Cartas de Sor María de Jesús de Agreda y de Felipe IV. Edited by Carlos Seco Serrano. 2 vols. Biblioteca de Autores Españoles, vols. 108–9. Madrid: Ediciones Atlas, 1958.

Cayetano Martín, María del C., Pilar Flores Cuerrero, and Cristina Gállego Rubio. "El Concejo de Madrid y las honras fúnebres en memoria del rey Don Felipe IV, Año 1665." *Hispania Sacra* 35 (1983): 723–38.

Cervera de la Torre, Antonio. *Testimonio avtentico, y verdadero, de las cosas notables qve passaron en la dichosa muerte del Rey nuestro señor Don Phelippe segundo.* Valencia, 1599.

Champlin, J. M. "Forty Hours Devotion." *The New Catholic Encyclopedia* 5:1036. N.p.: McGraw-Hill Book Co., 1967.

Corral, José del. "Felipe IV y el Real Monasterio de la Encarnación." *Anales del Instituto de Estudios Madrileños* 14 (1977): 203–40.

Covarrubias Orozco, Sebastián de. *Emblemas morales.* Madrid, 1610.

Cuartero y Huerta, Baltasar. *El Monasterio de San Jerónimo el Real: protección y dádivas de los Reyes de España a dicho Monasterio.* Madrid: Artes Gráficas Municipales, 1966.

Dávila Fernández, María del P. *Los sermones y el arte.* Valladolid: Universidad de Valladolid, 1980.

Deleito y Piñuela, José. *El Rey se divierte (recuerdos de hace tres siglos).* Madrid: Espasa-Calpe, 1935.

"Dia en q*e* murio nr̄o Rey q*e* Dios tiene el Gran Don filipo quarto." Madrid, Biblioteca Nacional, Ms. 1,000, fols. 5–6*v*.

Díaz de Ylarraza, Gregorio. *Relacion diaria de la enfermedad, y mverte del gran Rey Don Felipe IIII. Nuestro Señor. Y de los Oficios, y Exequias, Que la Serenissima, y muy Catolica Reyna N. Señora Doña Mariana de Austria Con Reuerente Culto, y Piadoso Zelo Ha mandado celebrar, En su Deposicion, Nouenario, y Honras. En su Real Palacio, y Conuento Real de la Encarnacion.* Madrid, 1665.

Díaz Padrón, Matías. *Museo del Prado, catálogo de pinturas. I: Escuela flamenca, siglo*

XVII. 2 vols. Madrid: Museo del Prado, 1975.

Elliott, J. H. *The Count-Duke of Olivares: The Statesman in an Age of Decline.* New Haven and London: Yale University Press, 1986.

———. *Imperial Spain 1469–1716.* London: Edward Arnold (Publishers), 1963.

———. *The Revolt of the Catalans: A Study in the Decline of Spain (1598–1640).* Cambridge: Cambridge University Press, 1963.

Elogios al Palacio Real del Bven Retiro. Edited by Diego de Covarrubias y Leiva. Madrid, 1635.

"Enfermedad, Muerte y Entierro, del Catolico Rey Don Phelipe quarto. Año de 1665." London, British Library, Ms. Add. 10,236, fols. 433–41.

Enríquez, Alonso. *Honras y obseqvias qve hizo al Catholico, y Christianissimo Rey Don Filipe Tercero nuestro Señor su muy Noble y muy Leal Ciudad de Mvrcia.* Murcia, 1621.

"Epitome de todas las cosas suzedidas en Tiempo del señor Rei don ph̃ quartto." Madrid, Real Academia de la Historia, Ms. 9-3-5-G-32bis.

Escrivense los svbcessos de Espana, Flandes, Italia, y otras partes de la Europa, desde Março de 44. hasta el mismo de 45. N.p. [1645].

España, Juan de. Untitled book of ceremonies. Madrid, Real Academia de la Historia, Colección Salazar y Castro, K-53.

"Etiquetas generales de la Casa R̃ del Rey ño. S̃ para el Uso y exerzicio de los ofizios de sus Criados." Madrid, Biblioteca Nacional, Ms. 10,666.

Fanshawe, Anne, Lady. *Memoirs of Lady Fanshawe, Wife of the Right Hon. Sir Richard Fanshawe, Bart. Ambassador from Charles the Second to the Court of Madrid in 1665. To Which are Added, Extracts from the Correspondence of Sir Richard Fanshawe.* London, 1829.

Flor, Fernando R. de la. "El jeroglífico y su función dentro de la arquitectura efímera barroca (a propósito de treinta y tres jero-glíficos de Alonso de Ledesma, para las fiestas de beatificación de San Ignacio en el Colegio de la Compañía de Jesús en Salamanca, 1610)." *Boletín del Museo e Instituto Camón Aznar* 8 (1982): 84–102.

Florencia, Jerónimo de. *Sermon qve predico a la Magestad Catolica del Rey Don Felipe Quarto Nuestro Señor el Padre Geronimo de Florencia, Religioso de la Compañia de Iesvs, Predicador de su Magestad, y Confessor de sus Altezas los Serenissimos Infantes don Carlos, y don Fernando Cardenal, y Arçobispo de Toledo, en las Honras que su Magestad hizo al Rey Felipe III. su padre y Nuestro Señor, que Dios tiene, en San Geronimo el Real de Madrid a quatro de Mayo de 1621.* Madrid [1621?].

———. *Sermon qve predico a la Magestad del Rey Don Felipe III. nuestro Señor, el P. Geronimo de Florencia su Predicador, y Religioso de la Compania de Iesvs, en las Honras que su Magestad hizo a la serenissima Reyna D. Margarita su muger, que es en gloria, en S. Geronimo el Real de Madrid, a 18. de Nouiembre de 1611. años.* Madrid, 1611.

Gállego, Julián. *Visión y símbolos en la pintura española del Siglo de Oro.* Madrid: Aguilar, 1972.

García de Escañuela, Bartolomé. *Penas en la mverte, y alivios en las virtvdes de el rey catholico de las Españas N. S. Felipe IV. el Grande. Empezadas a proponer en las Reales Honoras, que con Imperial demostracion de fidelidad, y grandeza celebrò la Coronada Villa de Madrid, en su Convento de Santo Domingo el Real, a 23. de Diziembre de 1665.* Madrid, 1666.

García Mahiques, Rafael. "Las 'Empresas Sacras' de Núñez de Cepeda: un lenguaje que configura al prelado contrarreformista." *Goya,* nos. 187–88 (July–October 1985): 27–36.

Giesey, Ralph E. *The Royal Funeral Ceremony in Renaissance France.* Travaux d'Humanisme et Renaissance, vol. 37. Geneva: Librairie E. Droz, 1960.

Gómez de Mora, Juan. "Aparato del tvmulo real que se edifico en el Conuēto de S. Geronimo De la Villa de Madrid para celebrar las honras Del Inclito y esclarecido Rey Don Filipe. III." Salamanca, Biblioteca Universitaria, Ms. 1,973 [Photographic copy in Madrid, Palacio Real, Biblioteca, II–739].

———. *Relacion de las honras fvnerales qve se hizieron para la Reyna doña Margarita de Austria nuestra senora, en esta villa de Madrid por su Magestad del Rey don Felipe nuestro senor.* N.p., n.d.

Heninger, S. K., Jr. *The Cosmographical Glass: Renaissance Diagrams of the Universe.* San Marino, Ca.: Huntington Library, 1977.

Herrera, Adolfo. "Rutilio Gaci." *Boletín de la Sociedad Española de Excursiones* 13 (1905): 57–70.

Hofmann, Christina. *Das Spanische Hofzeremoniell von 1500–1700.* Erlanger Historische Studien, vol. 8. Frankfurt am Main: Peter Lang, 1985.

Holweck, Frederick G. "Name of Mary, Feast of the Holy." *The Catholic Encyclopedia* 10 (New York: Robert Appleton Co., 1911): 673.

Hurtado, Luis. *La Philipica oracion, historico fvneral, en la mverte de la Catolica Magestad del Rey Nuestro Señor D. Phelipe Qvarto el Grande, Rey de las Españas, y Emperador de las Indias. Breve descripcion del tvmulo, que la Imperial Ciudad de Toledo erigiò en su muy Santa Iglesia, el dia veinte y tres de Diziembre, del año passado de M.DC.LXV. Para celebrar sus solemnes Exequias. Con algvnos de los gerogliphicos, y epitaphios, que estuuieron en su lienços, y vayetas, y otros escritos en la muerte, y para la sepultura del Eminentissimo Señor Don Baltasar de Moscoso y Sandoval, Arçobispo de la mesma Santa Iglesia.* Madrid, 1666.

Izquierdo Hernández, Manuel. "Bosquejo histórico del Príncipe Baltasar Carlos de Austria." Published lecture (January 11, 1968),

Sociedad Española de Médicos Escritores y Artistas. N.p. [1968].

Jacquot, Jean, ed. *Les Fêtes de la Renaissance, II. Fêtes et cérémonies au temps de Charles Quint.* Paris: Editions de Centre National de la Recherche Scientifique, 1960.

Junquera de Vega, Paulina. "El obrador de bordados de El Escorial." In *El Escorial 1563–1963,* 2:551–82. Madrid: Ediciones Patrimonio Nacional, 1963.

Justi, Carl. *Diego Velazquez and His Times.* Rev. ed. Translated by A. H. Keane. London, 1889.

Kamen, Henry. *Spain in the Later Seventeenth Century, 1665–1700.* London and New York: Longman, 1980.

Kantorowicz, Ernst H. "Oriens Augusti—Lever du Roi." *Dumbarton Oaks Papers* 17 (1963): 117–77.

Koenigsberger, Helmut. *The Government of Sicily under Philip II of Spain: A Study in the Practice of Empire.* Foreword by J. M. Batista i Roca. London and New York: Staples Press, 1951.

Krautheimer, Richard. "Introduction to an 'Iconography of Mediaeval Architecture.'" *Journal of the Warburg and Courtauld Institutes* 5 (1942): 1–33.

Kubler, George. *Building the Escorial.* Princeton: Princeton University Press, 1982.

Kuretsky, Susan D. "Rembrandt's Tree Stump: An Iconographic Attribute of St. Jerome." *Art Bulletin* 56 (1974): 571–80.

Lagomarsino, P. David. "The Habsburg Way of Death." Unpublished lecture, International Conference on Arts, Letters and Ceremonial at the Court of the Spanish Habsburgs, Duke University, April 3, 1980.

Ledda, Giuseppina. *Contributo allo studio della letteratura emblematica in Spagna (1549–1613).* Pisa: Università di Pisa, 1970.

León Pinelo, Antonio de. *Anales de Madrid (desde el año 447 al de 1658).* Edited by Pedro Fernández Martín. Madrid: Instituto de Estudios Madrileños, 1971.

Lezana, Mauricio de. *Memorial de las virtudes con que el Rey N. S. Filipo IV. (que* está en gloria) mereciô el renombre de Grande, no solo en la tierra, sino tambien en el Cielo. Para consvelo (en perdida tan grande) de la Reyna Nuestra Señora, de sus hijos, y vassallos. N.p. [1665].

Libro de las Honras qve hizo el Colegio de la Cõpañia de Iesvs de Madrid, à la M. C. de la Emperatriz doña Maria de Austria, fundadora del dicho Colegio, que se celebraron a 21. de Abril de 1603. Madrid, 1603.

López, Diego. Declaracion magistral sobre las emblemas de Andres Alciato con todas las Historias, Antiguedades, Moralidad, y Doctrina tocante a las buenas costumbres. Nájera, 1615.

López [de Hoyos], Juan. Hystoria y relaciõ verdadera de la enfermedad felicissimo transito, y sumptuosas exequias funebres de la Serenissima Reyna de España Doña Isabel de Valoys nuestra Señora. Con los sermones, letras y epitaphios a su tumulo, dilatado con con costũbres y cerimonias varias de differentes nasciones en enterrar sus diffunctos como paresce por la tabla deste libro. En el qual se Comprehende el nascimiento y muerte de su Magestad. Madrid, 1569.

———. Relacion de la mverte y honras fvnebres del SS. Principe D. Carlos, hijo de la Mag. del Catholico Rey D. Philippe el segũdo nuestro Señor. Madrid, 1568.

López Serrano, Matilde. "Reflejo velazqueño en el arte del libro español de su tiempo." In Varia velazqueña: homenaje á Velázquez en el III centenario de su muerte 1660–1960, 1:499–513. Madrid: Ministerio de Educación Nacional, 1960.

Manrique, Angel. Exeqvias. Tvmvlo y pompa fvneral, qve la Vniversidad de Salamanca hizo en las honras. Del Rey nuestro Señor don Felipe III. en cinco de Iunio de mil y seyscientos y veynte y vno. Salamanca, 1621.

Marías, Fernando, and Agustín Bustamante. "Apuntes arquitectónicos madrileños de hacia 1660." Archivo Español de Arte 58 (1985): 34–43.

Martínez, Juan. "Relación de la enfermedad del príncipe nuestro señor, escrita por el Padre Fray Juan Martínez, confesor de Su Majestad, para el doctor Andrés. (Año 1656.)" In Relaciones históricas de los siglos XVI y XVII, edited by Francisco R. de Uhagón. Sociedad de Bibliófilos Españoles, 32:338–55. Madrid, 1896.

Maura y Gamazo, Gabriel, Duque de. Vida y reinado de Carlos II. Rev. ed. 2 vols. Madrid: Espasa-Calpe, 1954.

Maza, Francisco de la. Las piras funerarias en la historia y en el arte de México: grabados, litografías y documentos del siglo XVI al XIX. Mexico City: Instituto de Investigaciones Estéticas, 1946.

Méndez Silva, Rodrigo. Gloriosa celebridad de España en el feliz nacimiento, y solemnissimo bavtismo de sv Deseado Principe D. Felipe Prospero, hijo del Gran Monarca D. Felipe IV. y de la Esclarecida Reyna D. Mariana de Avstria. Madrid, 1658.

———. Nacimiento, y bautismo del Serenissimo Infante de España, D. Fernando Tomas de Avstria. Madrid, 1659.

Morán, J. Miguel, and Fernando Checa. El coleccionismo en España: de la cámara de maravillas a la galería de pinturas. Madrid: Ediciones Cátedra, 1985.

Morena, Aurea de la. "El Monasterio de San Jerónimo el Real, de Madrid." Anales del Instituto de Estudios Madrileños 10 (1974): 47–78.

"Naçimiento y successos (Por mayor) Del Rey Don Phelipe Segundo nuestro señor, y su Testam[to] Muerte y Honrras." London, British Library, Ms. Add. 10,236, fols. 27–45[v].

Nájera, Manuel de. Sermon funebre, predicado por el Padre Manvel de Naxera, predicador de sv Magestad, En las svmptvosas lvgvbres exequias que hizieron a su Magestad en el Colegio Imperial de la Compañia de Iesus, los Estudios Reales, que su Magestad, que goza gloria, dexò en el fundados. Madrid, 1665.

Négociations relatives à la succession d'Espagne sous Louis XIV ou correspondances, mémoires, et actes diplomatiques concernant les prétentions et l'avénement de la

Maison de Bourbon au trône d'Espagne. Edited by François A. A. Mignet. Vol. 1. Collection de Documents Inédits sur l'Histoire de France, vol. 57. Paris, 1835.

Orso, Steven N. *Philip IV and the Decoration of the Alcázar of Madrid.* Princeton: Princeton University Press, 1986.

"Papeles varios" [*noticias* from 1637–1642]. Madrid, Biblioteca Nacional, Ms. 9,402.

Paravicino [Arteaga], Hortensio F. *Panegyrico fvneral a la gloriosa memoria del Señor Rey D. Filipe Tercero El Piadoso.* Madrid, 1625.

"Patrocinio." *Enciclopedia universal ilustrada europea-americana,* 42:872–73. Barcelona: Hijos de J. Espasa, n.d.

Pérez de la Rua, Antonio. *Fvneral hecho En Roma en la Yglesia de Santiago de los Españoles à 18. de Diciembre de 1665. A la gloriosa memoria del Rei Catolico de las Españas nuesro señor D. Felipe Qvarto el Grande en nombre de la nacion española Por el Excelentisimo Señor D. Pedro Antonio de Aragon Cauallero y Clauero del Orden de Alcántara, Gentilhombre de la Camara de su Magestad, Capitan de su Guardia Tudesca, de su Consejo de guerra, su Embaxador ordinario en Roma a la Santidad de Alexandro VII. y. su Virrey y Capitan General al Reino de Napoles.* Rome, 1666.

Pérez Sánchez, Alfonso E. *Historia del dibujo en España de la Edad Media a Goya.* Madrid: Ediciones Cátedra, 1986.

Pompa Fvneral Honras y Exequias en la muerte De la muy Alta y Catolica Señora Doña Isabel de Borbon Reyna de las Españas y del Nuevo Mundo Que se celebraron en el Real Convento de S. Geronimo de la villa de Madrid. Mandadas pvblicar por el Conde de Castrillo Gentilhombre de la Camara de su Mag.ᵈ de los Consejos de Estado y Guerra y Presidente del de las Indias. Que por orden particular de su Magestad (que Dios guarde) acudio y assistio a su disposicion y execucion. Madrid, 1645.

Praz, Mario. *Studies in Seventeenth-Century Imagery.* Rev. ed. Sussidi Eruditi, no. 16. Rome: Edizioni di Storia e Letteratura, 1964.

Quintana, Jerónimo de. *A la mvy antigva, noble y coronada villa de Madrid. Historia de sv antigvedad, nobleza y grandeza.* Madrid, 1629.

Quiros, Pedro de. *Parentacion real qve en la mverte de Felipe IV. el Grande Rey de España. Domador de la eregia. Vindice de la Fe. Celebro la mvy noble, y mvy leal Civdad de Salamanca.* Salamanca, 1666.

Relacion breve de la muerte del Rey N. S. Madrid, 1621.

Relacion de la enfermedad, mverte, y entierro del Rey Don Felipe Quarto nuestro Señor, (que estâ en el cielo) sucedida Iueves 17 de Setiembre Año de 1665. Seville [1665].

Relacion de la mverte de nuestro catolicissimo y bienaventvrado Rey y Señor Don Felipe Tercero de gloriosa memoria, que Dios tiene en el Cielo. Y assi mismo se dà cuenta de las rogativas que se hizieron por su salud, y de que enfermedad muriò, y en que dia, y el grandioso Entierro que se le hizo. Con vna breve Recopilacion de toda su vida y virtudes exemplares, y casos memorables que sucedieron en su Reynado. Y el principio del Govierno del Rey Don Felipe Dominico Victor Quarto nuestro señor, que Dios guarde. Y muerte del Gran Duque de Florencia. Seville, 1621.

Relacion de las Honras del Rey Felipe Tercero que està en el cielo, y la solene entrada en Madrid del Rey Felipe Quarto, que Dios guarde. Madrid, 1621.

"Relaçion de lo que paso a las honrras que su mag. mando hazer en Som gerᵐᵒ de madrid por el rrey nro Senor su padre que aya gloria domingo 17 de otubre de 1598." Madrid, Biblioteca Nacional, Ms. 18,718[78].

Relacion del feliz parto que tuuo la Reyna nuestra Señora, en 17. de Octubre de 1629. dia de Sāt Florencio Obispo, Miercoles a las siete de la mañana, y fiestas que se han hecho hasta 21. de dicho mes en la Villa de Madrid. Barcelona, 1629.

Relaciones breves de actos públicos celebra-

dos en Madrid de *1541 a 1650*. Edited by José Simón Díaz. El Madrid de los Austrias, Serie Documentación, no. 1. Madrid: Instituto de Estudios Madrileños, 1982.

"Resumen de la vida del Principe D. Baltasar Carlos." Madrid, Biblioteca Nacional, Ms. 18,718[130].

Ripa, Cesare. *Iconologia, o vero descrittione d'imagini delle Virtv', Vitij, Affetti, Passioni humane, Corpi celesti, Mondo e sue parti*. 1611. Reprint. New York and London: Garland Publishing, 1976.

Rodríguez de Monforte, Pedro. *Descripcion de las honras que se hicieron a la Catholica Mag.ᵈ de D. Phelippe quarto Rey de las Españas y del nuevo Mundo en el Real Conuento de la Encarnacion qve de horden de la Reyna ñra Señora como svperintendente de las reales obras dispvso D. Baltasar Barroso de Ribera, Marques de Malpica Mayordomo y Gentilhombre de Camara de su Mag.ᵈ que Dios aya y Gouernador de la guarda Alemana*. Madrid, 1666.

Rodríguez Villa, Antonio. *Etiquetas de la Casa de Austria*. Madrid, Jaime Ratés, 1913.

Rosenthal, Earl E. "The Invention of the Columnar Device of Emperor Charles V at the Court of Burgundy in Flanders in 1516." *Journal of the Warburg and Courtauld Institutes* 36 (1973): 198−230.

Sabatini, Rafael. *Torquemada and the Spanish Inquisition: A History*. New York: Brentano's, 1913.

Sáenz de Miera Santos, Carmen. "Túmulos madrileños del siglo XVII." *Anales del Instituto de Estudios Madrileños* 21 (1984): 37−42.

Sánchez Alonso, María C. "Juramentos de príncipes herederos en Madrid (1561−1598)." *Anales del Instituto de Estudios Madrileños* 6 (1970): 29−41.

Sánchez Pérez, Aquilino. *La literatura emblemática española (Siglos XVI y XVII)*. Colección Temas, no. 11. Madrid: Sociedad General Española de Librería, 1977.

Sariñana, Isidro. *Llanto del Occidente en el Ocaso del mas claro Sol de las Españas.* *Fvnebres Demonstraciones, qve hizo, Pyra Real, qve erigio en las Exeqvias del Rey N. Señor D. Felipe IIII. El Grande. El Ex.ᵐᵒ Señor D. Antonio Sebastian de Toledo, Marques de Manzera, Virrey de la Nueva-España, con la Real Audiencia, en la S. yglesia metropolitana de Mexico, Ciudad Imperial del Nuevo Mundo*. Mexico City, 1666.

Spear, Richard E. *Domenichino*. 2 vols. New Haven and London: Yale University Press, 1982.

Stradling, R. A. *Philip IV and the Government of Spain 1621−1665*. Cambridge: Cambridge University Press, 1988.

Stratton, Suzanne. "The Immaculate Conception in Spanish Renaissance and Baroque Art." Ph.D. dissertation, New York University, 1983.

Strong, Roy. *Art and Power: Renaissance Festivals 1450−1650*. Berkeley and Los Angeles: University of California Press, 1984.

Tervarent, Guy de. *Attributs et symboles dans l'art profane 1450−1600: dictionnaire d'un language perdu*. 2 vols. in 1. Travaux d'Humanisme et de Renaissance, no. 29. Geneva: Librairie E. Droz, 1958−1959.

Testamento de Felipe IV: edición facsimil. Edited by Antonio Domínguez Ortiz. Testamentos de los Reyes de la Casa de Austria, vol. 4. Madrid: Editora Nacional, 1982.

Thurston, Herbert. "Forty Hours' Devotion." *The Catholic Encyclopedia* 6:151−53. New York: Robert Appleton Co., 1909

Tormo [y Monzó], Elías. *Las iglesias del antiguo Madrid*. Edited by María E. Gómez Moreno. Madrid: Instituto de España, 1972.

Tovar Martín, Virginia. *Arquitectura madrileña del siglo XVII (datos para su estudio)*. El Madrid de los Austrias, Serie Estudios, no. 3. Madrid: Instituto de Estudios Madrileños, 1983.

———. "Juan Gómez de Mora, arquitecto y trazador del rey y maestro mayor de obras de la villa de Madrid." In *Juan Gómez de Mora (1586−1648)*, 1−162. Madrid:

Ayuntamiento de Madrid, 1986.

"Tratado de las ceremonias, o, culto, qve se dà a Dios en la Real Capilla de los Reyes Catholicos Nuestros Señores (Dios los guarde) Dividido en Dos partes." 2 vols. London, British Library, Ms. Egerton 1,822 and 1,823.

Trevor-Roper, Hugh. *Princes and Artists: Patronage and Ideology at Four Habsburg Courts 1517–1633.* The Yaseen Lectures, no. 1. New York: Harper & Row, 1976.

Ulloa, Luis de. *Fiestas qve se celebraron en la Corte por el nacimiento de Don Felipe Prospero, Principe de Asturias.* N.p., n.d.

Untitled *gaceta* of 1665. In "Sucesos del año 1665." Madrid, Biblioteca Nacional, Ms. 2,392, fols. 237–38^v.

Valgoma y Díaz Varela, Dalmiro de la. "Honras fúnebres regias en tiempo de Felipe II." In *El Escorial 1563–1963,* 1:359–98. Madrid: Ediciones Patrimonio Nacional, 1963.

Varey, J. E. "L'Auditoire du *Salón Dorado* de l'*Alcázar* de Madrid au XVIIe siècle." In *Dramaturgie et Societé: rapports entre l'oeuvre théâtrale, son interprétation et son public aux XVIe et XVIIe siècles,* edited by Jean Jacquot with Élie Konigson and Marcel Oddon, 1:77–91. Paris: Centre National de la Recherche Scientifique, 1968.

———. "Further Notes on Processional Ceremonial of the Spanish Court in the Seventeenth Century." *Iberoromania,* n.s., 1 (1974): 71–79.

———. "La mayordomía mayor y los festejos palaciegos del siglo XVII." *Anales del Instituto de Estudios Madrileños* 4 (1969): 145–68.

———. "Processional Ceremonial of the Spanish Court in the Seventeenth Century." In *Studia Iberica: Festschrift für Hans Flasche,* edited by Karl-Hermann Körner and Klaus Rühl, 643–52. Bern and Munich: Francke Verlag, 1973.

Velasco, Antonio L. de. *Fvnesto geroglifico, enigma del mayor dolor, qve en representaciones mvdas manifesto la mvy Noble, Antigua, Leal, Insigne, y Coronada Ciudad de Valencia, en las honras de su Rey Felipe el Grande, IV. en Castilla, y III. en Aragon.* Valencia, 1666.

Vera Tassis y Villarroel, Juan de. *Noticias historiales de la enfermedad, mverte, y exsequias de la esclarecida Reyna de las Españas Doña María Lvisa de Orleans, Borbon Stvart y Avstria, Nvestra Señora, dignissima consorte del Rey nvestro señor Don Carlos Segundo de Avstria.* Madrid, 1690.

Vicens y Hualde, Ignacio. "Arquitectura efímera barroca: un estudio de las estructuras funerarias españolas del siglo XVII." 4 vols. Ph.D. dissertation, Escuela Técnica Superior de Arquitectura de Madrid, Universidad Politécnica de Madrid, 1985.

Von Barghahn, Barbara. *Philip IV and the "Golden House" of the Buen Retiro: In the Tradition of Caesar.* 2 vols. New York and London: Garland Publishing, 1986.

Wittkower, Rudolf. "Eagle and Serpent: A Study in the Migration of Symbols." *Journal of the Warburg Institute* 2 (1938–1939): 293–325.

Yates, Frances A. *Astraea: The Imperial Theme in the Sixteenth Century.* London and Boston: Routledge & Kegan Paul, 1975.

Index of Symbols and Personifications

Palm: branch, 69; tree, 106
Parrot, 115
Peace, 29n6
Pelican, 86–87
Phoenix, 94–95
Piety, 29n6
Port, 103–5
Providence, Divine, 75, 89, 97, 100, 103
Prudence, 29n6, 68, 110

Rain, 108
Realms, Spanish, 35, 39
Religion, 29n6, 110
Ring, 64
River, 90
Robe, 64

Sandglass, 36, 67, 75, 102, 108–9
Scepter, 18, 19, 66, 67, 75, 85, 86, 89, 92, 97, 114, 122, 123
Scythe, 36, 66, 67, 100, 105–6
Sea, flaming, 90
Sepulcher, 89, 93, 102
Serpent, 102
Ship, 104–5
Silver, 61
Skeleton, 35, 75. *See also* Arm: skeletal
Skull, 35, 62, 67, 70, 75, 86–87, 89–90, 92, 108–9
Skull-and-crossbones, 19, 35, 36, 66
Spain, 48

Spheres, celestial, 86
Spring, 113–14
Star, 96, 104–5, 107–8
Storm at sea, 104–5
Stump, tree, 75
Sun, 41, 67, 72–74, 75, 77, 83–99 passim, 115, 121
Swan, 39–40, 84
Sword, 18, 19, 66, 68, 75, 95, 110, 115

Table, claw-foot, 109
Tablecloth, 109
Temperance, 68, 110
Thunderbolts, 115
Time, 66, 100
Tomb. *See* Sepulcher
Tree: stump, 75; unspecified, 89, 105–7; olive, 95; palm, 106; withered, 113. *See also* Branch
Trophies. *See* General Index
Trumpet, 69
Truth, 29n6
Tumba. See General Index
Turban-crown, 115

Victory, 29n6
Virtues, sets of, 29, 39, 40, 67–68, 110

Wind: South (Austro), 104, 105, 114; North (Boreas), 114
Wreath, 107, 114

General Index

Alcántara, Roque de, 69
Alcázar of Madrid: king's summer apartments, 1, 123; Royal Chapel, 3, 14, 15, 20, 20*n*29, 26, 59–60, 88, 99, 107; Great Hall, 5, 15, 78, 92; repository for collars of the Golden Fleece, 20, 50, 66; library of plans and drawings, 38; linked to La Encarnación, 60; in hieroglyph at Philip IV's royal exequies, 101; royal balcony, 101; Hall of Mirrors, 109; mentioned, 4, 13, 59, 80
Alciati, Andrea, 104
Alexander VII, Pope, 107
Anne of Austria, Queen of Spain, 17, 35
Antique precedents for royal exequies, 30–32, 91
Arce, Francisco de, 44
Audience at royal exequies, 8, 62–63
Avila, Clemente de, 65

Baltasar Carlos, Prince: last days and death, 14, 15, 77, 84; attends royal exequies for Isabella of Bourbon, 22, 45; Madrid's exequies for, 38; life, 73, 77, 91; referred to in hieroglyph at Isabella of Bourbon's royal exequies, 106
—royal exequies for: guards in church cloister, 26; financial constraints upon, 28–29, 55; coats of arms at, 33–34, 37; aftermath, 50, 51; project for documentary book, 55, 112; mentioned, 10, 17, 38
Banners. *See* Flags
Barrionuevo, Jerónimo de, 78
Bellefond, Marquis of, 80
Books: documenting royal exequies, 8–9, 25, 27, 31, 36, 38, 43, 51–55, 61, 62, 82, 111–16; precedent for royal exequies books, 51–52, 54
Buen Retiro, Palace of the: access to San Jerónimo, 16, 21, 22, 45; mentioned, 32, 59, 72, 78
Burgos, Juan de, 66*n*7

Cajés, Eugenio, 39, 71*n*3
Calderón, María, 81
Calderón de la Barca, Pedro, 73
Candles: feature of royal exequies, 8, 18, 27, 30, 32, 36, 43, 46, 119; when lighted, 23, 24, 63, 64; coloring, 24, 33, 69; quantities needed, 32, 70; smoke and fire hazard, 33, 45, 61, 70; types, 33; at Isabella of Bourbon's royal exequies, 32, 33, 44–45, 50, 70; disposal of remnants, 50, 51; at royal exequies for Philip IV, 61–70 passim, 86. *See also* Index of Symbols and Personifications
Capella ardente, 18, 29, 32

Carbonel, Alonso, 48
Cárdenas, Padre Maestro Fray Miguel de, 64
Carducho, Vicente, 39, 71*n*3
Carlos, Prince Don, 17
Carreño de Miranda, Juan, 71*n*3, 109
Castelo, Félix, 71*n*3
Castile, Constable of, 38
Castillo, Fray Antonio del, 4
Castrillo, Count of, 3, 43–44, 45, 48–49
Catafalques: feature of royal exequies, 8, 36, 50, 119; design criteria, 27–37 passim, 38; illusionism of materials, 28, 37, 44, 65, 66; dismantling of, 28, 50–51; origins of, 29–30; as baldachins for *tumbas*, 30; antique and medieval precedents for, 30–32; at royal exequies for Philip IV, 31, 61, 65–70, 85, 121–22; centralized plans in, 31–32; types of decorations on, 33–37; angels on, 35; women's decorated differently from men's, 35; construction of, 39, 43. *See also* Ceiling painting
Catalina Micaela, Infanta, 17
Ceiling painting: feature of catafalques, 30; at Isabella of Bourbon's royal exequies, 30, 39, 54, 67; at Philip IV's royal exequies, 66–67, 68, 98, 112, 127–28
Cerda, Padre Juan Ludovico de la, 52
Charles I of Spain: last days and death, 4, 14, 84, 96; life, 7, 13, 30; exequies for, 17, 29; referred to in an Alciati emblem, 104*n*51
Charles II of Spain: at Philip IV's death, 3, 4, 59; succeeds Philip IV, 5–6, 59, 70, 75–80 passim, 117; royal exequies for, 38, 60; physical frailty, 59–60, 61, 79–80; orders royal exequies for others, 60; attends Philip IV's royal exequies, 62, 63, 64; referred to in decorations at Philip IV's royal exequies, 74, 83, 84, 87, 89–95 passim, 98, 99–100, 101, 105, 106, 108, 122, 124, 128; birth, 79; proclaimed king in Madrid, 101
Charles V, Holy Roman Emperor. *See* Charles I of Spain
Churriguera, José Benito de, 38
Coats of arms: feature of royal exequies, 8, 18, 24, 27, 33–37 passim, 50; "full" royal arms, 18, 19, 21, 23, 33, 34, 35, 66, 114; of Spanish realms, 19, 33–36 passim, 39, 55, 62, 82, 84, 87, 101, 112; of grandparents of the deceased, 21, 23, 33, 34–35, 68–69, 119; of royal councils, 21, 33, 37, 39, 55, 63, 84, 95, 112; of individuals, 33, 35, 119; at royal exequies for Philip IV, 61–69 passim, 84, 112; of Madrid, 115
College of Cuenca, exequies for Philip III at, 98

Philip IV of Spain (*continued*)
at his royal exequies, 67, 68, 76, 81, 82–110 passim, 121–28 passim; epithets, 72, 74, 82, 86, 95, 109, 115; exequies in his honor staged outside the court, 72–73; birth, 73, 122; *juramento*, 73, 91; orders commemorative sermon for Philip III, 74, 83, 95; need for a male heir, 77–81; mentioned, 8, 74, 77, 99
Plaza Mayor, Madrid, 101
Príncipe jurado defined, 7–8
Processions: supplicatory, 3, 4, 14; bringing Viaticum to Philip IV, 3, 76; funeral cortege to El Escorial, 5, 15, 46, 53, 66, 111; royal etiquette for, 13, 22; of councils at royal exequies, 21; of king or prince entering royal exequies, 21–22, 23
Pueyo, Miguel, 39

Raising the pennon, 101
Riera, Antonio, 48
Ripa, Cesare, 40
Rizi, Francisco, 71*n*3
Rodríguez de Monforte, Pedro: interprets decorations at Philip IV's royal exequies, 31, 61–62, 66–71 passim; compiles *Descripcion de las honras*, 55, 68, 69, 71, 111–12
Rosende, Padre Antonio, 66*n*7
Rudolf I, Holy Roman Emperor, 76, 123

Saint Isidro, 3, 4, 14
Saint James of Alcalá, 4
San Andrés, church of, 3
San Benito, Valladolid, royal monastery of, 119
San Jerónimo, royal monastery of: church used for *juramento*, 8; church used for royal exequies, 16–27 passim, 43, 50, 52, 60, 62, 65, 70; history of, 16–17; cloister used for royal exequies, 22, 25–26, 43, 44, 45, 50, 53, 54, 106, 112; abandoned as setting for royal exequies, 59, 111
San Juan, parish church of, 88, 111
San Lorenzo at El Escorial, royal monastery of: Habsburgs taken there for entombment, 5, 6, 15, 18, 46, 53, 101; royal exequies vestments and *tumba* instruments kept there, 19–20, 66; lends candlesticks to royal exequies, 45; mentioned, 16, 74
San Lúcar and of Medina de las Torres, Duke of, 101

Santa María, parish church of, 3, 4
Santo Domingo, royal convent of, 17
Seating: practice at royal exequies, 18, 20, 21, 25, 27, 30, 32, 33, 37; at Philip IV's royal exequies, 62–63, 66
Semini, Giulio Cesare, 71*n*3
Sermon: feature of royal exequies, 23, 52, 54; at Jesuit College honors for Empress María, 52; at Philip IV's royal exequies, 64, 111–12; ordered by Philip IV in memory of Philip III, 74, 83, 95
Souvenir hunters, 50
Succession: general problem of, 5–6; concern in Philip IV's reign, 77–81

Tajara, Count of, 4
Texada, Miguel de, 80
Toledo, Juan Bautista de, 16
Torre, Jusepe de la, 51
Torre, Pedro de la, 65
Town Hall, Madrid, 101
Trophies: feature of royal exequies, 18, 27, 34–35; omitted from women's royal exequies, 35; at Philip IV's royal exequies, 61, 65, 69
Tumba and its instruments: feature of royal exequies, 18–20, 27, 30, 31, 35, 39, 45, 50, 54, 119; in catafalque at Philip IV's royal exequies, 66, 68, 75, 95, 127; in hieroglyphs at Philip IV's royal exequies, 92, 97

Ubilla y Medina, Antonio de, 60
Urban VIII, Pope, 88

Valencia, exequies for Philip IV in, 72–73
Valeriano, Piero, 36
Valladolid: capital, 7; Philip IV's birthplace, 73, 122
Velázquez, Diego de, 114
Vestments for royal exequies, 19, 23, 24, 50
Villafranca y Malagón, Pedro de, 54, 55, 61, 69–70, 71, 112–13, 114
Villanueva, Francisco de, 44
Virgin of Atocha, 4, 14

Yanguas, Domingo de, 71*n*3

Zaragoza, Baltasar Carlos dies in, 15